Field Guide to
THE AMERICAN
TEENAGER

Field Guide to THE AMERICAN TEENAGER

A Parent's Companion

Anne
Stay persistantly
patient !

JOSEPH DI PRISCO, PH.D.
MICHAEL RIERA, PH.D.

PERSEUS PUBLISHING
Cambridge, Massachusetts

Failing to fetch me at first keep encouraged,
Missing me one place search another,
I stop somewhere waiting for you.
—WALT WHITMAN, *SONG OF MYSELF*

Nobody is despised who can manage a crocodile.
—LEWIS CARROLL

A CIP catalog record for this book is available from the Library of Congress.
ISBN 0-7382-0267-3

Perseus Publishing is a member of the Perseus Books Group.

Find us on the World Wide Web at http://www.perseuspublishing.com

Perseus Publishing books are available at special discounts for bulk purchases in the U.S. by corporations, institutions, and other organizations. For more information, please contact the Special Markets Department at HarperCollins Publishers, 10 East 53rd Street, New York, NY 10022, or call 1-212-207-7528.

Text design by Jeff Williams
Set in 11-point Minion by Perseus Publishing Services

First printing, June 2000
1 2 3 4 5 6 7 8 9 10—03 02 01 00

To Megan,
with my deepest gratitude.
—*M. R.*

To Mario Di Prisco,
with thanks for guiding your father
through your adolescence
—*J. DP.*

Contents

Acknowledgments

We would like to express our gratitude to our colleagues, friends, associates, and family members who made invaluable contributions to the writing of this book. It would be impossible to single out every person who helped shape this book with an insight, a question, a critique, or a kindness, but here are some of them:

Francesca Applegarth. Dan Barrett. Laurie Bottoms. Bodie Brizendine. Betty Buck. Bill Bullard. Rick Clarke. Annie Condon. C. Slade Crawford. Nan Fredotovich. Tony Fredotovich. John A. Gray. Tucker Hiatt. Fred Hoerner. Elaine Howard. Robert J. Kelly. Khris Lundy. Craig McGarvey. Christine McQuade. Donald McQuade. Elise Miller. Samantha Sanderson. Carlton H. Tucker. David Wood. Samantha Weaver. Valerie Wright. Shafia Zaloom. The San Francisco Bay Area Deans' Group.

Elizabeth Trupin-Pulli, our wonderful literary agent and friend, without whom this book would remain merely an idea. Thanks for your timely words of wisdom and for keeping us on track throughout.

Marnie Cochran, our editor at Perseus Publishing, who understood this book from the beginning and whose energy, dedication, and intelligence spurred us forward. Also, Donna MacCletchie, Lissa Warren, Marco F. Pavia, and Chrisona Schmidt of Perseus.

Particular appreciation to Peter Beren and to Joan Ryan.

The teenagers and parents we have taught and worked with and learned from over the years.

The faculties and families of schools where we have worked and consulted, especially San Francisco University High School and Marin Academy.

Special thanks to our parents: Elizabeth and Pat Riera. Catherine and Joseph Di Prisco.

Finally, we want to thank most especially our families for their encouragement, their wisdom, their readings, their suggestions, their company, their conversation, and their faith. Megan Twadell-Riera and Lucia Riera; Martin, Ava, and Sharky. Patricia Ainsworth James and Mario Di Prisco; Abby, Jack, and Edwina.

Foreword

by Joan Ryan

Every Thursday morning, I walk with a small group of women through the wooded hills near my home. We like to think we do this for the exercise but mostly it's for the talking. We figure out all the important things, such as why our husbands can work a Palm Pilot with only a few minutes of instruction but still can't figure out how to switch on the dishwasher. But more times than not, the discussion turns to our children, the most confounding subject of all.

"You think the toddler stage is bad," my friend Lorna said the other day to one of our friends, the mother of young children. "Wait till you have teenagers." Lorna's son is thirteen. "He's home from school twenty minutes," she went on, "and you're ready to kill him. You can't say anything to him or he falls apart. You hate them but you love them so much. It's quite interesting."

My son is nine, inching toward his teenage years. Already he is becoming mysterious in the way that creatures on *Animal Planet* are. My husband and I observe him like documentarians, hoping to glean some clues as to why he crumples his homework in frustration one day and sticks with it like a beady-eyed accountant the next. Why he curls up next to us one night and won't tolerate so much as a kiss on the head the next.

My first understanding of what might be going on inside his head came when, in researching a newspaper story about boys, I attended one of Mike

Riera's talks to junior high parents in Marin County, California. He talked as if he were both fifteen and forty-five, describing teenage behavior to a tee—drawing howls of laughter from the parents—and then translating their behavior into adult language. Their teenager's behavior wasn't always about them as parents (a difficult concept for us baby boomers), and it wasn't always what it seemed to be. Once parents could start understanding how a teenager's brain worked, they could start communicating better with their child and ease up on being so defensive and judgmental and crabby.

I took notes furiously, as a parent more than a journalist. Mike's insights struck home. If I wanted to have an open, loving relationship with my son as he moved through adolescence, I'd have to be more clued in to the emotions, pressures, temptations, conflicts, and complex dynamics of the teenage world. Not long after that talk, two boys went on a killing spree at Columbine High School in Colorado, one of more than half a dozen deadly outbursts by teenage boys in two years. We already knew how girls struggled with body image and self-esteem as they hit their teenage years, how they can turn to cutting themselves, or something worse, to release their emotional pain. Now boys, too, were making us pay closer attention to how confusing and treacherous the teenage years can be.

Sometimes we dismiss the seemingly irrational behavior and moods of teenagers as normal kid stuff, the stuff we went through and survived just fine. And some of it is. But our children live in a different world from the one we knew. They know more. They see more. They are both more grown-up and more vulnerable than we were. They and their friends can make us feel like anthropologists in a baffling, unfamiliar culture. We try to be like our own parents, but their ways don't always work anymore. The game has changed, but nobody is out there handing out the new rulebooks.

Now somebody is. Two people, actually. Mike Riera teamed up with his friend Joseph Di Prisco, a longtime English teacher, administrator, and writer, to produce *Field Guide to the American Teenager*. I met Joe over a long lunch one day with Mike. He's wry and self-deprecating and passionate about his work. He's the kind of teacher who managed to present the tragedy and betrayal and passion of Shakespeare in way that tapped into his students' lives, helping them to understand what they already knew.

Field Guide to the American Teenager isn't a rulebook. It can't be. Every teenager is happy and moody and tense and confused in different ways.

The same can be said about every parent. What this book does is pull back the curtains on our children's lives. It is full of the conversations we as parents rarely hear: teenagers talking to each other and to other adults. We get to be flies on the wall, watching and listening and learning. We get to see how deeply our children love us despite acting as if we were mutant aliens. We see how much common sense they actually possess, how often our seemingly ignored advice floats into their heads when they need it most.

One of my favorite statistics in the book is that 80 percent of students in a *Who's Who* survey admitted to cheating. But 63 percent of parents thought their children never cheated. The *Field Guide* lays out why there is such a disconnect—and why so many kids cheat. (You'll be relieved to know it's usually not because we didn't bring them up well.) The book tackles all the issues we and our children face day in and day out: how teenagers process failure; how they confront the injustice of being cut from a sports team or left out of a party; how they struggle to please both parents and friends when the responsibilities to each relationship conflict.

Raising a child strips away all our masks. I thought I was a patient, mentally healthy person before my son was born. Now I find myself at times behaving like Elizabeth Taylor in *Who's Afraid of Virginia Woolf?* My Thursday walks help. My friends let me know I'm not alone. They tell me what has worked for them. They share everything they know. The *Field Guide to the American Teenager* is like that, only smarter. It's a wise companion, nodding its head, laughing in empathy and recognition, and sharing its experience and counsel. As a parent, I'm relieved and thankful to have a found such a thorough field guide to teenagers. I expect the only person more grateful will be my son.

Introduction

The fundamental fact about our experience is that it is a process of change.

—WILLIAM JAMES

– ONE –

Teenager. The word conjures up images of remoteness, irrationality, mystery, and even chaos in the minds of many adults. However slanted the associations, it is nonetheless a fact of family life that parents and their teenagers can, almost effortlessly, confuse or antagonize each other. They seem to speak at cross-purposes. They seem to value conflicting cultures. They seem to inhabit opposing worlds.

As parents you cannot afford to be discouraged. You *can* understand your teenagers. In fact, teenagers need more than ever before to be understood. The problem is, they need you to hear what they can't quite articulate and to see what they really can't show you.

Teenagers develop by growing up—and by growing up fast—just beyond your view. During adolescence, growing *up* goes along with growing *away.* That is in the nature of adolescence. At the moment when teenagers seem at risk of slipping away, and when you may very well feel frustrated enough to let them, though, *Field Guide* points in the direction of reconciliation. What makes life so hard for parents is that they find it hard to shake their memories of the child they once knew who has now grown up. But that child is no more. And now you need to re-learn who your child has become: a teenager.

This is why *Field Guide* combines stories of teenagers in their natural setting with compassionate, in-depth analysis and pragmatic counsel. It shows teenagers' living their lives on their own terms: for example, working a part-time job, taking a class, playing on a team, reaching out to an adult, saving a struggling friend, breaking hearts, falling in love, talking to the school counselor, driving around late at night. It illuminates the extraordinary in the ordinary reality of everyday teenage life. And it dramatizes teenagers' addressing the crucibles of their lives—sexual identity, drugs, divorce, mortality, and so on—through stories and conversations. Teenagers' lives, like adults', are series of stories and conversations.

This field guide may seem unusual insofar as it has no pictures or maps, and not much of a field, either. The conventional field guide informs your perception, training you to understand what it is you are seeing—and what it is you are missing. In a parallel way, however, this book invites you to glimpse aspects of your own children in these universal accounts of self-discovery and of family. It has often been remarked that, if you truly want to understand your teenagers, talk to their friends—not to grill them for inside information, but to gain an appreciation of their daily struggles and joys. Similarly, though your children may not be (to refer to a few chapter themes) depressed, anorexic, learning disabled, experimenting with drugs and alcohol, starring on a team, or losing a part-time job, you can be absolutely sure they brush every day against those who are, and these teenagers, who may well be their best friends, are central to their world and their self-conception.

Each chapter features three elements: a Narrative, at least one Conversation, and Notes Home. At the heart of each is a representative tale, based upon real-life incidents and experiences of teenagers' confronting risks, challenges, and opportunities. There are no compact allegories, as befits such real-life fables. The information can be ambiguous and multi-leveled, the participants muddled, the choices unclear or hard to make. In short, an episode in the life of a teenager. Here is where readers will *overhear* the voices of teenagers growing up. They can also hear those voices in those conversations that take place between a teenager and a trusted adult, such as a teacher, a coach, an adviser, a guidance counselor, a family friend, an employer. This is a freeze-frame instant of a teenager reaching out for clarification, insight, support, and relationship. Such reaching out occurs daily, probably hourly, wherever teenagers and adults converge. In their talking, we watch them take a turn, usually inward. This is where you can see how teenagers think, dream, imagine, and cope, and yearn to work out conflicts, internal and external. (Teenagers are the emperors of self-revelation, but always on their own terms, and usually gradually, partially, obliquely.) In the notes home we expand upon each chapter's subject, explicitly and tangentially. We point out the principal developmental issues at play in the experience and the deeper levels of meaning and significance. (In addition, in the Appendixes we provide for reference purposes description and analysis of adolescent development year by year.) We also provide in the notes home practical suggestions for parents to improve their relationships with their teenagers.

In some parenting books, anecdotes and dialogues are simply in the service of illustrating a point or two about a major topic, like depression, anorexia, athletics. Ours is different. *Field Guide* models the messy reality of parents and of teenagers. In the life of any family, experiences seldom arrive in neat packages. Sometimes with our teenagers we get more information than we want, and sometimes we get less information than we need. The same is true with these narratives.

The art of parenting begins with knowing how to read kids in between the lines of their lives. Teenagers don't fall in love, or grieve, or smoke, or play soccer in a vacuum. We only know what these experiences mean for them, and for us, when we grasp them in the context of their tribulations, aspirations, and dreams. Their decisions and choices, their weaknesses and strengths, are interconnected.

What sort of guidance do you as parents desire? Naturally, you might wish that there were surefire do's and don't's and a set of foolproof, unambiguous prescriptions. At the same time, however, all parents know that their children are nothing if not complex and, therefore, that absolutes are either unreliable or in short supply. When it comes to parenting, context is paramount, because just about every conflict between a teenager and a parent boils down to a dispute as to context. (She wants the car so that she and her friends can go to a party, but you are worried about her driving at night and who those friends are.) This is the reason that you can use, not a manual, but a field guide. You will grow to appreciate the complexities of teenagers in general and will empathize with and influence your own children in particular. One further consequence is that you will realize how your children are, despite contrary signals, committed to a relationship with you—but committed to a *redefined* kind of relationship.

–TWO–

How familiar are these exchanges?

"What happened at school?"

"Nothing."

"How was your day?"

"Fine."

There does not seem to be much of an "exchange" going on in this archetypal moment in the life of a teenager's family. On the surface these inquiries certainly seem reasonable, hardly intrusive. And perhaps some parents somewhere will hear the news pertaining to the periodic table or *Romeo and Juliet*, or stand informed by a colorful accounting as to what took place at the coffee house or in the tryouts. But we all know the chances for that outcome are only slightly less remote than Jupiter.

Imagine, though, how the question is heard by some teenagers: roughly tantamount to a shot across the bow. How in the world can a teenager rationally explain that . . . *you know, everything happened, at least twice, including once to my best friend who's still not over it, and, hey, that was before lunch period, you wouldn't have believed it, it was so incredible, so weird, only now it's too boring to go through again, and, besides, what time's dinner anyway?*

Yes, teenagers may be shutting themselves off from their parents with a one-word screen, but more likely they themselves are, long after the fact, still interpreting and assessing, consciously and unconsciously, what happened today, still coming to terms with what it all means. By *Nothing*, by *Fine*, they could easily mean, *I'll get back to you later*. Which itself might really mean, *Could take a few hours—or days—or years, to figure that one out*. Adolescent development is neither linear nor progressive; it is more like a spiral, around and back, elliptical, not quite circular, usually passing through similar points on different planes. Or as the novelist A.M. Holmes once said, "The thing about adolescence that interests me is that it's the time when people are most themselves. It's also the time you re-live for the rest of your life."

What happened at school? How was your day? The problem with such questions is that they are central, and too provocative. Every day, often within the flick of an eye, transformative moments routinely occur in the lives of teenagers. These moments are sometimes mysterious and even risky. How can they possibly summarize the experience? Everything *did* happen, and they don't know quite how they feel about it yet, let alone how to explain it to their parents.

And yet all the participants in the family drama are lurching toward each other. In our seemingly different languages, we are communicating as urgently and as articulately as we can. Recent research empirically supports this view. The groundbreaking National Longitudinal Study on Adolescent Health indicates the primacy of the influence of parents and other adults—and downplays the authority of peers. In the end, in the words of the study's director: "We invest heavily in rule development, but that's not where the action is. The action is in adults' connecting with kids."

Adolescence can be shocking, uncomfortable, and painful to endure, as well as to observe. In nature the caterpillar creates a cocoon, where, hidden from view and over time, it grows into a butterfly. Then, when the time is right, a miracle occurs: a butterfly, suddenly using its wings. For human beings, there is no similar refuge. Astonishing growth takes place in plain view. In puberty, the body undergoes a series of hormonal and physical changes. The teenager is really along for the ride. The body becomes larger, it sexually matures. Rarely do any of these changes take place on an orderly path. Some thirteen-year-old girls have the bodies of women, and some seventeen-year-olds have yet to show signs of physical maturation. Some boys are six-feet tall and shaving by the time they are fourteen, while others have minimal body hair at eighteen. Throughout, teenagers are painfully and self-consciously aware of how they are shaping up—and, especially, of how they are deviating from the imaginary norm. (Of course, no teenagers can identify with confidence and precision the nature of the supposed norm.) Even so, the quest for normalcy makes them feel desperate, and nothing like normal, whatever that may be. Teenagers wrestle with these internal pressures even while they manage their lives in school, on the field, on the stage, at work, and in all the places in between.

It is no coincidence that a classic literary work often taught in high school is Kafka's "Metamorphosis." The story begins, chillingly, with young Gregor Samsa waking up one morning to discover that after a night of upsetting dreams he had been converted into a gigantic, repulsive insect. In the rest of the story, before he is thrown onto a dust heap, he struggles to survive, to communicate with his bewildered family, all the while yearning for love and understanding. All teenagers share with Gregor the shock of their own development. Their hormonal development unleashes feelings and ushers in a sexual blossoming; it rings in profound changes in the workings of the brain. Becoming a teenager is nothing less than waking up one day with a revised consciousness in an altered body. Teenagers experience this thunderbolt, too, but they do not know what has hit them. After all, it's never happened before.

Though teenagers seem to be a mind-boggling mix of drives and motivations, they are not opaque. This may be surprising to some. It is certainly good news for everyone. *Field Guide* addresses the isolation, fear, and silence you endure at this stage by showing you how to interpret the often bewildering changes and behaviors of your children. The reality is that teenagers are *there*, present to adults. Though in ways that are not initially clear or convenient, they are continually reaching out to us—for talk, friendship, knowledge, support, consideration, and wisdom. These moments are golden opportunities. We need to recognize and seize them. This is finally why this book is unabashedly hopeful. Because parents and their teenagers are growing alongside each other, there is, we believe, even in those inevitable dark moments, always and ever the possibility of regeneration.

1
Drinking and Driving

....

... when most adults look at their own lives, they place heavy emphasis on the combination of two factors . . . : choice and chance. We do not tell our life stories as examples of determinism of any kind. What is the last memoir you read whose author sees himself as a hapless actor playing out the lines and stage directions encoded in his DNA? Or as a blank slate on which his parents drew the road map?

—PERRI KLASS

Opposition is true Friendship.

—WILLIAM BLAKE

The Undesignated Driver

– One –

Last summer King High School was rocked. A car full of teenagers, most under the influence, plowed into a telephone pole, an accident that took the life of the driver, who was twice the legal limit. Why didn't anybody take the keys? Why didn't one of the sober kids take the wheel? Why didn't somebody call home?

At Josh's school across town, JFK, the faculty and administration stepped up alcohol-awareness programs. In addition, the Parents' Association resolved to reduce the chances of such an occurrence at their school. Most senior parents signed contracts not to allow drink to be served in their homes to teenagers. They also agreed that there would be no questions asked if their kids called for a ride home at any time. They didn't enjoy thinking that their kids were drinking on weekends and they didn't want to endorse it, but they were realistic, too. The seniors also signed contracts. They agreed to having a designated driver and pledged to call if they ever found themselves over their heads.

It was weird, and largely unspoken, but some JFK parents might be forgiven for thinking that, awful as the accident had been, maybe their own kids would take it as a screeching wake-up call. No one would call that a silver lining. At the same time, maybe their kids would be more careful than ever before, and maybe their parents could sleep better at night.

– Two –

The three boys flipped coins, and Josh came up heads and the others tails, which made him the designated driver. Steve and Dex did not bother to fake disappointment. Of course, they were major stars on the party scene, while Josh, even though he was also a senior, was a newcomer—and, honestly, he didn't drink much. Still, he was resolved to try a few things at this late stage in his high school career, and going out with guys like Steve and Dex constituted a dramatic change. Besides, at school and in classes the three of them got along pretty well, and when they mentioned the party to him on Friday, Josh saw no reason not to go: his social calendar wasn't what anybody would call busy.

Not long after the three arrived at the party, Josh was surprised for lots of reasons. For one thing, he found himself having a pretty good time. Being known as the designated driver was a kind of badge of honor—in a funny way. It certainly set him apart from most kids at the party. And yet it put him in with the other designated drivers, drinking Coke and watching the wheels come off the other kids as they drank and drank. It was like there were two different parties going on simultaneously. It was also, well, interesting to be stone sober and see how the other kids' true selves seemed to be coming out. True selves weren't always a pretty sight.

All right, self-righteousness did come easy to him. At least that's what his big sister always seemed to mean when she was angry with him, which was quite often. "Josh, you can be such a jerk without even trying hard." He was glad she was away at college. If he went to a local college, maybe he could talk his parents into giving him her room, which was bigger and nicer than his. Then again, maybe she had the right idea, taking off for school.

Several hours later, Josh was sipping mineral water and feeling superior when Dex stumbled over to him, eyes glazed and wearing a T-shirt he didn't have on when he came to the party.

"Louie Louie, we gotta go, party sucks."

"Really? It's early, it could get better." Not that he could testify from first-hand experience.

"OK, give me the keys, then, you can stay if you want."

"You're wasted, Dex."

"Joshua! Don't be like you always are."

"Still not giving you the keys." Josh did not know where he was getting the strength to stand up to Dex, but he couldn't stop doing it either. He looked for help from Steve, but he was dancing like a maniac with three girls, and it didn't look like anyone could get his attention. "We had an agreement," Josh said. "Don't do this, Dex."

"Don't do this, Dex," Dex mimicked. "Hey, Designated, we friends or not?"

"What's that got to do with anything?"

"Friends trust each other. I can drive. Plus, it's my car."

He did have a point about the car: it was his. Still, Josh held his ground: "I'm not going anywhere, and you're not going anywhere, we had an agreement. I'm the designated driver."

"Consider yourself undesignated. Give up the keys, now."

"No."

"Don't make me come over there. You're not my jailer, and not my mom."

"Just calm down, OK? Stay here, I'll get Steve and we can go, all right?"

"I don't want to go anywhere with you. It's my car."

"I can't give you the keys."

"You're going to make me do something I don't want to do."

"That's what I'm trying to stop you from doing."

"You are such a donna." Then Dex took a swing at Josh but didn't even come close to grazing him. That's when everybody in the party rushed up and separated them. In all the commotion and shouting, Josh heard a few things from Dex he wished he hadn't heard, but in a minute they were dragging Dex outside to calm down.

It all happened so fast that Josh didn't realize till after it was over that he was still shaking. Dex was a strong guy, and he tried to hit him and . . .

"Man, bummer," said Stacey, a girl Josh knew only from a safe distance in Physics class, where he used to watch her secretly most of the period when he wasn't contemplating gravity and the formula of 9.8 meters per second per second. She was somebody he yearned to talk with if she ever cut him a lucky break. Till now that moment had never arrived. "That wasn't right what Dex did," she said. "I know you were just trying to do the right thing." Her gravelly drawl made him feel itchy inside.

"I was?" Then he added. "I *was*, I guess. He OK?"

"Dex can get a little crazy at parties, is all. He'll be all right when he gets some fresh air. You'll see, he'll come back and give you a hug and apologize like mad, you wait. I'm glad you showed up at the party; I didn't expect you. Want *this*?"

This? That would be the joint Stacey was offering him with a smile.

"What?" Sure, he had tried it once before, but . . .

"It's pretty lightweight, go on. You deserve it, it'll calm you down."

Josh rolled around in his mind those notions she had broached: he did deserve it after what happened, and it would calm him down. *Time for changes, Josh, or what?*

– Three –

After midnight, Josh, Steve, and Dex stood alongside the car. They kept their eyes on it, as if they were afraid it could spring to life and drive itself away. Dex was in a more malleable mood and in yet another T-shirt, Steve was still flying, and Josh was spacey after a couple of tiny hits a few hours ago.

"Now what are we going to do?" Josh said out loud. He also wondered what happened to Stacey and if he had said or done something weird that accounted for her sudden disappearance tonight. Maybe Monday in class he might just look at her and tell by the look in her eyes if he was the dead meat he suspected he was.

"What do you mean?" Dex fumed. "You're driving us home."

"Stacey—"

"Was she there?"

"Stacey—I think I might be a little stoned, a little."

"Josh," Dex said, "the foot looks like it's on the other shoe now, Mister Designated."

"Maybe I should just call my dad." Josh and his family had talked about alcohol, yes, and they had their agreements, but he wasn't completely sure those agreements transferred to smoking dope.

"Maybe *you* can call *your* dad—no way I'm calling mine."

"Or maybe," Josh wondered, "maybe I'll just throw these keys into the bushes and we can walk home." He'd seen something like that once in a movie, and he always fantasized about how a gesture like that would feel.

"Let's not get carried away. Just drive. You're not that stoned, I can tell. Now *Steve*, he's that stoned. Besides, sometimes you can drive better if you're just a little stoned."

"Maybe I'm not really all that stoned. I probably can drive."

"Well," said Steve, "you can sure drive better than either of us."

"That's not much to go on, is it?" For Josh it wasn't a rhetorical question.

"I got to get home, Josh," said Steve. "I'm freezing."

"What Steve means," Dex explained, "is he's got a one-o'clock curfew, no excuses."

Steve's Conversation with His Math Teacher, Ms. Siegel

—That's some story, Steve. I'm relieved you got home safely.

—Yeah, that would have been a bad ending to a good night. It was a great party. I had a great time. I think I was doing my rendition of the Whirling Dervish.

—Why are you telling me all this?

—Not really sure. You seem cool, I thought you'd understand.

—OK. Maybe you're telling me because you're concerned about Dex and Josh? Dex did take a swing at him.

—No big thing. Dex blows up and five minutes later he's your best friend, no big deal, especially when he's drinking.

—Well, in my book that's a problem, but then again I don't know Dex that well.

—Not many people really know Dex, but I do. He's been my best friend since eighth grade. He'd do anything for me.

—And you'd do the same for him.

—Absolutely.

—How about Josh? Do you feel like he let you down and put you in a cross by getting stoned?

—Who am I to judge? We got home safely, and that's all that matters. Right?

—OK, but it seems to me that there was a problem when you guys decided how you were getting home.

—Yeah, they kind of got into it all over again.

—*They* got into it again? What about you?

—What do you mean, what about me? They were the ones getting into it with each other. And Josh was the one who got stoned.

—Funny, I see all three of you in the same boat. You had to get home too.

—Well, yeah, but it wasn't my boat and I wasn't the designated driver.

—Right, you were just an innocent bystander. Though if things had turned out differently maybe you would have been an innocent victim.

—It was between those two guys, and besides, I don't get in the middle of other people's problems. Why are you looking at me like that?

—Now I get it.

—Get what?

—Now I know why you're telling me all this.

—You do?

—I think when you thought about it afterwards is when you got scared. You were standing on the sidelines while your two friends decided your fate.

—It was a freaky way to end the night, and I don't want to go home that way ever again.

—And the reason you're telling me this is, you're worried you might do the same thing next time.

—Probably.

—Which kind of probably? Probably you're worried or probably you might do the same thing?

—Probably both.

Notes Home

The Good News, the Bad News,
and Some of the In-Between

Nothing arouses our anxieties quite like the car. Of course, the importance of the car to a teenager is impossible to overestimate. It is a safe haven, a ticket to fun and friendship, an apartment on wheels, a magic carpet that needs only half a tank of gas. It is a vehicle to an alternative world—games, parties, dating—places where the standards, the values, are nothing like home. And this is what scares us most, especially when alcohol is part of the equation. It is a fact, however, that most of our teenagers will, sooner or later, make potentially life-and-death decisions pertaining to driving and drinking. Alarmingly, "alcohol is the single biggest factor behind the leading cause of death among teenagers—traffic accidents."[1]

In a recent study of teenage drinking, the American Academy of Pediatrics concluded that "more than half of the youths ages 16–19 said they drank during the preceding month, but nearly two-thirds said they always appointed a designated driver."[2] The study also reported, however, that 80 percent of those surveyed thought it was fine to drink as long as there was a designated driver. And that's not all: nearly half thought designated drivers were still able to drink. Most parents who stumbled across the bulletin in their morning papers probably felt their stomachs take a roller coaster ride as they calculated the good news/bad news content of those mixed messages.

When it comes to teenagers, we as parents need to try to adjust to hearing less than 100 percent good news. That won't ever be easy, of course. But maybe those categories themselves are a little simplistic. And maybe theirs is a reality that stubbornly resists either/or categorizations.

Speaking of the story of Josh and friends, can we derive any good news? Of course: sometimes Josh did the right thing and somehow (as we find out through Steve's meeting with his teacher) they all got home safely. Is there bad news? Plenty. It is a possibility, verging upon a certainty, that somebody who was impaired drove that car home.

Let us cut to the heart of the parental hopes and anxiety generated by this narrative: Is there anything those boys' parents could have done to *guarantee* that they would not drive off in a state of diminished capacity? No. None of their curfews and agreements and contracts and conversations will necessarily preclude the teenager's making a serious error in judgment. And there's nothing you will find in this book, or in any responsible book, that will offer such vain assurance. The worst indeed does happen to normal kids like Josh, Dex, and Steve. Those arrest and accident statistics are haunting and depressing and real.

Now let's ask the hard question in a more pragmatic way. If the parents could not have ensured that their children would do the right thing, is there anything they could have done that would have *improved* the chances of their making a wiser choice, such as calling home or catching a cab or walking? (Or staying sober in the first place?) Yes. To explain why this is so, we will examine adolescent logic and decisionmaking, discuss parental influence during adolescence, and then spell out the best approaches for parents.

Are Teenagers Scared Straight?

When the nearby King High School suffered its tragedy, many parents at JFK believed that maybe their own kids would hear a wake-up call. But how useful are such cautionary lessons? In the short term, certainly, they can have an impact. If you are like most people, after you pass a gruesome car wreck on the highway, you drive very cautiously for a while and you solemnly resolve to keep within the speed limit and drive defensively. But how many of us forget that resolution within the week?

Not one of the teenagers in this story gives any indication of being "scared straight." Tonight, in the moment, those recollections of contracts and community meetings and alcohol education seem to be a million miles away from Josh and friends, and seem downright irrelevant to the problems at hand. Perversely, awareness of that other tragedy could even embolden some teenagers. They hear that that the driver who perished was totally drunk, and, really, all they've had is a few beers or a couple of hits. In other words, that experience has nothing to do with them, finally. Their case is unique. What's more, the community has suffered one tragedy this year, and there's no way a second one can occur. And besides, nothing really terrible can happen to them: they've got big plans for college and the whole world eagerly awaits their arrival.

The decision to use (or to refrain from using, for that matter) is complex. The allure it holds for a teenager can transfix them. Never underestimate the complexity of your teenager's social existence and private desires. Remember the antidrug campaign of some years ago, Just Say No? It's a strong and clear message, no doubt about it, and it may prove fairly effective for younger children. But the appeal of the idea for teenagers can be decidedly mixed. Nevertheless, parents may believe that memorizing this mantra will protect their teenagers from temptation and opportunity. Adolescents simply don't function that way, however. They don't automatically rally to a slogan predicated upon negation and a battle cry whose essence is denial. Madison Avenue lives off the susceptibilities of teenagers, but no company is going to cash in on Just Don't Do It. Affirmation of their individual selves and their personal values—that is what teenagers need and it does not easily reduce to sloganizing.

Living in the Moment

Probably none of those involved in this story started the night with the intention of getting into trouble, or at least into more trouble than they could deal with. What's more, if each had been individually interviewed by his parents before leaving the front door, each would likely have said nothing to inspire unease. "Yes," we can hear them pledging, "we'll be careful and we'll drive safely. We've got a designated driver." And yet before the night is through things will happen that would cause parents sheer dread and terror if they knew.

So how did they get to the point of taking such risks? This is not easy to analyze because every one of them in the course of the evening makes complicated decisions that are, though ultimately questionable, defensible *in the moment*. And *in the moment* is teenagers' home base.

Begin by putting yourself in Josh's place and Dex's place and Steve's place. If you think that any of them had a simple choice to make and that sensible alternatives, like calling home, were irresistible, reconsider. In their individual ways, each is trying to do the best thing possible under the circumstances. Josh, for instance, admirably stood up to Dex when he demanded the keys but then did a wrong thing when he smoked the joint, effectively undesignating himself. It's clear why in the second instance he might have been swayed to do exactly the thing he would never have expected himself to do. A temptation offered by a girl he is attracted to is hard, if not impossible, to pass up. Dex was generous with the car from the outset, and he invited Josh as a friend to come along, but then he got out of control after drinking. Stacey was kind and supportive of Josh, and of Dex, even as she was unintentionally derailing Josh and rationalizing Dex's pugnaciousness.

Steve, in a way, is the most complicated case of the three. He is a good friend and a good companion for a party, but he appears passive, even when his safety is at stake. But that's not quite it. He's all too ready to let Josh and Dex work out the situation, not because he is passive but because he is their friend and wants to pay them the respect friendship entails. He is the one who is later haunted by the experience of the night, so much so that he talks with Ms. Siegel, for reasons he cannot really articulate. Eventually, he concludes, with prompting, that he is very, very lucky he is alive to tell the tale. As we overhear his conversation with his teacher, we detect him in the act of growing up. Steve is gradually coming to terms with the role he played that night, as well as the more challenging role he declined. As a result, he has an invaluable opportunity to reflect on real friendship and responsibility. And that's something that deeply shakes him up, as it should—and as his teacher intends.

For a teenager, the contexts of decisionmaking are always shifting. That's what it means to be *in the moment*. A teenager's world is complicated, a series of fast-changing expectations, and his choices are tough to balance. Every move means a loss of one type or another. He can with absolute certainty and goodwill subscribe to contracts with his parents, can take in his health education, and can make resolutions to do the right thing. But none of these abstract positions will *necessarily* carry the moment. It is not all a matter of peer pressure, either. Josh, for instance, does not take the joint from Stacey because he fears that his peers would mock him otherwise. He takes it because this is the best invitation from Stacey he has ever received. It's just the opposite of group thinking: it is altogether personal and individual thinking.

What's a Parent to Do?

One key for parents in this vexed and anxious arena is not to make alcohol the subject of a power struggle. You should assert your authority, but that is only the first step. The problem is very similar to the one involving grades: if teenagers acquire the sense that they are merely players in your drama, that good grades are mainly a mechanism to please you and not themselves, they have no way to be themselves. In the long run, they will get good grades (or better grades) when they care about getting those grades. And they drive safely and make sound choices when they see that it is in their power too. This is why it is invaluable to communicate care to your children and a respect for their complexity. Do that, and you and your children are partners in—and for—life.

We are not in any sense minimizing the dangers of drinking and driving. Just the opposite. The truth is that your imagination of your child's predicaments, and your compassion for the difficulties his life poses, enables you to play a decisive role at a most urgent time.

Do Parents Matter Anymore?

Judith Rich Harris is the author of *The Nurture Assumption: Why Children Turn Out the Way They Do*, a best-selling work controversial for the counterintuitive thesis emblazoned on the book cover: "Parents matter less than you think and peers matter more." Harris argues that a candid scientific reconsideration of the research shows that there exists no causal connection between the parenting of children ("nurture") and the eventual adults these children grow into: that's why for her the supposed fruits of parental "nurture" are merely the illusory product of an unconvincing "assumption." For her, what matters most is the "group socialization" that takes place in the "environment" of peers.

Instantly, the theory elicited fervent denunciations from eminent authorities and equally impassioned testimonials from comparably credentialed readers. Even some of those troubled by the argument found it a timely, useful corrective of parenting books, or at least those that suggest some magical formula for raising happy, successful children. Perhaps this theory could relieve some anxiety or self-recrimination on the part of parents; after all, if parents don't ultimately matter, they can't be blamed for whatever goes wrong.

Yet psychologist and author Howard Gardner, among others, adduced a danger: Harris's book could be "potentially harmful" if it discouraged "parents from promoting their own beliefs and values, and from becoming models of behavior, at a time when such values and models should be clearly and continually conveyed to children." And he suggested that the book was, on the whole, irresponsible.[3]

We think that some of the vitriol aimed at Harris's book is unwarranted. For one thing, although her critics usually missed this, she does not contend that it's acceptable to mistreat or abandon your kids. Hardly. In fact, she argues in several places that it is extremely important to treat your kids respectfully, kindly, and generously. Why? Because they are human beings and deserve no less. In other words, she invokes the "moral imperative" as being "good enough reason to be nice to your kid."

Make no mistake, though. *The Nurture Assumption* is a fascinating work and a bracing read for all parents—and bracing in particular for those parents who are authors of parenting books, such as we are, even if we do not traffic in parenting formulas, magical or otherwise. Throughout this field guide we show how teenagers grow up just outside the purview of their parents. To some degree this seems to align us provisionally with Harris, but in most crucial respects—that is, in most practical respects—we must part company with her. Here's why we do, and why we believe parents do deeply, broadly, intensely matter both in the short- and long-term.

Parental Influence, Reexamined

Parenting is not a science; it's an art. Like the other arts, it resists codification and quantification. After all, we don't rely upon epidemiological or biogenetic or anthropological research to illuminate definitively the effect of, say, music on our lives or to explain the love and responsibility we individually affirm for our children or our spouses or our friends. Why? Because our feelings and our commitments are mysterious and difficult to speak about in the abstract, much less to quantify for statistical tabulation. That is ultimately why any so-called parenting style could never consist of a set of rules and injunctions. One day, for example, raising your voice in exasperation might be the right thing to do, though on most other occasions it would spell disaster.

Parents can effectively influence their teenagers only when they better understand the worlds their teenagers inhabit. Yes, peers are crucial. And though genetics is easily misunderstood, let's never lose sight of it: kids are not their parents even though they share their DNA. Yet everyone is familiar with the pervasive stereotypes suggesting that parents are fundamentally clueless about their kids' formative experiences (which are often assumed to be taking place in their peer groups). These stereotypes also suggest that when kids reach out to their parents (which happens continually) or vice versa, when parents reach out to their kids, they are stretching out from opposite sides of the Grand Canyon. We believe these stereotypes are dangerously misleading. So what is *influence* anyway, and how would we know we have—or had—any?

Take our story of the "undesignated" driver as a case in point. If you are a perfect role model of abstinence or temperance, will your child automatically follow suit? Of course not. All the human beings we know, and all the human beings who are your children, are too complicated for us to predict their behavior. We teach our children, we guide and support them, but we do not control them and their destiny. For that we should be glad. Because we cannot control them, they are free not only to love us and respect us but also to take responsibility for their own lives. And that is the essence of being a parent: letting your adolescent children go, but carefully, by stages and degrees (though by no means abandoning them), so that they may become who they are.

But in terms of influence, consider this. If you *don't* talk about alcohol, *don't* discuss responsibility behind the wheel, *don't* give them an out by establishing a no-questions-asked policy, *don't* assure them you will support them in complicated circumstances, and *don't* show them your willingness to listen to their side, what alternatives do they possess? That is, you influence them when you give them a way to cope and a chance to do the safe thing. It is not a cognitive matter, either, although cognition is not irrelevant (that's why you pitch your conversation on this topic differently, depending on age). For teenagers, knowledge of where their parents stand on crucial issues is hardly academic, and it is certainly more useful than ignorance. If teenagers are faced with risky possibilities and can conceive of no safe alternatives, what can we expect that they will do? Can you *control* them and their decisions? No. Can you *influence* them and their decisions? Definitely.

Again, it's essential to reimagine the terms, scope, and shape of our influence. Just keep in mind that parents who aren't from time to time surprised by their children simply aren't paying attention. Now let's go into a few areas where you might do something that will increase the chances of your teenager making sounder choices than those made by Josh, Dex, and Steve.

The Time for More Conversation About Alcohol Is Now

Like the sex talk, the conversation about alcohol is one that few parents look forward to, yet it is the conversation we all must have, again and again. Initiating the dialogue sends the message that you care, that you are clued in, and that you are realistic. On this issue, as well as sex, a vague, dreamy parent is exactly the parent a teenager does not need.

What is it that you are saying to yourself? *My teenager and I have always had a good relationship and she will come to me if she needs information.* But that's what probably will not happen. You need to meet her more than halfway. Why? For one thing, you know better than to take any chances. And for another, your kids need you to understand that they don't know everything without having to reveal their blind spots to you.

Or maybe you are saying, *Unfortunately, I should have had the conversation already, but I missed the opportunity in the distant past.* Forget it. It is never too late. Of course, it is not the same approach for a fifteen-year-old who is not going to parties or driving yet and an eighteen-year-old who is; and for that matter, it is not the same for your child and his best friend.

Or maybe you are thinking, *The school's health program has already covered this ground.* Good for the school. They are taking their job seriously, your child stands to benefit, and you should deeply appreciate it. They have done their part; now you do yours.

What? You're Not Perfect?

Suppose you, like most people, are not a teetotaler. Do you think that because you drink your authority on this topic is undercut? Well, it isn't. You are an adult, and there is a difference. You do have authority, you do have knowledge, you do have experience, you do have perspective. These are all powers that your child is acquiring. But do not be surprised when your teenager reminds you: "You did x, y, and z when you were in high school, and you turned out all right, so why can't I?" Or: "You drink wine at dinner, you have a cocktail when you come home from work. Why can't I have a beer on the weekends?"

Teenagers, especially older ones, do have that uncanny ability to zero in on our illusions, don't they? Maybe you do drink a little bit more than you should, who knows? Well, be advised, there are some who believe that they do know: your own kids. They are keeping extensive mental notes on your activities, choices, and decisions. And if you find yourself taking a hard look at your own habits after such a conversation with your teenager, consider yourself one with most other parents.

How much personal revelation is worthwhile? To be specific, how *useful* is it for your teenagers to know about those wild times in high school or college? (Or those mild times, for that matter?) Ultimately, you are the best judge, but such information should generally be disbursed on a need-to-know basis. That is, figure out how much you are comfortable with sharing—and then don't even get close to that amount. Is it all right not to answer a direct question? Yes. And it is also all right to give an indirect answer. *Did you smoke marijuana in high school, Dad?* "None of your business" won't be a good answer, but others might be: "That's not something we need to talk about right now." Or: "There are some things I used to do I wish I hadn't, and that might be one of them." Or "I've learned from my mistakes, but you don't have to make my mistakes in order to learn what I learned." That is, draw a limit you can live with and be honest within it. After all, nobody needs to see somebody else's dirty laundry. Remember, your teenager thinks he understands you and, at the same time, is pretty sure you are operating under a few misconceptions about him. In other words, your teenage children really don't need (or want) the details. Too much information is as bad as not enough. Don't worry: by the time he is sixteen or so, he will see your clay feet and love you anyway, or maybe love you even more because of your imperfections.

A few other words about this conversation. It needs to be honest, personal, forthright, and compassionate. But it needs to be centered on your teenagers and their experience. This can be more likely achieved if you avoid the old chestnut *do as I say, not as I do*—the formula for hypocrisy your kids will deplore. After all, it's their health, experience, and risk at the heart of the conversation, not yours. Before you clear your throat with them to start this conversation, it will help you to ask yourself hard questions, such as, "Why do I not want them to drink?" How you answer that question will enable you to shape an approach that will carry you to the high ground, where you should stay whenever you can. For one thing, it's absolutely OK to admit how terrified you are when you think about your child drinking, about what can go wrong. That in itself is a kind of reality check for them, even if they do fundamentally count themselves immortal. Your telling them that their lives are precious and that they are not immortal could help them down the road.

In addition, discuss the law and the legal implications of alcohol consumption, but don't make law the centerpiece of the conversation. Why? There's never been a rule, an injunction, or a law that a teenager can't debate. More important, the law is impersonal, whereas these conversations must be personal if they are to work. That is, your concern is about the health and safety of your son or daughter, not about some generic teenager. If you focus on the law, too, you are emphasizing compliance and obedience with regard to alcohol at the moment when your teenager is thinking about alcohol in very different terms: freedom and choice. At bottom, when you stress exclusively the law, you are relying on external authority just when your teenager needs to hear your individual voice of authority and wisdom.

If it's appropriate for you and your teenager, involve an expert or the school or a book that makes sense. Ideally, these conversations should take place well in advance of driving or well in advance of applying for a permit, for that matter. As we said earlier, however, it's never too late.

"Got a Minute?"

There is no correct way to have the conversation. If you are clear about what you are saying and if you listen, however, you will not go far astray. Now, at the risk of oversimplification, here are the essential points:

1. Get their attention in a place where they can be receptive, like the living room with the phone turned off or taking a ride or in their room just before bed. In other words, not just before leaving the house on a Friday night or as you are all rushing off for the day.
2. Be clear about the topic. *I want to talk to you about drugs and alcohol. I want to talk to you about drinking and driving.* There's no perfect segue to this conversation, so don't wait for one. And don't try to append this talk to another one, say, about grades, chores, or summer plans.
3. You go first. For one thing, once you announce the topic, he will be watching for the cues as to where this is headed, and he won't tip his hand until he knows for sure. You establish the tone and the boundaries.
4. Acknowledge reality. Drugs and alcohol are easily accessible, and both of you know it. "By age 13, half of the nation's teens say they can buy marijuana and 43 percent of them say they can buy acid, cocaine, or heroin."[4]
5. Make it safe for them to be honest. Let them know that their honesty may make you uncomfortable but that you want to hear from them anyway.
6. State your views. *I don't want you to use or drink, and here's why* . . . Only you know the reasons why you don't want them to experiment. And it's definitely all right to say something like *Because it scares the hell out of me.*
7. Listen.
8. Listen some more when they are silent. Silence speaks volumes.
9. Tell them you love them.

That Other Conversation: Alcohol and Driving

As your common sense and your selectively unforgetful teenagers remind you, what you teach about drugs and alcohol is expressed through your actions as much as through your rules and boundaries. Some parents fear, however, that they are sending a message encouraging drinking when they endorse the idea of a designated driver. But the message is not mixed, and here's why: *this* message is ultimately about safety and responsibility, and it's rooted in teenage reality. And you can send no mixed message as long as those issues are uppermost. In the last analysis, of course, though it is tempting sometimes to contemplate, you cannot shackle them to their bedposts and you cannot monitor their every activity outside the home.

The phone call late at night: every parent's heart skips a beat. Please don't turn off the phone—and please don't leave your children without the means to reach out to you for help on weekends, or any other time. But if the phone call wakes you to ask you to pick them up because they're unable to drive, or if their designated driver is unable to drive, it doesn't mean there aren't consequences. No questions may be asked that night, all right, but the next day should be dedicated to having a family conversation. Do so without forgetting that ultimately they have shown themselves—by virtue of that phone call—responsible. Teenagers have the knack for being responsible about being irresponsible; that is, it's irresponsible to drink at a party, but it's responsible not to drive or not to be driven by somebody else who has been drinking. Kids need to see you grasp the levels of responsibility. If they don't see that you can make the distinctions, they won't trust you. And that trust can save their lives.

Curfews are similarly tricky, involving the ways in which kids can be alternately responsible and irresponsible. You know what hour you are comfortable with, and you need to explain your reasoning and your feelings as fully as you can. But to be blunt, you don't want them to risk their lives to make a curfew. (Notice that a strict curfew may have contributed to Steve's disposition to go along with Josh and Dex.) Are you supplying them a free pass to ignore their curfew? No. You will sense if they respect the curfew, and you will know if they are taking advantage of your flexibility. Teenagers are experts at manipulating rules, however, so try to keep your rules simple and sensible. Mutual trust will solve the vast majority of anticipatable problems.

How Do You Know If Your Teenager Has a Serious Drinking Problem?

You can never know for sure. But never ignore the evidence. Are grades drifting? Are behaviors changing? Do you find strange bottles in the garbage or recycling bin? Are their excuses and their tales getting more and more convoluted? Who are these new best friends you've never heard of before?

Two types of parents have problems here. One overreacts and the other underreacts. Neither will help. Don't expect perfection unless you enjoy disappointment. And don't expect the worst, because you will bring it about. You don't have a teenager—whoever you are and whoever he or she is—who won't be tempted to drink, and only a few rare kids won't test you and themselves. Also rare, however, are those teenagers who won't eventually rise to the level of your trust and your honest, unsparing concern about their lives when you communicate it to them.

What to do if the day comes when you have caught your teenager drinking? You should realize the following: 99.9 percent of the time a parent catches a child it isn't the first drinking incident for him or her. (As scary as it sounds, it is fairly easy for teenagers to use alcohol without getting caught. So by the time you catch them you have an indication that they are probably experimenting regularly.) This is the time to consider a professional assessment. Here's why.

Assessment is not punishment. When you suspect your child has a learning disability, for example, you consult a professional diagnostician. When your child complains of low energy and flulike symptoms, you take her to the pediatrician. For the same reasons, you call your community counseling center and receive a referral for an assessment from a drug and alcohol counselor. All you are looking for is guidance and information. You may discover that your intuition was correct: it was an isolated incident that probably will not be repeated. On the other hand, you may learn that your teenager has a problem with alcohol. While this is difficult to hear, it is more difficult (and dangerous) not to hear.

A professional counselor will interview your teenager about his habits and attitudes. (Your teenager may undergo urinalysis, but not necessarily.) In any case, you will receive confidential, candid information about the depth of his problem. If appropriate, the counselor will issue recommendations for further treatment, from periodic check-ins to participation in a time-limited group program to, in extreme cases, residential therapy.

But don't dismiss your own knowledge. That is, keep in balance your own *expert* assessment. You have access to your children that is not available to professional evaluators: you see them day in and day out. You have a history and you have a future. And because of that, you should never take their drinking lightly and never downplay its significance. When you catch your kids drinking, it's time for the full-court family press. And by the way, that's exactly what your teenager has been hoping for. That's why you were able to catch him in the first place, though this is something he will not acknowledge until he is, say, well into his twenties. It is not that he is masochistically seeking punishment. Instead, he may well be relieved to bask in the attention that comes with being caught, which he otherwise does not know how to ask for, or receive.

Beyond that, however, it is a fact of parenting life that you will probably never hear about the near misses. For instance, if Josh had driven home that night, neither his parents nor the other boys' parents would have heard that information. Because teenagers live in the moment, last night is already ancient history for them. In truth, parents are usually in the dark about what happens in their children's daily lives, experiences at tryouts or in the election or on the field trip. When it comes to romance, they will usually be about half a relationship behind. And so on. What does this mean? For one thing, it's not easy being a parent of a teenager. For another, it's not easy being a teenager either.

The Last Word

There is one parent we know of who captured the essence of this chapter's message in a deceptively simple way. When he would see his daughter the morning after she went out with her friends, he would look her in the eye and say, "I'm glad you're here." At first she would respond, "What are you talking about? I'm always here for breakfast." "That's not what I mean," he would say, conveying somehow that he had spent an anxious night and that he was glad she was safe and in his life.

Focus on what's important. Look your teenagers in the eye. Let them know you are glad they are alive. That's one message they can't hear often enough.

2

Motivation and Success

Without Contraries there is no progression.

—William Blake

Even the sudden, tumbling finches
have fled into smoke, and the one road
whitened in moonlight leads everywhere.

—Philip Levine, "Ask for Nothing"

Participate in Your Own Experience

Miki's favorite restaurant was the Green Glen, a popular sandwich and salad place. One night, when she and her father were walking the dog, they noticed a Help Wanted sign hanging on the window. Miki balked at first when he suggested she apply for the job, but she eventually figured it wouldn't kill her to put away a few dollars for college. And she liked the idea of having her own money too. Even so, she was surprised when she was hired despite having no experience. Still, as soon as she was assigned her own sections, she informed her parents and her stepparents they were not to show up during her shifts—unless they were prepared to leave outrageous tips.

During the school year Miki could only work weekends, of course. Management was accommodating. Most of the employees were her age or a little older. In fact, one of the assistant managers was a student at the university and the other was a senior at her own school. The tips beat baby-sitting money (no more diapers or two-year-olds having tantrums either), with the added bonus that she wouldn't have to give up her weekend nights to work. During the upcoming summer she was counting on making lots of money by being scheduled every day.

Lately, though, Miki had a problem, a problem by the name of Sooner, the assistant manager. She had an attitude.

"Hey, order's been up there a while." That was Sooner to Miki, who was working the left side today, usually the tougher part of the floor. Working? She was chatting with some customers who sat at the counter, obviously her friends.

"OK, OK, OK." Miki's tone was a little chilly, which Sooner didn't miss. All Miki could think was, couldn't the girl see she was doing the best she could? If it was so important, she should go and deliver the pastrami on rye and tuna melt herself. She had to embarrass Miki in front of her friends too.

Later, when Miki checked out at the end of her shift, Sooner asked to talk. They went out back, where the walk-in and dish room were.

Miki was a little irritated. She had places to be. It was soon going to be Saturday night and, as usual, she had plans. Probably that wouldn't matter to somebody like Sooner, though, who lived for her job.

"You OK, Miki? Is there something bothering you?"

What was wrong was that Sooner was bugging her. "Everything's just fine, but I really need to get going. There's this great concert at Jansen Park I need to get ready for."

"You do seem to be in a hurry."

Perceptive—for an assistant manager, thought Miki.

"You know, you didn't do all your side work."

This came out of right field. "I did everything I was supposed to." What the hell was she talking about?

Sooner ticked off the duties Miki was supposed to complete before closing out. About half were completed, while the other half were either done halfheartedly or not at all, she claimed.

Miki shot her a look that was intended to singe her stupid bushy eyebrows. Didn't she have anything better to do? Of course not, this was the girl's life, her job. She used to be cool when she started. Maybe not cool, but certainly all right. It was Sooner who first interviewed her, she recalled. How come she couldn't cut her a break lately?

"I know you don't respect *me*, Miki, but you should respect your job."

That was a leap, but Miki didn't have time to deal with Sooner's personal problems. "What's to respect? It's a job, it's not my life. I get through it."

"OK, what about respecting yourself? Don't you care if you do a good job? Doesn't this job mean anything to you besides the measly paycheck?"

"This job has nothing to do with me." At the same time, from Miki's point of view, the paycheck wasn't so measly.

"You're right about that."

"What's that supposed to mean?"

"I mean that if you don't shape up in a hurry you could lose this job."

"Are you threatening me? Don't you have anything better to do with your time than get all over my case?"

"Listen, this isn't about you. It's about the job. People are tired of picking up after you."

"Do what you got to do. I'm not going to beg for a job."

"Nobody's asking you to beg, Miki."

"Listen, this greasy spoon is the high point of your life, not mine." Miki decided right then and there that she could easily avoid Sooner when she ran into her at school. And for sure, none of her friends were friends with Sooner. "Maybe that's why you are hassling me? You jealous?"

"Wow, are you ever off base. Are you really that blind? Miki, if I were you—"

"Which you aren't." Thank God, she said to herself, or I'd—

"Hey Miki, you want to keep working here it's pretty simple. Act like you care."

Miki's Conversation with Her Stepfather

—Hey, Phil, don't you hate it when people just lord it over you? They're such pathetic tiny people.

—I can't follow you all the time, Miki. What are you talking about?

—People with a power complex, with an attitude. Like they have a badge on, and you're the perp.

—You're the what?

—Don't you ever watch TV? The criminal, like, the perp.

—Oh, the *perpetrator*.

—Didn't I just say that?

—Go back to people lording over it over you. What are you talking about?

—The assistant manager where I work. Or maybe where I used to work.

You'd think she was God, telling me to do things.

—Like what?

—Seat those people. Serve those dishes. Pick up those plates. Do your side work. Smile.

—Smile?

—OK, I was exaggerating about the smile part. But you get the point.

—Sounds like what she's asking you . . .

—Telling me!

—OK. What she is telling you is to do your job. And isn't that what she's supposed to do as assistant manger? And aren't these things you're supposed to do on your own? What am I missing?

—Just about everything so far. First, respect. Second, what am I, an airhead? Third, I really like the money. Fourth, that job is not my life, but losing it is going to really screw things up for me.

—Are you thinking about quitting your job because you don't like it?

—It's not about liking or not liking. It's about showing up and getting paid.

—You get paid for showing up?

—I'm not employee of the month but I pretty much get around to everything, I guess.

—OK. If the assistant manager didn't remind you to seat, serve, pick up, or whatever, you would do it on your own?

—Well, sure. It's just that they all don't have to be done the second a person walks into the restaurant or the very instant the food comes up. I mean nobody is perfect.

—Hmm.

—Don't hmm me. You sound like Mom after she takes one of her classes in Creative Listening to Teenagers. I mean, I work hard enough, usually, but Sooner's still on my case. Who made her the work police anyway?

—The owners, maybe? Didn't you say Sooner's a senior at your school?

—Hey. Whose side you on? Now I'm going to have to find another job this summer. I mean, I don't really mind the restaurant. But I would hate getting canned.

—Is it too late to turn it around? You know, change the manager's mind?

—*Assistant* manager. Plus, you don't know her. Besides, I'm not even sure I could or would want to please her. Like she watches the coffee machine all day long. I don't even drink coffee, let alone know how to make it.

—They didn't train you?

—Even if I could make coffee she wouldn't be happy with me.

—Am I hearing you say you want to do a good job?

—I just want to keep the job.

—Well, good workers are always hard to find.

—Why, you know any?

—Seriously, you want to be a good waitress, or not?

—Sometimes.

—Sometimes? You think that's what Sooner's getting at?

—I guess.

—Who're you upset at, Sooner or yourself?

—Sometimes you sound like one of those radio therapists.

—Is that good?

—You'll have to check with Mom.

—Whatever, but what exactly is your status at work?

—Officially? Probation.

—So there's still time to save your job.

—Technically you could say that.

Notes Home

The Mystery of Motivation

Prominent motivational speakers are always in demand. These celebrity coaches, politicians, artists, and leaders deliver messages valued by corporations, educational institutions, and other organizations. All of them emphasize similar themes: *Success never comes without a dear price . . . Life is hard . . . 1 percent inspiration, 99 percent perspiration . . . Each of us has a unique and valuable contribution to make . . .* It is a rare speaker, though, who says something we haven't already heard more than once before. In a sense their real worth consists of reminding us what we have known all along about ourselves but have managed to forget over time or have had drained out of us. (Curiously, "dis-motivation" is generally better understood. At one time or another we have all been discouraged by a mentor or an authority. A word, a gesture, or even a non-remark was all it took to get us *not* to do or try something. These experiences account for some of our most painful memories of growing up.) Even though the lasting impact of motivational speakers is unclear or hard to explain, many would testify that afterward they are indeed inspired to work harder, be more sensitive, and do more—at least in the short term. At the same time, even though we do not know for certain what motivates people, we all agree it is a good thing—and much better than the alternatives.

Teenage motivation, though, remains one of the most inscrutable mysteries of the universe. Some kids seem to have it, others don't, and others seem to pull it out of their hats at the last second. It is what makes an athlete of lesser natural talent sometimes outperform the more gifted one. It is what makes average students excellent ones. And, as in this story, it is what differentiates dependable employees from unreliable ones.

Motivating a Teenager

All parents wish to see evidence of drive in their teenagers. When it is lacking, most parents worry. They strive to inspire their kids. Usually they employ rewards and punishments to do so, which may work in the short run but actually inhibit self-motivation over the long run. As Alfie Kohn writes in his groundbreaking book *Punished by Rewards*, "What rewards and punishments do produce is *temporary compliance.* They buy us obedience. If that's what we mean when we say they 'work,' then yes, they work wonders."

> But if we are ultimately concerned with the kind of people our children will become, there are no shortcuts. Good values have to be grown from the inside out. Praise and privileges and punishments can change behavior (for a while), but they cannot change the person who engages in the behavior—at least, not in the way we want. No behavioral manipulation ever helped a child develop a commitment to becoming a caring and responsible person. No reward for doing something we approve of ever gave a child a reason for continuing to act that way when there was no longer any reward to be gained for doing so.

Of course, it grates when a teenager underperforms. We think about why, of course, but mainly we think about how to correct the situation and turn the teenager around. The key, however, is to realize that the why and the how are absolutely, if mysteriously, connected. If we do not understand this, we make all the conventional mistakes.

For example, parents who see their children's grades plummet think they have to do something, anything, to get their message across—as if the child could be unaware of the gravity of the situation. The standard response, for instance, might be to ground the teenager or to limit participation in supposedly distracting extracurricular activities and sports. And yet studies of the connection between academic performance and interscholastic sports demonstrate that grades rise during the season of participation. A moment's reflection will convince you why this is true: the teenager is more likely to use time prudently because there is less to squander. A student who does not have practice and game commitments could be prone to procrastinate. During the season he is operating out of a consideration of achievement and his incentive is deeper, borne of the desire for success. He is also engaged in an activity that makes him feel good about himself. As a result, he has more to give. As the adage suggests, if you want something done, give the task to a busy person.

Nonetheless, many parents out of desperation will use this threaten-and-deny approach. The teenager may not go to a movie on Saturday night and she must be in her bedroom at four o'clock every day. But there is no way to guarantee that homework will be done or, more importantly, done well. After all, a teenager who has been underperforming may now grow bitter and angry. How can that be a formula for success? Yes, family or school can claim, *At least we're doing something to address the situation.* Or, *Now she knows we take these matters seriously.* True enough. And there may even be some short-term changes (though even this is not a good bet). We may hear the tapping of the keyboard from outside the bedroom door, we may see books and not CDs piled up on the bed. For an hour, a week, or a month, we may detect signs of improvement in grades and so on. But the threaten-and-deny strategy begins at the wrong end of the problem. Here's why.

There is an assumption that the specter of loss and the inculcation of fear will somehow right the course and force a teenager to be productive. After all, adults know how at times they motivate themselves by imagining bleak consequences for failure or procrastination. Many use the dread of ruin in order to inspire them to finish that project on time or make that call. An edict from on high—*Finish the project!*—can also generate productivity. But tasks completed under those circumstances will not be as satisfying. Ultimately, excellence, creativity, and passion follow from the pursuit of personal satisfaction. The same is true for teenagers.

Consider this analogy. When your one-year-old is crying and won't go to sleep, you do everything you can because you know that she needs her sleep, that she wants to sleep, and that she needs some encouragement. You hold her, you walk her, you lie down next to her. She sleeps eventually. That was then. Eventually at some point, though, she needed to learn how to put herself to sleep. It wasn't pleasant to watch her learn; there were hours of crying when you wanted to go into her room and pacify her.

When it comes to responding to your teenagers' shortcomings, the same is true. They, too, need to teach themselves. (Or are you planning on moving into their college dorm?) Does that mean, for instance, you should not offer help with homework? Of course not, but it doesn't mean you do it for them. If there is a word in the night's reading assignment that they do not understand and they ask for your help, go to the dictionary with them and look it up together. If they cannot solve an equation, invite them to articulate their confusion and to ask questions. Teenagers need your support, but it is a fine line between supporting them in learning these skills and taking over their problems. In this way, you are reprising your earliest role in your child's life: teacher. Similarly, your teenager is reprising her role as a child. Was she ever tired of learning how to do something? Did she ever say, I already know everything I need to know about the clouds in the sky, the pretty bugs under the rocks, the way appliances work, how birds fly, and if fish sleep?

But wait. Perhaps you are a pragmatist who values results more than anything. And suppose you say, Who cares if my teenager is enjoying her work, just as long as it is being completed? The problem with making such a move is that, ironically, you are not seeing the bottom line. Why? Because without personal satisfaction she cannot conceive of any results as being worthwhile. Never sever success from satisfaction. If you do, you have given her a recipe for cynicism and, a little bit down the road, depression too.

Self-Motivation

Motivation is not a constant. That is, teenagers are not uniformly, coherently, absolutely motivated (or unmotivated) all the time about everything. Like adults, they have bad weeks or bad semesters. Beyond that, life keeps getting in the way, sending up new priorities and occasionally erasing all priorities for a while. Falling in love may cause soccer to pale in comparison. Getting the lead in the school play may lead to paring down the list of friends. Needing to make money for car insurance may mean that homework suffers. A crisis in the family may divert your teenager's attention away from writing papers and toward spending time with friends. Keep things in perspective. For example, getting unsatisfactory grades in the ninth grade (for the student who previously performed well) probably predicts little for achievement in the twelfth.

This is what you can do as parents. First things first. No one can make anybody else self-motivated. That does not mean, however, that our hands are tied. Instead, we need to ask a different set of questions. Not, What are the surefire things *I* can do to get my child working up to her level? But instead, Based on my relationship with her and based on who she is, what will help *her* see not only that she is capable of better work but that better work is in her best interest? These are convoluted, vast, and complicated questions. And importantly, they are all based on being in relationship with your teenager. The stronger your relationship, the more you can do.

Motivation and Relationship

When we find ourselves dealing with a complicated, difficult teenager who evinces no motivation to succeed (or even survive) in school, on the team, or at work, it is important, first of all, to acknowledge to ourselves, and to the teenager, that we are in deep waters. If we are seeking some tried-and-true strategy, we are doomed. If we presume that a rational, cognitive approach is always effective ("you are very bright and very talented but you are undercutting yourself by not living up to your potential"), experience will disabuse us. We need to address the underlying reasons for the absence of motivation. But that means we need to address the character and personality of the teenager—a daunting prospect but, then again, the soundest prospect we have. That also means altering the discourse. Instead of restricting our attention to objective measures—grades, minutes on the court, or restaurant side work completed—we need to lead our teenagers to connect success with self-satisfaction. It's not a matter of pointing out, for instance, that Cs or Ds are intolerable to you; it's a matter of showing her what she can gain when she invests herself: knowledge, power, confidence, security, excitement. This conversation is the best game in town, and it's the only kind of conversation that is not demeaning or antagonistic. What's more, it builds on the expectation of success as it fosters your ongoing relationship.

Do we mean that if your child has three Ds, for instance, and is verging on probation that the conversation still needs to be about satisfaction and success? Yes. For a teenager, grades or related incentives are not adequate motivators. The payoff must be deeper.

The more profound incentive is to see the image of the person she desires to be—capable, competent, responsible—reflected by an adult she respects. One teacher gives a D, and the student sees only his inadequacy and limitations. Another teacher gives a D and leads that student to see a way to grow and improve. One coach criticizes a player's overhead serve in volleyball and the player feels miserable. Another coach points up what's wrong with the serve but explains what's going right, too. The struggling math student and the volleyball player both know they need to improve. But teenagers respond productively to adults who hold them accountable while simultaneously sending positive, supportive signals. That is, the student struggling with his math homework sees hopefulness and effort confirmed, not inadequacy. Or the volleyball player who feels awkward learning the overhead serve sees herself advancing in the mastery of a difficult skill. Struggle can be good for teenagers, but only if they see the struggle as leading somewhere they deem worthwhile.

Bear in mind that your children have relationships with other adults, such as teachers, coaches, and managers. Reach out to these adults. They can help, for the same reasons you can—they matter to your kids and your kids matter to them.

A danger lies herein, however. Teenagers are susceptible to manipulation. For example, they play in pain to impress the coach and are injured as a result; they listen to a cultic pitch from someone they find charismatic and become enthralled; they plagiarize a paper in order to live up to the expectations of their favorite teacher and find themselves in trouble. A famous gymnastics coach once said he "had no idea he might be damaging his young pupils by calling them idiots and imbeciles."[1] These are examples of motivation and motivators gone insane. Know the people coaching and teaching your teenager.

Finally, the one thing that has any chance of inspiring teenagers to do better, to go beyond themselves, is conveying that they and their work matter to you personally. This has nothing to do with being prescriptive, and it does not subvert your encouragement of work for its own sake. When you look at a report card, for instance, your conversation should be about learning and working, the effort and the interest, the high points and the low. When a parent says, "I don't care what your grades are as long as they represent your best effort" and means it, a teenager trusts his parent and feels encouraged to love learning. Grades are signs and measurements, but they are also educational tools. They are not the end of a conversation but the beginning of one.

Another Look at "Role Models"

As a matter of course, teenagers have lots of role models. None are drawn to a role model who is a miserable success or one who is a happy flop. Instead, teenagers are compelled by the intellectual rigor exhibited by a math teacher, the commitment they observe in a swimmer, the compassion they sense in a minister, or the beauty represented by a painter. They fashion an idea of their ideal self out of their relationships with many people. What role models have in common is that they appear to integrate accomplishment and joy. Because teenagers are idealistic, a life created around accomplishment and joy is the only one worth aspiring to. (Consult the Appendixes for an overview of how teenage idealism evolves over the years.)

Of course, such integration can come at a high price, and as parents we need to understand how teenagers seek out and make use of role models. Say your teenager becomes enamored of the idea of being a champion swimmer because she has recently met one. Say she is serious enough to begin a rigorous new workout regimen. Soon she realizes that she must practice twice a day for hours at a time and that her whole day, her whole life, in fact, has been reorganized. At first, this is exhilarating because such a new life feels so clear and pure. She imitates her role model as faithfully as she can. When reality kicks in, however, a week, a month, a semester later, maybe she will reconsider. She may start to think about the freedom she has lost in the pursuit of her new goal and the restrictions it has imposed on her life. She may realize that a champion swimmer is not who she is after all. Perhaps she was drawn not to the swimming but to what the life of a champion swimmer represented. Once she grasps this, she will be free to look for meaning elsewhere, and a more genuine expression of herself, instead of an imitation of another, may emerge. Whether or not it turns out that she is destined to be a champion swimmer or not, what matters is that she responded to the appeal heard within herself. Coming to terms with the reality is nothing less than a step toward her becoming an adult. She is now free to try something else, something closer to her heart. Through attempting to emulate the swimmer, though, she learned about passion and commitment—which is what role models teach us. At this point she may well be drawn to something quite different, say, the violin. In this sense, then, one of the role models for her new interest in the violin, in addition to her music teacher and the Bach her mother plays, may turn out to have been indirectly that swimmer. And out of her "failure" as a swimmer may come greater success elsewhere.

Miki's Conversation with Her Dad

—Hey, I passed by the restaurant Saturday but didn't see you.
—Actually, I wanted to talk to you about that. I wasn't on that shift, and I won't be on any others either.
—Meaning?
—Meaning, I got canned. Please don't get mad.
—You got fired?
—The owner, Patsy, called me last week and asked for my uniform.
—What went wrong?
—I don't think I'm cut out to be a waitress.
—I was a waiter once. It's hard work. People are demanding when it comes to food.
—I didn't mind the people, it was all the other stuff. The time clock, setting up, clearing tables, working the register, making coffee.
—Getting fired, though, was it a surprise?
—Sooner did warn me. She's the assistant manager. But I didn't listen to her. I never saw myself as the kind of person who'd get fired from anything.
—Did you deserve it?
—Sorry. I'm going to start looking real soon for another . . .
—I remember the time I got fired . . .
—You got fired? My dad got fired? How come you never told me?
—I was a bagger at a supermarket. I came to work late one day, and the boss got all over me. I must have been—your age, I guess. And I was so irritated I took it out on the first customer. I put her eggs and bananas in the bottom of the bag.
—DAD!
—Out of nowhere the guy swoops down on me. He must have been watching. And he tells me to follow him to his office. He told me he was about to

do me a big favor. This is a day you're never going to forget, he said. From here on in, you're going to be a better employee. You're going to value your next job, because you're done here. Then he fired me.

—You should have sued that sucker.

—Actually, after I finished graduate school, I was passing by the store and I saw him in there, same apron, same bow tie. I almost went in there, just to thank him. I wish I had. Because he was right. From that day on, I never took any job I ever had lightly again.

—Dad, is this another of your Life Lesson Stories?

—I guess that was a big lesson of mine. What about you?

—You know, Patsy did say something interesting on the phone at the end. She said she wished she could have gone along with Sooner and given me another chance.

—What's interesting about that?

—I had Sooner figured wrong, that's what. Turns out, she was really standing up for me all along. Probably means I had the job figured wrong too. I thought I was too good for that job.

—This one of your Life Lesson Stories, Miki?

—I hate these lessons. I'm not even sure what they are.

—Sure you do. You learned that you took your job lightly, but you also learned you took yourself lightly, too.

—Worst part is, it wouldn't have taken much. I could have done a better job. But I had no idea it mattered so much, just to try. I kind of miss the greasy spoon.

—Someday you can tell your own kids.

—Think it'll do any good?

—Probably not, but I wish I had told you.

—Speaking of which, Dad. Did you really put those eggs in the bottom of the bag?

—You've got to make mistakes to learn something. Your mom and I, we made some mistakes. Things have turned out all right, I guess, but it took a long time, and it's still hard to take sometimes. We're all still learning. Welcome to the club, Miki.

—Not bad for a guy who couldn't even bag groceries.

—Not bad for a girl who couldn't . . .

—Too soon, Dad.

—Maybe I shouldn't have brought up the divorce.

—Like I don't think about it every day? Welcome to the club, Dad.

More Notes Home

Sooner's So-Called Life?

Miki was wrong in her assessment of Sooner. And she was probably wrong to think that the restaurant was Sooner's whole life. Yet it's true that the Sooner she came to know in the restaurant was different from the Sooner at school. Miki did not understand, possibly until she got fired, how and where she could develop commitment and responsibility, and why this is important to her.

For a teenager, this development can take place in virtually any context, but it usually happens in one of three areas: in the classroom, at school but outside of the academic arena, or at some sort of job, paid or unpaid. Surprisingly, however, responsibility in one area hardly guarantees responsibility in the others—at least not in the short term. Although Sooner was reliable and accountable at work, she may well have been unaccomplished in other areas of her life: schoolwork, cocurricular activities, friendships. Once teenagers get a taste of competence, pride, and self-motivation, however, it is usually just a matter of time before these behaviors expand to other areas of their lives. But it doesn't happen overnight or as a result of prodding by others. This motivation must come from within.

In the story told here, Sooner seems to have risen to the challenge and responsibility of her job. In fact, as evidenced by her position as assistant manager, she has likely shown extraordinary diligence. For her the job is much more than a "measly paycheck." In the context of the restaurant she is competent, responsible, and self-directed. These are all wonderful attributes, and wherever they occur in a teenager's life it is important to go out of your way to acknowledge them. To miss this development is to miss an essential part of the person.

Authority and Peers

As with any social grouping, some teenagers have more influence than others. These are the ones who determine fashions, agendas, humor. They define the boundaries of the popular culture of a school. It is different, though, for a teenager who has officially sanctioned responsibility for her peers. She walks a tight rope indeed. This is true for class officers, team captains, camp counselors, newspaper and yearbook editors, and, yes, assistant managers, too. The captain of a team, for instance, is by definition an equal member of that team but is also by definition more than equal. Captains are formally responsible for more than themselves, which can lead to some rather unexpected and disheartening interactions. How does a teenager confront a close friend on his lackadaisical attitude in practice while both motivating him to do better and not sabotaging their social relationship? How does a captain console a friend who was just benched even though she agrees with the coach's decision? How does a captain influence his friends' social doings on Saturday nights in order to set a good example for the younger players, even as he maintains connection to his group of friends?

Teenagers in leadership positions risk periods of loneliness and alienation from their peers. If they cater to their friends, they suffer the guilt and angst that comes with not living up to the responsibilities entrusted to them by both peers and adults. The problem is that adults and peers may have different standards for fulfilling the obligation of leadership. If they falter on the side of overresponsibility, they suffer the incomprehension and disdain of their teammates and friends. No wonder some kids (and adults) shy away from leadership. Not everyone can balance competing priorities. And not everyone cares deeply enough to risk going out on a limb.

Failure As Not Knowing How to Ask for Help

Sometimes teenagers appear unmotivated simply because they are not trained properly or because they are too self-conscious to ask for assistance. No matter how often a teacher says that "there are no stupid questions," most teenagers secretly fear the teacher is being disingenuous or is setting a trap for the unsuspecting. But it takes strength to reveal ignorance and self-confidence to convey insecurity. In this story, Miki is short on both, like the overwhelming majority of teenagers. Clearly, she never learned how to make coffee. Possibly she was never taught or was instructed in a manner that she did not understand. The mature response for Miki would be to ask somebody to teach her how to do this side work. Yet she didn't do this. Why?

For many teenagers, working around the not-knowing is more congenial than exposing their vulnerability. Even though compensatory strategies are doomed (she will never make the coffee and she will keep out of the work station), they are less threatening than opening themselves up to the potential rejection of others. Miki is self-conscious that she does not know how to make coffee and her not asking for assistance is a sign that she fears belittlement, which is an archetypal adolescent anxiety. This fear may be distorted, but for her it is very real in its consequences: because she does not ask for the basic training, she cannot perform her job satisfactorily. Her attitude is alienating her fellow workers, who have to cover for her. For Miki, more than trouble with the coffee pot is brewing.

Is Miki herself the kind of person who responds graciously to requests for help? If so, she would probably ask for assistance readily when she needed it. ("It is tricky, this coffee machine. Let me show you.") If she is not that kind of person, she could see herself responding to another's problem in exactly the belittling manner she fears. ("We went over that already. Were you paying attention, or what?")

Teenagers miss opportunities to learn when they do not give themselves enough credit. The truth is that they are better than they know they are. This is exactly what Sooner tells Miki, and what Miki, in her narcissism, cannot yet hear. This is a typical bind for many, many teenagers. Because they hate humiliation they set themselves up for humiliation.

Family Expectations of Motivation and Success

Is success good for teenagers? That depends on how success is defined.

Once one of the authors accompanied a fourteen-year-old to the hospital emergency room. The boy had been seriously injured during basketball practice—on the day he made the final cut. He broke his arm when he hustled to make a difficult defensive play and collided with the gym wall. This was especially galling for him because he had made the team against the odds. As he sat in the waiting room, the season seemed lost and all the effort wasted. The orthopedist on call was a famous surgeon whose name was often in the sports pages for his career-saving operations on famous professional athletes. The doctor knew the boy's high school well; in fact, his daughter had graduated a few years ago. "I see more kids from your high school in the emergency room than any other school around," he said. "I think these kids feel pushed to succeed, and they're hurting themselves." His was the voice of a father remembering his own child. He was concerned about the pressures these teenagers felt—the message that there was no alternative to winning or playing beyond their capacities. This surgeon had a perspective on what might be called the dark side of motivation.

Are we sending mixed signals to teenagers? We say, "Be adult and take pleasure in your work for its own sake. Don't worry about being first violin or getting an A in the course, just do the best you can." At the same time we also say, "Why aren't you doing the solo? Of course you should be getting an A, if you only tried a little bit harder. This is your life, these are your grades. Now's the time for you, if you want a scholarship, if you want to get into the college of your dreams, not that these should be your goals, but still . . . "

The narrowly defined drive to success is apparent to all of us every time the Olympic Games are held, when we as a society imply by our adulation and love of cereal box pictures that anything less than a gold medal constitutes failure. Do we really value success at any price? Is that what we want our children to feel?

How families define success, and how they connect success to satisfaction and effort, is vital. In doing so, you are making boundaries and living your family values. For instance, if we send the signal that nothing less than admission to a certain college is acceptable, a teenager could justify doing anything—perhaps even cheating—to achieve the goal.

As parents, we should always take the long view.

Do you recall that high school or college reunion at which you encountered somebody you once effectively dismissed? Now all of a sudden you see that she is fabulously successful in her demanding profession, that she is extraordinarily witty, intelligent, perceptive, and interesting. Did you change or did she? More than likely it was a combination of both. Yes, you may very well have missed her strengths and virtues, but she probably did not realize them herself at the time.

This moment of recognition gives us a clue as to what is going on with those teenagers who are so opaque to us during high school. Often we know little about what drives teenagers to step forward or what pushes them to slink into the background, to take chances or to take the safe path, to yearn for excellence or to settle for getting by. Developmentally speaking, of course, each human being is a mystery. For some, high school is their time to shine, and the remainder of life seems only a dim recapitulation of past successes. Many students perform much, much better in college. For others, middle age is the period of expansion and creativity.

Perhaps the teenager struggling through adolescence is establishing the ground of future success, integration, and achievement.

A family that expects more than a child can deliver is doing as much of a disservice as one that expects (or settles for) not enough. In one, the teenager is asked to exceed himself; in the other, to ignore his abilities. Both messages amount to dismissal. The teenager will feel expendable and irrelevant not only to the family but also to himself. Of course, knowing when to push and when to back off is the ultimate challenge for you as a parent, and it will require all of *your* motivation to help your child thrive.

In survey after survey of teenagers on the subject of role models, parents are always the top vote getters—though few, if any, of these kids will come home and announce their rankings to Mom and Dad. Whether they tell you or not, you and your belief in them are central.

3

Date Rape

If a story begins with finding, it must end with searching.
—Penelope Fitzgerald, *The Blue Flower*

I went to the Garden of Love.
And saw what I never had seen:
A Chapel was built in the midst,
Where I used to play on the green.

—William Blake,
Songs of Innocence and of Experience

Sex, the Prom, and Other Misunderstandings

– One –

Jessica used to exude plenty of confidence. Confidence is rare in a ninth grader. But she looked you in the eye, she spoke her piece, and she didn't usually let people interrupt her when she was talking. She had plenty of friends and did well in her classes and on the playing field. She also attracted more than her share of attention from the boys, especially older ones. It had been that way since the beginning of the year. At first she didn't know how to handle the attention. She seemed startled and then confused, and then embarrassed. Still, she seemed capable of seeing things for what they were. She didn't seem ultimately susceptible to flattery.

Here's one image of Jessica. She once did a parody of the expansive, mature young woman, lecturing a friend as to how truly transparent boys were and how they were really out for only one thing; so keep your eyes open. Then almost immediately, as on cue, the two of them giggled like middle-schoolers until they collapsed onto the floor. Here's another image: excitedly telling her friends she had been asked to the prom by a senior.

No question, she shocked her world by accepting the prom invitation. In fact, what was more shocking was that her date was one of the same boys she used to make fun of during first semester for famously having only the one thing on his mind.

Jessica going to the prom? Some of her teachers doubted that this was a welcome development for any ninth grader. She was mature for her age all right, but was she mature enough for this? Anyone with experience in high schools might reasonably worry that nothing but complications could result from the age difference and the unrealistic expectations engendered by the prom. But what if Jessica could go and have a perfectly wonderful evening? Her adviser, in particular, couldn't shake her uneasy feelings. She caught herself hoping Jessica would get a slight case of the measles.

Jessica picked up on the mood. No wonder she avoided her adviser the week leading up to the prom. She wasn't being cunning and she wasn't hostile, exactly. In fact, she respected her adviser too much to be alone in the same room with her. She didn't need to explain the prom right now. All she needed was to go and have a good time.

– *Two* –

Saturday night was the prom. Monday, Jessica didn't show up for school.

A week after the prom another image of Jessica emerged: now you see her, now you don't. Only now she seemed a little bit harder, a little sadder, a little more cautious and controlled. Crazy rumors were going around. People noticed that she and her date didn't spend time together on campus; in fact, they seemed to shun each other. Even more troubling was that Jessica often huddled in a corner with a few friends. She was clearly the focus of their rapt attention. But whenever anyone approached, they all got self-conscious and studied their fingernails.

One day her adviser almost tripped over Jessica sitting on the ground between two cars in the parking lot. "What are you doing?"

"Nothing."

Her adviser couldn't help noticing Jessica's tears. "You OK?" Sometimes even when she knew the answers she asked the questions.

Jessica wiped her face with the sleeves of her oversized sweatshirt. She smiled distantly and fought off another round of tears.

The adviser bent down toward Jessica. "Anything I can do to help?"

"Can you turn back time?"

"You haven't been yourself since—" She didn't need to finish the thought.

"I got to go now. Maybe later." She stayed put.

"Later's good."

"Nothing's good."

The adviser sat down on the ground next to her and waited. Suddenly she wasn't in a hurry anymore.

Jessica's Conversation with Simone, Her Big Sister

The school year came to an end. Simone, the oldest of the three sisters, has just returned home from her first year away at college and was settling back in her room when Jessica entered and stood by the window.

—Hey, Jess, what's that in your hand?

—Prom pictures.

—Cute. Let me see.

—No.

—Come on, nobody ever looks good in a prom picture, don't worry.

—Why you want to see a picture of a jerk?

—I felt silly looking at my first prom pictures, too. You'll get over it.

—Not me. Him.

—Give it up.

—Well, I knew you were waiting around for my report, so I thought I'd come in and tell you the old prom sucked. Well, not the prom exactly—my date. I don't feel I really went to the prom. He. Is. Such. A. Jerk.

—A jerk how?

—In every way, that's how.

—Details.

—How could I know he was a jerk until the prom? Before he was sweet and nice. He was different from other boys, at least I thought he was. I mean, we went out a couple of times before, movie, pizza, like that. He never even tried to kiss till the third date, and that was a little kiss good night. Which was when he asked me to go to the prom. I was so stupid, I said yes.

—So what happened at the prom?

—Started before the prom, when he picked me up. He was in a stretch limo with his buddies and their dates, which he never told me about, and none of whom I knew. Whatever, I said, but the whole limo reeked of alcohol. I should have turned around right then, but I could see Mom and Dad through the tinted windows and they were waving me good-bye, and they'd just taken all these cheesy snapshots, and Carrie was there, too, smiling like a ten-year-old maniac. How could I go back?

—Did you say anything to him?

—It was happening all too fast, plus everybody in the whole car was a senior, and they were all his friends, what could I say, there was nothing I could do. And it just got worse. He was all over me before I knew it. It was like he was showing off. Then at the prom, he ignored me, sneaking to the rest room with the other guys. Only when the music slowed down and the lights dimmed, he'd come back. It was terrible, but there was nothing I could do. None of my friends were there to help me out.

—Sounds awful.

—I don't even want to talk about how it ended.

—I had a date like that once.

—It was like in a dream, a terrible dream. It was weird. I saw him show something to his buddy and they high-fived each other. And I realized it was a condom. Which is when I lost it. I wasn't going to get together with him, and there was no way in hell he was going to rape me.

—I remember that voice going off in my head, too.

—You know I think that's the first time, *just now*, the first time I let myself say *that* word out loud.

—First week at college, we had acquaintance-rape workshops, and I couldn't believe how many girls told horror stories.

—Yeah, but that night . . . that night, that minute he turned around, and I caught his eye and I gave him the dirtiest look I've ever given anybody in my life, and then I walked right to the pay phone and called Mom and Dad. I told them come get me and if they asked me any questions, I was going to jump out of the car. For once in their life they finally shut up.

—But have you talked with them since?

—Little. They've been all right. They want to know more, but they're not in my face. Dad did pick up the phone that night to call that guy's parents, but I talked him out of it. He may have called since, but I don't care anymore. I'll never speak to that guy again.

—It all sounds awful, Jess. Except there's one thing. At least you showed you could stand up for yourself. I wasn't as strong as you were.

—But how come I feel so lousy?

—What else do you expect?

—I'm just so embarrassed. He played me, which is exactly what everybody said he would do. Even Mom and Dad. I can't believe I was so stupid, so naive! I thought for sure that they were all wrong, but it was me who was wrong. I never want to date again.

—That's a big leap. I thought that once.

—Tell me all guys aren't jerks.

—All guys aren't jerks.

—Say it like you mean it.

—I did meet somebody this year. He's going to visit. He's not like our prom dates.

—Yeah, well, I just don't know what I'm going to do with these prom pictures.

—Let's light the barbecue.

—Think that'll help?

—Who knows? It will be fun. Which is something you could use.

—OK. But Simone, the hardest part? It's like I can't trust my own instincts anymore. But one thing's for sure. I definitely won't let anything like that happen to me ever again. You get the matches, I'll get the lighter fluid.

Notes Home

Two Steps Forward, One Step Back

We should never underestimate how subtly teenagers change over the course of a year, and how precariously they shift into and out of vulnerability during these fluctuations. Predicting the stock market is one thing, but charting the emotional and psychological growth curve of a teenager is far more intricate. We also must remind ourselves that teenagers change as a result of experience and that most of these learning experiences come at a price, some at a high price. In this story Jessica is changing and changing fast, right before the eyes of her parents, her sister, and other adults. Of course, she is also changing outside their field of vision. If we are not watchful, we can miss these changes.

Girls arrive as ninth graders developmentally ahead of boys, and this is one of the reasons that they often gaze romantically upon the older boys— and why the boys gaze back. Another reason is that they recognize the status that comes with going out with an older boy, especially if that boy himself possesses high status. Curiously, these girls are more immune to these influences at the beginning of the school year than at the end. After two semesters they would seem to have grown more savvy. But the reality is that in the fall they do not yet fully appreciate, for instance, that Tyler is an incredible athlete and an A student destined for great things. Or that Jamal is a fabulous guitar player and poet. Or that Cecil is the big party animal on campus to whom everyone flocks on weekends. But once girls see these boys reveling in their element and see firsthand their status, they become more susceptible to advances from them. Even though in most other respects girls are more insightful, they are too immersed in adolescent culture to see through the veil of status.

In addition, at the end of the ninth grade, girls (and boys, too) are enduring onslaughts of acute self-doubt. They are still adjusting to high school socially and academically. Relationships at home are changing, their bodies feel out of control, and friendships are shifting more quickly than they can articulate. In particular, a ninth-grade girl who sees the world clearly and accurately in October may lose her focus by May. True, not every ninth-grade girl is guileless before older boys. Some, however, are susceptible to being blinded or distracted by the extravagant attention boys expend upon them, the clouds of flattery, the envy of friends, the boyfriend with his own car, in sum, by the spectacle of all the signs and symbols of conventional high school success and élan. In this state, ninth-grade girls are most apt to mingle with upperclassmen, hoping that their status and apparent self-assurance will rub off on them. And in some cases this is exactly what happens. But teenagers' idealism is fragile and it makes them vulnerable. For many young women this moment ends in disappointment and heartbreak, sometimes worse.

A fourteen- or fifteen-year-old like Jessica being invited to the prom by a seventeen- or eighteen-year-old is by definition not going to think very rationally. This occasion is usually the stuff dreams are made of. As we can see, though, and as we (along with her adviser) might have anticipated, such dreams can turn into nightmares. (See Appendix A, "Where Am I? Being 14–15" and Appendix D, "Where Am I Going and Where Have I Been? Being 17-18.")

A Boy's Life

What about *him*? The boy who invited Jessica (whose name she is too disgusted to utter) is conceivably in crisis too—and a good thing it is if afterward he felt shame and guilt. He should feel bad because he crossed many lines—starting with the alcohol and ending with flashing the condom. He acted insensitively and threateningly.

In recent years, predatory boys have been excoriated. Yet the caricature of boys' being casually, universally violent is as far from reality as girls' being helpless. These days our gender stereotypes are under reconsideration. William Pollack's *Real Boys,* for instance, is a sympathetic portrait of boys, who are thwarted by "gender-straitjacketing." Routinely, pressures are placed upon them to have sex before they are ready, to boast of sexual conquests (even fabricated ones), and to remain aloof and indifferent to girls. At the same time, they are not encouraged to express the tender feelings they do indeed have, their yearnings for connection and relationship.

Let us examine Jessica's prom story from the boy's point of view. It is conceivable that he had never behaved like this with any other girl. After all, he had never made Jessica uncomfortable before, and they had gone out a few times, not merely uneventfully but pleasantly. So who was the *real* boy? The one who treated Jessica respectfully on their dates or the one showing off for his buddies? He himself might not know for sure. What upset Jessica, in particular, were the limo and all the other arrangements, his "being all over her," and, most dramatically, his flashing the condom to his buddy. Seen through his eyes, however, his actions might mean something different from what Jessica thinks. Here's what might be going on for him:

This is going to be a great night. I really like this girl. I won't tell her about the limo and all because there's no need to get into it with her and her parents. Besides, these are my buddies, and they're great guys, and we've been talking about the limo and prom for the whole year. Besides, it'll all work out, and before the night's over she's going to have a great time.

What about the condom, which struck Jessica as crude and threatening? That might have been a gesture to entertain the guys, to live up to a desirable public image. He might have thought he was a guy acting the way guys are supposed to act with other guys. Of course, we want him to learn sensitivity and understand how his macho bravado disturbs girls. Nonetheless, forcing himself on her sexually or even exerting sexual pressure on her might not have been his plan.

Then again, maybe that was the plan. Or maybe that would become the plan before the night was through. Still, what is frightening about adolescence is how close to the margins of irreparable damage and loss teenagers routinely place themselves, how close they come to the shore of no return.

Luckily for both of them, Jessica drew on reliable resources, her confidence and her trust in her family, to resist the pressures she perceived. Interestingly, though, she hates herself for being so stupid as to have thought well of this boy. But her judgment may not have been wrong at all; maybe he was indeed a good kid who in a bad moment, in a pack of guys, temporarily discarded or misplaced his moral bearings.

All this is not to say that his behavior is remotely excusable. Jessica and he may never talk again, and perhaps they shouldn't. But it would not be surprising if he himself felt mortified afterward and wished he could do something to undo the whole night. An eighteen-year-old boy is susceptible to just the sort of fantasy making that can violently collide with a younger teenager's dreamy notions of romance. This is another reason age differences between teenagers accelerate tension and risk. A fourteen-year-old and an eighteen-year-old are not speaking the same language. Although their mutual insecurities compel them to fill the void between them, they tend to talk over and past each other.

Intuition and Self-Consciousness

Every person has an accurate voice of intuition, the part of ourselves that recognizes when something is wrong and works to make itself heard. Whenever we trust this voice and act on its message, we are usually glad we did and, more important, we trust our intuition the next time it speaks.

In this story Jessica's intuition was keen. From the moment she set foot in the limousine, she recognized that something was awry. Unfortunately for her, it took her most of the night to act on her intuition. Similarly, there is the chance that the same is true for the boy. He may have sensed something was wrong as he attempted to be both the young man Jessica had come to know on successful dates and the guys' guy that his buddies knew. If he did have this intuition, however, he failed to take heed.

Whenever we make an error in judgment, we usually look back and ask ourselves, *How come I didn't see it coming? Why didn't I act on what I was sensing?* These are critical questions for growth, the very questions Jessica started to pursue with her adviser, and certainly with her older, more experienced sister. In this way, her growth is a matter of taking one step backward (realizing she did not act soon enough on her intuition and working to understand why), followed by two steps forward (greater trust in her intuition).

For teenagers, one of the primary inhibitions to trusting their voice of intuition is their self-consciousness, which is frequently overwhelming. That is, under the spell of self-consciousness teenagers dismiss intuition as an intrusion on the self they are working to present to those around them. For example, Jessica aspires to the status of affiliating with seniors, even as she senses the danger awaiting her. Remember, more than anything, adolescents want to fit in. Because intuition told her to move away from the crowd she yearned to be a part of, Jessica may have had a hard time listening to it.

If Jessica had acted on her initial intuition, she would have never driven off in the limousine with her date and his friends. What would have transpired instead? It is likely that her decision would have brought on the sort of attention she didn't want. Jessica is fourteen or fifteen, and she needs to demonstrate nonchalance over the twists of social logistics. In this context, it is almost too much to expect Jessica to listen to her intuition, which is telling her to beware.

No teenager, no human being, makes consistently good decisions. In general, good judgment comes from making poor decisions and understanding why they were poor. On the way to learning wise decisionmaking teenagers go through different levels of understanding and, ultimately, maturity:

Level 1: Teenagers do not struggle with making a tough choice.
Level 2: Teenagers play back their memories of decisions made and acknowledge what they did wrong.

Level 3: Teenagers recognize a bad decision while they are in the act
of deciding but feel powerless to make a different decision.
Level 4: Teenagers identify a decision as a bad one before they act on
it and choose an alternative.

Jessica has experienced three of these levels. Clearly she made what
turned out to be a bad choice to go to the prom with this boy and made
another bad decision to ignore her intuition and ride away in the limousine. During the course of the evening, she recognized her poor decisions
while she was making them. Yet she stayed at the prom despite his behavior in ignoring her except for the slow dances, when he was all over her. By
the conclusion of the evening she let herself fully recognize where things
were heading and acted on her insight before letting the evening deterio-
rate even further.

It is important that teenagers recognize and acknowledge each of these
levels. In this case, Jessica would otherwise have felt guilty and stupid, in-
accurately chalking up a terrible night to one poor decision, the decision
to go to the prom with this boy in the first place. When all is said and done,
Jessica needs to realize that, yes, she made an unfortunate decision, but she
also learned something over the course of the evening and, in the end,
acted in absolutely the best manner possible. In this way Jessica can walk
away from the memory of this prom night with the knowledge that she
can listen to and act on her intuition in the future. In other words, she
once again can trust her own judgment.

Relationship Through Crisis

Perceptive adults who work with teenagers undergoing crises often struggle over what to do for the kids in their care. Here Jessica's adviser worries
before the prom. But if she had confronted Jessica, she would have risked
being placed in the category of the typically prying, intrusive adult authority figure. The difficulty here lies with her identifying and then coming to
terms with the true problem, not how to stop Jessica from going to the
prom (without school or family intervention, her attendance is a fait ac-
compli) and not now how to assume responsibility that rightfully belongs
to Jessica.

Instead, all along the adult's challenge is to maintain integrity in her relationship with Jessica. Because she did not panic before the prom, she can

assist her in the crisis that resulted. Maintaining integrity requires patience and fortitude, and it involves much more listening than talking. More than almost anything else, at this time in their lives teenagers need adults who will want to understand them, adults who are, in a manner of speaking, *safe*. In any case, her adviser probably has the chance to be one of those adults for Jessica. If she can stay *safe*, that is, receptive, accessible, available, throughout a burgeoning crisis, Jessica can turn to her for advice, solace, or assistance when she gets into other, perhaps even more difficult, scrapes. So when Jessica sits weeping on the ground, the adviser joins her and waits for her to take the lead. And because she does not force a conversation and listens for cues, the adviser is likely going to prove very useful for Jessica. At the same time, the student–adviser relationship is going to be rewarding for the adult too.

The Prom Next Time

The prom will not be the last challenge of Jessica's high school life, and it will not be the last time she faces complicated adolescent problems. In other words, she is not done growing up. What happened for her at the prom (not to mention what might have happened) is not necessarily the defining moment for Jessica. If the adults in her life had panicked and conveyed to Jessica that her life had careened out of her control, *that* disappointment would itself have constituted the defining moment. Fortunately for Jessica, her parents, despite their anger, behaved wisely. It could not have been easy for them to restrain themselves. They came close to intervening by calling the boy's family that night, but instead held back, listening to Jessica and trusting her when she said she could take care of herself. At some point in the future, it will be appropriate for them to inform the boy's parents of what Jessica has told them. In the short term, however, her parents need to concentrate their efforts on Jessica and her well-being in order to help her understand what has happened and to limit the chances for anything like that from ever happening again.

In seeking counsel with her adviser and her sister, Jessica made an attempt to come to terms with her experience and began claiming the limits of her responsibility. She was angry and hurt, of course, but she also seemed resolute in her conviction that she would overcome this ordeal and not become a victim. Jessica will likely revisit the prom in her imagination, in her future conversations with her adviser, and in her relationships with other boys and girls, for a long time to come.

In the meantime, the key for an adult is to keep the relationship alive and growing. This does not mean a direct, interrogating conversation, which, in this case, may have been off-putting for Jessica, but it does mean the adviser's going out of her way to make herself seen as both responsible and safe by Jessica. This might mean a casual walk alongside Jessica just to let her know that she sees her as a bit removed and troubled as of late. When she stays silent or asserts that she is fine, the adult is still allowed to say, "Well, just wanted to let you know that I care about you. If ever you need to talk, let me know. I'm a pretty good listener, even if I am your teacher." Then see where the silence goes. It may lead to her opening up instantly, but it probably will not. Months from now, even years, may be the time they can talk candidly.

Teenagers take notice when adults go out of their way for them, even if they do not show it at the time. Or, more accurately, especially *if* they do not show it at the time. Finally, it never hurts to remind ourselves that teenagers are both more capable and less capable, more resilient and less resilient, than we might assume.

Parents' Intuition

All of a sudden, you feel an aching intuition about your teenager: something's off.

Your first inclination is to ask directly what's wrong. Sometimes a teenager will tell you, though usually not. You will feel inclined to manufacture theories at this point and then test them out. All of this is understandable, but it is often better to try another tack. If answers aren't forthcoming, sometimes giving your teenagers the opportunity to come to you with their problems is more effective.

Still, that suggestion sounds a little bit hollow, doesn't it? The truth is, however, all your questioning is not necessarily going to further your cause. And all your worry is not going to encourage your teenager to come forward. And neither are your attestations that, despite evidence to the contrary, you were once a teenager yourself and you know exactly what teenagers are going through. In these kinds of moments parents earn their hazardous duty pay, when they pace around the house just as they did when their children were infants and suffering from an ear infection. It's altogether different now, of course. You just know something's troubling them, but no antibiotics, no cradle rocking will do the trick. You want to keep pain away from your child, of course, but she wants to handle it her-self—for now. Even if evolution was shrewd to make it this way, the anxi-ety is no less easy to bear.

Hang in there. In a famous line by Emily Dickinson, "Tell the truth, but tell it slant." In other words, declare your concern, but declare it *slant*. Try to get your teenager to shoot some hoops with you or cook dinner with you or walk the dog with you. Just about any activity will do, anything that doesn't seem to hold out the immediate prospect of intimate revelation. (A car ride is especially useful; moving together, perhaps in darkness, in an enclosed safe space might provide the perfect conditions for conversa-tion.) If you remain receptive and do not ask explicit questions, who knows, you might eventually hear all you need, and your teenager might admit he has been seeking just this opportunity. If you're lucky, you might even be the stunned, happy beneficiary of that wondering look in his eyes that says, *I have no idea why, but I'm glad we talked.* Just don't wait for him to say that in so many words.

Self-Consciousness, Intuition, and Personal Safety

As we have seen in Jessica's story, self-consciousness clouds the vision of the best kids, especially when their intuition is screaming to go against the prevailing direction of the crowd. Granted, this is how teenagers come to learn about and trust their own intuition. But still, as a parent, you need to do your best to hasten that learning curve when it involves personal safety.

In this regard encourage and support your teenage sons and daughters to attend a weekend workshop on self-defense and personal safety. All teenagers, not just those in an urban environment, can use this kind of training and exposure. Most importantly, they need the actual role playing and experience that come from these workshops. They need to hear them-selves shouting, "Get away from me!" or "Somebody please help me!" If the real need ever arises, this action will not be a foreign experience to them. They also need to recognize that there are bad people in the world who do terrible things—not many, but some. And when they encounter this kind of person they are equipped to take care of themselves.

Date Rape

Teenagers know that date rape happens. It occurs more often than anyone wants to believe and has traumatizing repercussions for individual victims and for whole communities. And yet kids are not always sure how to talk about it, and neither are adults. What is date rape? Everyone agrees that date rape is a crime, but what makes it difficult to define is that it involves acquaintances and sex that one party contends is consensual. If you gather a group of teenagers, you will hear a dozen different interpretations. Is it simply not listening to "no"? Is it not saying no assertively enough? Are all boys potentially predators? Are all girls potentially victims? How does one take responsibility for one's desires? And who is in control of one's body?

Kids need to talk through their questions, confusions, and assumptions. The obvious point about date rape is how boys push past no. The subtle question is, What pushes them to go past no? Are hormones to blame? Or the prevailing cultural stereotypes and pressures of masculinity? Are boys acting on what they believe girls really want? And what leads girls not to say no assertively enough? Is it self-image? Is it fear for their safety? Is it fear of rejection, or a vain hope for acceptance? Or is it what happens when boys think they have been led on?

Date rape relates to all of the above, and more, which is why it is such an uncomfortable topic, which is why you must talk about it with your teenagers now. You need to know that your teenagers, both boys and girls, have grappled with the topic. With your active engagement they might be able to anticipate a problem before it arrives. This kind of engagement has nothing to do with lecturing. It is an ongoing dialogue that evolves over years. Your teenager's comments and answers may well shock you at first, but you need to hear them. And get ready, here comes the mirror. Some of their values and attitudes—and not only the best ones—they may have mislearned from you.

4

Integrity

Going out into the fields of learning,
We shake the dew from the grasses.
All is new.

—Josephine Miles, "Paths"

Most people are motivated to justify their own actions, beliefs,
and feelings. When a person does something, he or she will try,
if at all possible, to convince himself or herself (and others) that
it was a logical, reasonable thing to do.

—Eliot Aronson, *The Social Animal*

Be Prepared

At last school was out for the summer. The mood in the administration
building was slow and lazy, and the June sky was blue and clear. As anyone
would expect, there were few students on campus these days. Danny was
one of them, and he was sitting in the dean's office, as no one would have
expected. Nobody who was required to meet with the dean at this time of
year was there to chat about summer jobs and vacation plans.

Danny was a student who had received (from this dean, in fact) numerous academic awards in the spring assembly. His grade point average
placed him at the top of his freshman class. But now he was in trouble.

Danny clasped his hands tightly in his lap and jiggled his legs as he leaned forward in the direction of the dean's cluttered desk.

The problem was that his algebra final examination was clouded by suspicious circumstances. It seemed that a cheat-sheet had been discovered beneath Danny's desk. It wasn't the cheat-sheet itself that staggered the teacher or the dean (neither of them was that naive), but that it seemed to belong to Danny. Before the test, the only question left with regard to him was whether he was going to receive an A or an A+ for a semester grade.

The dean tried to make small talk, but he was getting nowhere. Danny's voice was muted and every response so far consisted of exactly one word. He was clearly waiting for the proverbial other shoe to drop.

The dean decided on an indirect approach: "You know, Danny, sometimes we make mistakes, sometimes even serious mistakes, and somehow we can't even stop ourselves. It's not that we're bad people. We just make mistakes."

"I didn't cheat. I don't need to cheat. I told Miss Wheatley. I can't believe she didn't believe me. I thought we were friends. I thought she trusted me."

"If she was wrong, I'm sure she'll be the first to apologize to you, Danny. Heck, I'll be right with her, begging for your forgiveness. She's only human. She makes mistakes, too, just as you and I do."

"Good, because it's not fair to send somebody to the dean when you're not sure."

"But going back to what I was talking about a second ago. Sometimes, for some reason we just make a bad decision. When it's over, we think back and wonder who took over our minds and bodies for a second, you know what I mean?"

Danny warily nodded.

"We've all been there," said the dean. "Including me."

Danny moved forward in his chair. "You? For real?"

"Let's just say that I did things when I was in school that I am not particularly proud of. You can see the sign on the door outside says there's a dean inside this office, not a saint or some kind of hero."

"You know how many people cheat in this school who never get caught? Man, you know how many people cheat in Miss Wheatley's class?"

"That's another topic for another conversation. Right now, let's stay on Danny. Remember what I said. Everybody makes mistakes. It's one thing to make a serious mistake, but it's much worse not to take responsibility for that mistake. Danny, now's the time to be honest. Now's the time to take responsibility. Let me ask you: Did you make a mistake?"

"Besides, that test was so easy, I could have aced it in my sleep."

"That's still another subject. Let me ask you again, and I want you to think about this very seriously now: Everybody makes mistakes, and it's hard to admit it when you do. But that's exactly what I'm asking you to think about. Did you make a mistake you're ready to admit?"

"The only mistake I made was getting caught."

"Danny, you know better than that. I don't call that a mistake, I call that good luck. If you didn't get caught, you'd never have the chance to never cheat again. Tell me what happened."

He did. It took a minute, but he began speaking through flowing tears. He had acted alone, he said. He didn't help anybody else on the exam, and he couldn't explain why he did it. "I feel like such a dope."

"This a new experience?"

"Now I know why they say you're a wise guy. My father's going to kill me."

"And that, too . . . "

"Please don't say that's another subject, too. But he's going to be mad I won't get into a good college."

"Why won't you get into college?"

"Don't you have to tell the world?"

"Your problem stays right here, with you and me, Miss Wheatley, and your folks. If you do it again—that's a horse of a different color. Meanwhile, everybody at school knows the consequences for first timers. The handbook's crystal clear."

"From now on, you're going to see me walking across campus and say, *There goes Danny, the Cheater.*"

"It doesn't work that way. You cheated, all right, but that doesn't mean you're a cheater. Everybody gets a second chance. This is yours."

"That's what my father'll say, *Danny, the Cheater.*"

"I will talk to him, I promise."

Later, while Danny walked up and down the hall, the dean called his father. He always dreaded these calls. This one went better than most, however. He only had to repeat the story once. His dad conveyed sadness more than anything, not the more typical rage and disappointment and hostility that many parents exhibited. When his dad heard that Danny was taking responsibility for his actions, he said, "That sounds like Danny." Good, thought the dean, they had something to work with. Tomorrow they could have a family conference.

Danny came back to the dean's office. "How did he take it?"

"Funny thing. You know, that's what he asked about you."

Notes Home

When Is Cheating, Well, Just Cheating?

Sometimes cheating is just cheating: a kid panics and takes the easy way out.

Much more often, however, cheating means more than that. Some teenagers cheat because they cannot see any other way to bring up a grade, some to compete with their peers, some to meet the expectations of their teachers or parents. What is always true, however, is that cheating lies close to the source of teenagers' deepest, most intense conflicts and doubts. This is why cheating and being caught threaten a teenager's fragile conception of himself and his worth; curiously, though, a student whose cheating goes undetected may not experience anything like a crisis. Believe it or not, altruistic, ethical, and intelligent teenagers can rationalize cheating—and barely register the internal conflicts. They will remain immune to these shocks, unless and until they are held accountable. Such turmoil, though, is essential to their growing up and to their conception of integrity, identity, values, morality, community, and family.

Regardless of the mountain of evidence looming over him, a teenager's first response to being confronted with a charge of cheating is usually *I didn't do it.* This kind of denial is vehement, accompanied by oaths, expletives, and the occasional reference to lawyers. As with all unfounded denials, this is an attempt to knock the accuser off balance. After that response becomes untenable (hard to knock down that mountain), there comes an avalanche of justifications along the lines of *Everybody cheats* or *It was just homework* or *What's the big deal?*—followed by *It's not like I'm a criminal or anything.* The next line of response (because that mountain still won't budge) is to assail the assignment or the teacher: *He's a terrible teacher! That test was impossible, we all gave up and cheated.*

Faced with these desperate self-justifications, and because the stakes are so high, as parents and teachers we must ask hard questions and resist settling for easy answers. Doing so, we will enter into the heart of teenagers. Here's the surprise: they let us in.

The School Where Nobody Cheats (and Other Utopias)

A survey of teenagers listed in *Who's Who* indicated that 80 percent of these high achievers admitted to cheating. As many asserted, for them the ends—college, success, and so on—justify the means. Fundamentally, this is what the culture at large often tacitly condones. Of course, academic dishonesty is a perennial problem in most if not all schools, and this has more to do with the nature of teenagers than any school's mission and philosophy, or any school's shortcomings for that matter. All the rules in the world will not make this problem go away. Still, for excellent reasons, each institution will take its own approach to addressing academic integrity. Some adopt an honor code. Some confront it exhaustively in handbooks or through faculty-led discussion groups at the start of the school year. All discussions about integrity, however, should ideally begin with a candid recognition as to how hard, how psychologically and morally demanding, it is to be honest all the time. Any adult who thinks otherwise is deluding himself, and this is why a parent or anyone working with teenagers will locate academic integrity in the largest, most comprehensive context. Integrity is not about whether or not to use a cheat-sheet, it's about how to lead a moral life.

How do adolescents develop integrity? They learn the value of integrity through experience. They discover that integrity is not an acquired thing or something to be preserved intact, forever. Only experience can teach them this lesson. There is a knotty complication with adolescents, however. Although there is nothing more precious than their personal integrity, they must sometimes be pushed to make the connection between academic integrity and the affirmation of their personal integrity. That is, they can be taught that being dishonest in their academic work means that they are misrepresenting themselves, compromising their integrity. Though such a connection would seem self-evident, this is not a simple, immediate, or guaranteed link.

Academic dishonesty is different from, say, shoplifting or sneaking into a movie or walking out without paying the restaurant check. All of these actions are indefensible, but the stakes with regard to cheating are more personal. It's one thing to steal a sweater from an anonymous department store, but it's another to betray a teacher, one's classmates, and oneself, and reap unearned rewards for doing so. Similarly, honesty in one realm of a teenager's life does not automatically translate into another. To echo *Anna Karenina*, every act of dishonesty is different, and every act of honesty is the same. Herein lies a clue for parents: stress not only *dis*honesty, but honesty too.

"My Child Would Never Cheat"

Let us return to that *Who's Who* survey. Although most teenagers admitted cheating, 63 percent of parents thought their own children never cheated. What does this disconnection teach us? Among other things, it suggests that we as parents need to rethink the topic of honesty as it pertains to the daily lives of our kids.

Teenagers' parents are their first teachers in regard to integrity. Does that make parents accountable for any acts of their teenagers' bad judgment? Absolutely not. Yet teenagers are acutely vulnerable to a temptation to cheat: after all, they are experts at maintaining the appearance of knowing much more than they actually know. Given the stage of their development, they will intermittently test limits. Cheating, then, is not a mark of depravity or criminality so much as a testing of themselves, their schools, their families. Teenagers in effect are asking themselves: *Is this an act I am capable of doing? Something I can get away with? Does the school care if I try? And what will the school do if I am caught?*

Teenagers would not bother to test the limits unless the testing and the limits themselves were crucial. That is, they want to find out, *What do these adults ultimately stand for? What is right? Will anybody step forward to act on what they say is right—and how will they act? And if they won't act at all, why should it matter to me?* Understanding this, parents can view cheating, for instance, as a golden opportunity to reinforce values. Far from taking teenagers off the hook, that recognition amounts to the strongest response on the part of adults.

Any teenager who cheats for the first time faces a major moral crisis. He will worry about having cheated and sweat it out until he gets back the plagiarized paper or the copied test. At that point he will feel relieved to know that his deception has not been detected and he will be pleased with—and perhaps not too guilty about—the results. Consequently, he is more likely to cheat again, but without all the moral tension. In so doing, he falls into the habit of self-evasion, which contaminates much more than his academic life.

Cheating is seductive and it can easily worm into a teenager's way of life. The truth is, teenagers may cheat at any stage, from a homework assignment in the first week of ninth grade to the last exam they take before graduation. They may be admitted early to college or they may have no plans for continuing their education after high school—it does not matter. Some will cheat according to opportunity; in fact, some cheating can be attributed, superficially, to faulty faculty supervision, vague assignments, or fuzzy expectations. Some cheat according to need, that is, to obtain a better grade, to compensate for poor preparation, to maintain a friendship, to placate others (teachers, parents, and peers), or to buttress a shaky self-image. Most students, whatever their GPA, will muse about or even plot cheating at some point or will allow themselves to be manipulated into helping another student cheat. In other words, good kids do cheat. Good kids whose families promote honesty. Good kids who are worried about their friends' staying in school or getting suspended from the team if they don't pass a course. Good kids who cheat once and then never cheat again. For parents to imagine otherwise is yet another type of self-deception.

Go Beyond Blame

Assigning blame and spelling out the repercussions for any single act of cheating is not the ultimate quest. We as parents must search for an understanding of our kids' misguided motivation. We must search for the reason for dishonesty (and honesty, too) in the home, in the school, in the heart of the adolescent, or, most likely, in some combination. Why did this teenager cheat? And why now? Answering the latter question may be more compelling than answering the former.

In this story, a teacher has reported an incident of academic dishonesty to the dean. Parents sometimes complain that a school is ganging up on their teenager or is overreacting to a once-in-a-lifetime indiscretion. Certainly, a heavy hand is not necessarily the wisest approach here (or on most occasions for that matter). Yet just as parents have a responsibility to define the moral parameters of their family, the school has a similar obligation. Thus reporting Danny's offense to an administrator was appropriate. The school must communicate the gravity of cheating and underscore what is at stake for the individual and the community—no matter how much the teenager minimizes what he has done. Some may believe that the stronger the response the less likely the chances of a repeat offense, and the greater the opportunity for education. In reality, though, consequences do not have to be severe in order to be effective. Consequences do need to be real enough, however, that a teenager pauses and willingly engages in self-reflection and self-criticism. But they should not send him reeling in resentment and anger, thereby bypassing the opportunity to understand the implications of his behavior.

Of course, many times teenagers never admit culpability, despite the trace existence of incriminating information. They deny their guilt and the evidence is not irrefutable. What happens here? The school still has a responsibility to disclose to the family what it knows and reasonably suspects. This is not done to tarnish a student's reputation—though it may appear that way at first—but to allow parents to take the lead in the discussion of integrity.

Back to Danny. After failing in several attempts to distract the dean, each of which the dean duly notes, Danny bares his soul, at the same time obliquely pointing the finger at unrealistic parent expectations. He is an A student who fears the disapproval of his father, who worries, according to Danny, that his son won't get into a "good" college and seems to demand what Danny has just demonstrated that he cannot deliver: perfection. This is actually the ending of one story (the determination of facts) and the beginning of another, deeper one (the search for motivation), which, unlike the first, has no absolute truths. Unrealistic parent expectations? Is Danny unrealistic about his parents, or are they unrealistic about him? Or are both conditions true, as they more than occasionally are? All we know from the story is that we don't know, which is the typical setup for a family conference with the dean.

The Family Conference

Everybody knows this conference will not be easy. By the very nature of the occasion, Danny, his family, and his school are vulnerable. The goal of the family conference is to absorb the shock of the cheating incident and to understand how the school and the family can work through this episode—together. Some participants will attempt to put this experience behind them or shift the conversation to ensuring that cheating never happens in the future. These are worthy goals, to be sure, but they are in the distance, at least a few conversations away. Now is the time to stay in the present and bring to light the underlying reasons for the cheating.

When discussions proceed well, and even sometimes when they do not, they can ultimately disclose the dynamics of the teenager. If a teenager is to learn and move on, these dynamics must at least be identified and addressed (as in outlining consequences). Unless this happens, Danny will probably return to the dean's office to answer for some equally serious offense in the future.

It is always worthwhile to assume that reasons exist beneath the surface, and beyond Danny's conscious mind, too. We can be led to understanding by listening to what he does and does not say. Danny is our best resource for understanding what his actions mean. With that insight, we can serve as a resource for his growth.

Consider what might have motivated Danny to cheat. For example, suppose Danny's parents do indeed afflict him with unrealistic expectations. Even though they may not be conscious of conveying this feeling, they have given Danny the sense that not even being an award-winning student at the top of his class is good enough for them. What then? First, though Danny may be suffering from the imposition of such expectations, the school needs to exact consequences for cheating—an essay on plagiarism, an apology to the teacher, a zero on the assignment, or whatever the school community has deemed appropriate practice. Second, Danny's parents have work to do. They need to shed their illusions about Danny. They also need to see how their son is suffering, and making poor choices, in response to their projections. In the end, if Danny can acknowledge that his parents' expectations were irrational, his perceptiveness may be in and of itself sufficient for him to move confidently ahead. As a result, he might even come to view the dean or the teacher who "caused" him so much grief as an ally.

Suppose, on the other hand, that Danny's parents are themselves in the dark regarding harsh expectations Danny has placed on himself. It is now the parents, not Danny, who want to make use of the teacher and dean as allies. This requires, after the imposition of consequences, an altogether different follow-through with Danny. Now the goal of the family conference is to help Danny understand the connection between these self-imposed expectations and his sense of his own identity. This is not therapy. It is simply delving into the motivation for the behavior. As before, acknowledging the existence of underlying forces may be adequate for Danny.

Notice that the dean, at the outset, did not push Danny into a corner, even though he had plenty of evidence. He did not want to prove that Danny was guilty; rather, he wanted to free Danny to assume responsibility by inviting him to take a look at any possible hidden forces in his life. Notice, too, that Danny, when he was first called into the dean's office, began to acknowledge responsibility once he heard the dean admit his own imperfections. This self-revelation by the dean allowed Danny to uncover the camouflaged parts of himself that he had struggled so hard—and until now, apparently, successfully—to keep concealed. As a practical matter, a little bit of self-disclosure by an adult goes a long way with a teenager, who will sooner or later, with an adult he respects, probe for personal information.

Now suppose the meeting exposes domestic discord. Perhaps Mom and Dad are in the midst of an ugly separation that will likely lead to divorce. Perhaps there is alcoholism, compulsive gambling, neglect, or financial instability at play. Danny is caught in the middle and hasn't told anybody about what is going on at home. While still working out the consequences of cheating, the teacher and the dean can reach out to offer a completely different kind of support for Danny and his family. Furthermore, they are now in the position to serve as translators to, or mediators with, other teachers who may be dealing with any changes in Danny. Here everyone can help Danny resist self-destructive behaviors, which teenagers perform to deflect their attention away *from* their pain—and to call others' attention *to* their pain. One place to begin is with everyone's acknowledgment that Danny *is* suffering for an understandable reason, that it is difficult for any teenager going through what he is going through to navigate his way around his life, and that erratic and self-destructive behavior is a reaction to his current home life.

Whatever it was that drove Danny to cheat, an absolute moral limit must be set for him: it is wrong to cheat and there must be consequences for such choices. At the same time, Danny's action must be seen, in its completeness, as symbolic: he did one thing that meant another thing. He didn't need the higher grade, but he did seem to need to do something that might (and in this case did) upend his world. The trick for parents is to combine understanding with sympathy and resolution. Danny's action, they must communicate, was indeed understandable (and perhaps in some sense psychologically inevitable, given the particular circumstances of his life and family), but is not to be condoned.

Consequences and Support

Consequences and support not only *can* but *should* go hand in hand. Consequences without support merely add up to punishment, which breeds resentment. Support without consequences finally trickles down to condescension, which makes for cynicism. Without consequences the teenager becomes jaded; the community does, too, because no limit has been established. As a result teenagers may be implicitly encouraged to test further. But when families and schools strive to work together—and it is hard work—with clear eyes and open hearts, the chances for hostility and cynicism diminish appreciably. And when consequences and support reinforce each other, there is the possibility of regeneration. This is why such crises as Danny's, which burst to light in sorrow and bitterness and crashing disappointment, can usher in transcendent hopefulness all around.

Cheating and the End of the World

If the day comes that you find out your teenager has cheated, you will likely go through many painful emotional stages. Anger. *My kid is a good kid; something must have pushed him over the edge. The other kid's to blame. The teacher's to blame.* Panic. *Will she ever get into college now? Will this be on his record?* Defensiveness. Protectiveness. Humiliation. Embarrassment. Righteous Indignation. *You are grounded until graduation.* Sadness. *Where did I go wrong?* Discouragement. *Do I know who my child is anymore? Can I ever trust her again?* Guilt. You may recall when you yourself once cheated in high school and feel mortified, either for having gotten away with it or for having been caught. And you're afraid your teenager is going to probe your past because you are not sure how you are going to respond. In truth, these stages will overlap, and it will take all your love and wisdom to think clearly in and through the crisis and to act appropriately.

What your teenager needs from you is very simple: to establish moral limits. As simple as this is to say, though, it is every bit as hard to accomplish. Articulate the natural consequences of their action; that is, suit the response to the points you are trying to make. Raking leaves for a month and waxing the car would not be natural consequences of being dishonest, but writing a letter of apology to the teacher and serving as a math tutor for younger kids might be. Working along with the school, you can make the consequences meaningful but not draconian. Even while you are making clear that you reject cheating, you must embrace your teenager with love and support. This is the message you must convey: you love your child so deeply that you must hold her accountable.

Sometimes, though, we may fall into the habit of delegating to the school and to the teachers responsibilities to instruct our children on some of those hot issues we may feel unprepared to handle ourselves. Sex and sexuality is one issue. So is personal integrity. If this describes your tendency, rethink your position as soon as possible. As with sex, integrity is going to be a crucible for your teenager. Remember, articulating consequences is not a simple matter of lecturing or hectoring your teenager with moral injunctions. Moral injunctions are crucial, of course, but it's more complicated than that. The key in this situation is to have an open discussion (an *honest* discussion) about honesty. Share what you're comfortable with sharing, and avoid at all costs if you can the "When I Was in High School" speech (that approach will work *maybe* once or at the most twice in the four years you have, so time it carefully and use it wisely). Talk together about what both of you stand for and why. Acknowledge the omnipresence of temptation, and be realistic and pragmatic. The more work you do here, the less surprised your teenager will be when she's under a deadline to write the paper or when he's asked to let somebody see his answers on the quiz. Reflect on the deepest underpinnings of moral action. Isn't representing oneself honestly and accurately as important as anything could be? No matter what they say, your kids know that they risk their moral integrity by cheating. Look together at the biggest possible picture and examine what is important to you as a family. Then affirm it, together.

Danny's Conversation with the Scoutmaster

—I've been thinking. I don't know if I'm cut out to be an Eagle Scout.
—What are you talking about, Danny Boy? You've got Eagle Scout written all over you.
—That's what I'm talking about. I'm worried about what's inside of me.
—You embody what the Scouts are all about. We need more guys like you.
—But a Scout is trustworthy, loyal, helpful, friendly, courteous, kind, obedi-

ent, cheerful, thrifty, brave, clean, and reverent. Some days I might be some of that, and other days I might be none of them.

—You left out one thing, the unstated thing. A Scout is human. That means you don't have to be perfect to be the perfect Scout.

—You don't get merit badges for screwing up.

—Is there something you want to tell me?

—School was tough this year, and I made a mistake that I regret. I feel I let everybody down. It makes me wonder if I'm the kind of guy who can set a good example.

—Your dad talked to me, you know. He didn't tell me what was going on in school, just that he's worried you're being pretty hard on yourself.

—Really?

—I think he might be right, too. You push yourself and you have high standards.

—I just don't live up to them, is the problem.

—Nobody can live up to the standards of perfection.

—People have been telling me that. Like my dad the other day. After it all happened, he and I spent some time just talking. We threw the baseball around a little, and talked some more. You know, I'm not even sure what we talked about. About his work, I think, a little. That's not the important part somehow. He was telling me in a between-the-lines kind of way something I already knew. That he loved me anyway, I think.

—Had you forgotten?

—Not exactly, but it's good to be reminded.

5

Drugs and the Family

....

The art of being wise is the art of knowing what to overlook.

—WILLIAM JAMES

It's amazing that anyone teaches, that anyone wants to, or can. And so it seems nearly miraculous that the best teachers can somehow accomplish what's required and still have the focus and concentration to help students discover what they are destined to do and magically, in the process, change entire lives.

—FRANCINE PROSE,
"AN APPLE FOR THE MIRACLE WORKER"

Fear and Loathing in the Parking Lot

– One –

There it was: a new red sports car, gleaming and sleek, the top invitingly down. Mr. Salinas wished it were his car. He wished he could be driving it down the coast highway along about now. He also wished somebody hadn't taken his parking space—again. Parking is at a premium around his school, and that's why every space in the faculty lot is assigned and numbered. But how could a school guest know he wasn't supposed to park here? Unless, of course, he actually bothered to glance at any one of the dozen or so posted signs directing him to the visitor's lot. Still, there was nothing for Mr. Salinas to gain by giving over to his road warrior alter ego. Instead he would be philosophical; he would be the understanding citizen of the school community. Besides, he figured that was what he got for going off campus for a late lunch.

In any event, parking well is the best revenge. He prowled the student lot, hunting for a space. He got lucky and found one. After he stepped out of his car, though, he discovered that his good fortune came at a price. He saw something he wished he hadn't. To be precise, he *thought* he saw something.

There they were, Julia and Talia, getting out of a car. These were students of his, and he would have said he got along with them. From his vantage point forty or fifty feet away, it was obvious that they were enjoying themselves—his colleagues in the English Department might label that an example of understatement. Their voices were strident and their laughter slightly manic.

Wait a second. Was that the scent of marijuana wafting through the parking lot?

His choice was a tough one: confront them or keep moving. He didn't have any proof that they were smoking marijuana. Besides, he told himself, he hadn't chosen law enforcement as a career. He was a teacher. Perhaps just a couple of sophomores with a case of the giggles, right? Even though he had doubts, by this time he had pretty much decided to go the enlightened path of least resistance. So he kept his head down and moved along. The trouble was, nobody would accuse Mr. Salinas of being very Zen about anything.

At that moment Julia caught him looking at her. He must have been studying her more intently than he realized. She froze. Her jaw dropped, her eyebrows rose, and her cheeks flushed the color of the school mascot, which was the devil.

"Oh, hi, Mr. Salinas," Julia blurted out.

Talia swiveled her head past Mr. Salinas and seemed to be scanning the parking lot for the nearest boulder to crouch behind.

He said hello and together they walked back toward the main school building. The girls were jittery, and they vacillated between chummy chatter and clunking, self-conscious silence.

"What were you doing off campus, Mr. Salinas?" asked Talia, in the spirit of slightly forced friendly conversation.

He answered in a kindred spirit.

About one heartbeat later, Julia asked, "So, where have you been, Mr. Salinas?"

All right, he thought. There was no question now. Besides, he was sure he smelled something not sold at the cosmetics counter. His role was becoming more and more complicated by the second. The three of them marched farther, grimly. He finally asked them to stop, peered into their camouflaging sunglasses, and asked if they had just been smoking dope. Julia histrionically protested her innocence—"Are you crazy!"—as Talia looked down, studying her shuffling shoes.

He scratched his head: "OK, ladies, follow my train of thought. Once I started walking through the parking lot I smelled the pot, just as I observed the two of you sauntering back to main campus in an intensely cheerful mood. Nobody else around and when I got close to you I could smell it on both of you. Yet when I ask you about this, Julia, you deny it and call me crazy, and, Talia, you look like you ate the canary. Tell me what conclusion you would draw?"

"I don't care what you think you smell," insisted Julia, "and you can draw whatever conclusion you want. I didn't smoke pot! And neither did Talia either. Right, Talia?" Talia shook her head dubiously, in mournful accord. Then Julia added, "You know, this is America, innocent until proven guilty, not the other way around."

If he kept up this questioning much longer he would be late for class and probably wind up too frazzled to teach coherently. So he told them they would be talking again. "Tomorrow, my room, lunch time, be there."

He hoped that when that time came he would have something to say.

As he went through the motions for the rest of the day, he found himself harking back to this incident and imagined ways to deal with the problem—that is, to deal seriously and professionally with two students he liked.

On the one hand, he was tempted to tell the vice principal of his suspicion and let *her* deal with it. But without proof he knew there wouldn't be much she could do. But the main reason he didn't go to the vice principal was that, given his knowledge, the kids, and their reaction, he saw no usefulness in escalating this into an official disciplinary inquiry. If they had admitted they had been smoking dope, of course, he would have advised the administration. But as it stood, everything was a he-said, she-said blur.

But then again he didn't want to let them get away with this either. It was simply too important to ignore. That wouldn't teach anything. And that wouldn't work to anybody's advantage, especially his. After all, by smoking marijuana on campus they were being bold to the point of stupid, careless to the point of reckless. Kids usually don't do something that doesn't make a lot of sense—unless it makes a kind of sense. And kids usually don't get caught by you unless they want to, or need to, get caught by you.

After talking with his wife over dinner about what had happened, he passed a restless night. As he thought about his own two-year-old daughter and about being a parent himself, he wondered what he might find helpful in a situation like this—if it ever came up, say, in about fourteen years. That train of thought gave him an approach that he thought just might work.

– Two –

Julia told Talia they had to get their stories straight. So they talked on the phone that night, to prepare for, as she termed it, Salinas's inquisition.

"Such a major dork," said Julia. "It's none of his business. I tell you something, I don't need this, not now, I've got too much going on, not that it matters to him, because he's a teacher and he doesn't have a life."

"He's really not so bad," Talia offered, tentatively. She was thinking about how many times Mr. Salinas had stayed after school to help her with her homework.

"What are you talking about, girl! He's a pathetic narc. Which isn't his job. He's supposed to be a teacher."

Talia didn't know what to say. All she kept thinking about was how much homework she wasn't going to get done tonight. That, and the voices of her parents echoing downstairs in the living room.

"Talia, it's very simple. Like my old man says, Nobody ever got hanged for something he didn't say. We're kind of taking the Fifth Amendment, that's all. It's our constitutional right."

"He's not that stupid, you know. He smelled the dope."

"Stop using the word already. Besides, if he knew what it smelled like, it means he's probably no saint himself, right? Be strong, girl, hold your mud."

"That sounds like your dad, too."

"Well, sometimes he almost can make a little bit of sense." Julia laughed one second too long to be convincing.

"OK."

"So, we're together?"

"You and me, Julia."

"*That's our story, Mr. Salinas, and we're sticking to it.* Go ahead, say it, for practice."

"I've got to finish this paper."

"OK, be a good girl. You watch, we keep our stories straight and all this is going to blow over. Trust me, I've seen it happen a dozen times before."

– Three –

The three of them met in his classroom the next day at lunch, just as Mr. Salinas had requested.

"Well, ladies, given yesterday's problem any additional thought?"

"Which problem would that be, Mr. Salinas?" said Julia.

"You're not going to help, are you?"

"Wish we could," said Talia. And meant it, too.

"Let me rephrase that. You sure you don't want to help yourself?" He addressed Talia, whom he sensed was wavering a bit.

Julia took no chances and jumped in. "Sounds more like you want us to help you, Mr. Salinas."

"OK, that's enough for now. If that's the only alternative you're giving me . . . "

"You could decide to believe us," Talia suggested.

"I suppose I could tell myself I didn't see and smell what I did." But he shot her a look that indicated the probability was low.

What followed was silence, lots of it. The three of them glanced up to stare up at the clock over the classroom door.

Eventually, Mr. Salinas said he gave up, told them that he was going to contact each of their families tonight to tell them what he thought may have happened. This was not, he explained, to make any formal accusations or to initiate disciplinary measures, just to inform them. Their families had a right to know, and he had an obligation to inform them. He suggested that each girl talk to her parents before he called, which would be about eight o'clock.

Julia was outraged and Talia began to cry. If they were innocent they had nothing to fear, he said. And if they weren't, then their parents needed to be involved. Taking the high road didn't seem to be impressing either of them. Still, he felt he had no choice, and he left it at that.

That night, he called Talia's parents first, as he had gotten to know them a little the previous year. Both of them got on the line. They seemed to be listening intensely, not interrupting him, taking in the news. Then when Mr. Salinas was done, Talia's father said, "That's pretty much what Talia told us." He then said that they were still talking with Talia and asked if he could call Mr. Salinas later that evening.

Relieved, Mr. Salinas hung up the phone and said to himself, *There, that wasn't too bad, was it?* He was therefore feeling pretty good when he dialed Julia's number. He had never met her parents and had never spoken to them before. Her mom seemed shocked to be hearing a teacher's voice on the telephone. Clearly, she hadn't been prepared, and she wasn't happy one bit. He wasn't quite finished with his account before she was interrogating *him*, focusing on his *so-called* account of the *so-called* incident.

Then the conversation turned ugly: "How dare you call our home and tell me my daughter has a drug problem? How dare you accuse my daughter? And by the way, who appointed you drug czar, Mr. Salinas?" Julia's mother then assured him that her daughter would never, ever smoke pot and that, furthermore, he should just stick to his job. Finally, for good measure, she added that she was going to lodge a formal complaint with the vice principal first thing the next morning. She may have hung up. He didn't recall hearing or saying good-bye.

Almost immediately his phone rang. It was Talia's dad. It took the teacher a second to register what he was hearing. Mr. Salinas was being thanked for taking the risk of confronting Talia on her behavior and for phoning home. Talia's father assured him that they had had a good, if not altogether pleasant, family talk and that everyone had learned from the experience. While the parents weren't overjoyed with everything Talia had said, they felt that their family relationships were stronger as a result of the discussion.

"Would you mind if I send a note to the vice principal about the fine job you're doing?" He would like to leave out the details of the incident, though.

His exchange with Talia's father was small consolation for Mr. Salinas, however, because he couldn't get the conversation with Julia's mother out of his head.

Talia's Conversation with Her Aunt Leah

—Talia, could you hold on for a second, please? I'm confused.
—Sure. About what?

—The whole lunch we've been talking and I still can't tell. Were you and Julia smoking pot, or not?

—What'd Mom tell you?

—She's my big sister, so she always needs my help.

—Oh, you're the authority on teenagers now?

—Nobody's an authority on teenagers, but I haven't hit the Big Three O, I still remember high school, and I do know you pretty well. So Talia, come on, did you get high or not?

—Well, guess you could say so, technically. Only, I wasn't high. Get it?

—So. You smoked pot but you didn't get high? I'm lost.

—Listen, come on, you've known me since I was born.

—I changed your diapers.

—I'm eating lunch, Leah. But I always thought kids who get high at school were stupid. Classes are hard enough, especially Salinas's, without being stoned. It's a loser thing to do.

—So what happened this time? Did you go against what you believe? Or did you change your beliefs?

—No. I still believe it's stupid to get stoned at school. And I know this is going to sound crazy, but I didn't smoke pot with Julia to get high. In fact, I didn't really even get high with her that day, I just sort of faked it.

—What are you running for president?

—Exactly. Anyway, well, Julia's cool. Everybody thinks so. I hardly know her, but in the past few weeks we've been hanging out a little bit, and we're in English and Geometry together. But still, I never spent a whole lot of time with her, other than going to and from class. She seemed nice.

—You look up to her?

—I don't exactly look up to her, but she's very cool.

—So how did you go from hanging out to getting stoned at school—all right, all right, check that—to not smoking pot with each other at school?

—We both have a free period after lunch and that day I saw her waving to her friends as they went to class. She seemed pretty down, so I kind of went up to her. Then she just sort of launched. All these family problems she was having, it was incredible. I thought my house was a zoo, but hers, man. Her parents are fighting all the time, pretty scary, too, maybe they're even breaking up, which wouldn't be the worst thing, she says. It was cool, you know what I mean? Not her problems, but the way she trusted me. All of a sudden she goes, "Hey, want to go for a ride? I got to get away from this crazy place for a minute; it'll clear my head. Come on, would you?" We had a free period, nobody was cutting. I didn't think twice. I didn't realize she was old enough even to drive, but turns out she has her own car and everything. But then when we were driving off, she just pulled out a joint, took a hit, and passed it over. What could I do? Plus, she was counting on me. So I took a tiny hit, or so, and sort of faked it. I don't think she could tell. I'm pretty sure anyway.

—How much of that did you tell your mom and dad?

—All of it, and that's what really pissed them off. Not the dope but that I was a dope, trying to please somebody else.

—Keep it up and they'll make you do a public service announcement.

—Right: This is Talia's brain not on drugs.

Notes Home

Being On and Being Off, Being In and Being Out

Some teenagers get high for the same reasons they study hard, run for student office, do community service, or play the guitar. That is, they do it for love, for joy, for fun, for friendship, for the education, for the pure experience of it. They do it to please others, to earn status, to test themselves, to make a statement to others (and themselves). In other words, they do it in and out of the fullness of their still evolving selves.

But let's be careful. No one should ever be pollyannaish, not for a second, on this topic. In addition to the legal issues involved, marijuana, beer, cocaine, heroin, acid, inhalants, speed, ecstasy, and so on, carry special risks and dangers and can lead to addiction and death. For a long time a debate has raged over the gateway theory of drugs: how marijuana, for instance, leads to other more serious drugs and addictions. Research is inconclusive, however. Yet "marijuana is a gateway drug in the sense that if people smoke it, they will probably associate with others who smoke marijuana, or use other drugs, so the opportunities to experiment are greater. Incidentally, the history of most addicts clearly demonstrates that the first drug they ever used or abused was either tobacco or alcohol—the real gateway drugs."[1] The fact remains, though, that a one-time experiment in drugs or alcohol can kill. If parents discover that their teenagers are experimenting occasionally with marijuana or alcohol, they have legitimate cause for concern. If they are experimenting with the more hard-core substances, they have cause for alarm. These teenagers require immediate assessment and professional treatment.

Still, the truth is, teenagers do experiment, and they do take their chances. Experimenting and chance taking are the very keys to their growing self-knowledge. All experiments and all chances are not equivalent, however, and this is where families, schools, and good friends can make a difference, helping teenagers make better experiments, take wiser chances, and learn from them. It goes without saying that living with teenagers embarked on this leg of their journey to adulthood is never easy.

Still, the good news is that the overwhelming majority of substance experimenters will never devolve into addiction or even lapse into drug abuse. The overwhelming majority will never get high and crash a car, will never be arrested, and will never flunk out of school. There is even compelling research suggesting that some kids who experiment but do not become dependent are psychologically healthier than both those who abuse *and* those who abstain altogether.[2]

For a few teenagers, grim eventualities do come to pass. Should parents sit back and wait out this season of experimentation? No. Or not quite. As they respond to their changing children's changing needs, there will be tears, there will be intensity, there will be breakthroughs, and there will be setbacks. The key to family success here is for parents to stay relentlessly engaged in an ongoing dialogue about such issues and, above all else, carve out the time for these tough encounters.

In this arena parents are likely to sense in a fresh, poignant way the limitations of their power. Unlimited parental control and protection is neither possible nor desirable, but parental *influence* is both possible and desirable. Your teenagers need you—even while they insist that you give them space to work things out for themselves and even while they say to you, often vehemently if not rudely, that they don't need you at all.

In order to support your teenagers when they are struggling over their independence, you must take the long view and be available and be together with them in *mutual* vulnerability. The fact is, you are never going to be present when the beer is being passed around in the car or when the joint is fired up. Nonetheless, how you prepare your children for those conceivable situations can make a difference. That is, you cannot spare them from making mistakes. At the same time, don't you make the mistake of abandoning them to their own devices. For one thing, at a bare minimum, make sure they have sound, detailed information about drugs and alcohol, from you or school or a health professional, preferably from all of you. That doesn't mean handing them a book and hoping for the best or asking how health class went today. It means checking in with them meaningfully and continually—but securely this side of haranguing them.

Drug Testing and Complexity

Teenagers don't use drugs or drink alcohol for no reason, and self-destruction is normally the farthest thing from their minds when they do. Each kid is different, and so is each occasion. In other words, there is no manual of standard response. In Julia's case, desperation and avoidance are spurring her on to drinking and using drugs. In Talia's case, this instance of using stems largely, it seems, from her concern for social status, or as a feature of her quest for personal identity, or as a means of solidifying and expressing love and friendship. It's rare to find one of these motivators not in the company of the others. No wonder using is a reasonable and even attractive risk. At this stage of her life, the fifteen- or sixteen-year-old experiences these issues as portentous. Besides, in Talia's mind, she was only pretending.

Nonetheless, you are right to be terrified when you see your children coming home Friday night under some degree of influence. But remember, that may be the *only* time your children ever do it. On the other hand, it may be the first signal of a serious drinking problem. Only honest conversation, vigilance, and the passage of time will tell. It may be wise, depending on what you learn, to consider assessment.

Breathalyzers and urine samples, hysteria in the home, and recrimination and accusation—all may be counterproductive. Not so incidentally, on the topic of drug testing, parents are often confused and divided. On one level, the tactic seems desperate and cynical and untrusting, but on another, the risk of temporarily alienating teenagers seems worth it if it means saving their lives. That's why testing might indeed be appropriate in a *few* cases—for instance, with a teenager who has been using regularly or one who is in angry denial. But testing for no specific reason, without precipitating cause, will naturally lead to bitterness, suspiciousness, and, almost inevitably, exactly the sorts of deceptions that will promote even more serious problems. Remember, for a teenager, testing without specific cause is rooted in mistrust, and mistrust is what neither you nor your teenager can afford to have in your relationship.

Instead, parents must come to understand the drive behind the risky behavior. This is not a matter of being either soft or naive; this is being practical and visionary. As you set a boundary, do so with love and respect. Don't miss the opportunity to support your teenager. You have the chance to show your teenager how to answer the challenges of growing up in less destructive and dangerous ways. That seems exactly what took place in Talia's home during the conversations that were precipitated by the phone call from her teacher.

In general, though the downside of using drugs or alcohol is perilous, the corresponding upside for a teenager is magnificent, as Talia communicated to her Aunt Leah. She can cement Julia's friendship by sharing the joint (or by appearing to do so) and by standing with her in the pact of dishonesty. Is it worth it? At her stage of development, that would be a definite maybe; certainly not a clear-cut no, but not an absolute yes, either. Talia's not a druggie and she's fond of her teacher, yet she stands ready to risk her reputation as well as the approbation of those she loves and admires because the allure of Julia's friendship is so tantalizing. The temptation a parent may feel to overreact in a situation like this, to not listen to the whole story, and to take a teenager's poor judgment personally must all be resolutely resisted. Why? Far too much is at stake.

What Is Truth?

Just about every experienced teacher has probably faced a dilemma similar to Mr. Salinas's. (As have most if not all parents, for that matter.) He confronted certain circumstances in which facts were impossible to lock down. Not only that, he was dealing with teenagers, who are, by nature, experts at fashioning ambiguity and instilling confusion. The problem is that the teacher had excellent cause to believe something serious took place, but he could not be absolutely certain.

So what is a teacher to do when the stakes are significant, or possibly significant, and when remaining passive is an untenable option? He is a teacher, not a criminal investigator; that is, he is working with teenagers in the interests of their own education and he is tuned in to their development. Beyond that, he knows that families deserve to have all the important information they need to raise their children—even if that information is not crystal clear and even if it is hard for him to impart and harder still for them to take in.

This predicament illustrates that in the long run teachers have only their own integrity to guide their judgment. If they keep the education of teenagers in mind, and if they give them the chance to take responsibility for what they do, teachers, like parents, will not often be off the mark. It would be wonderful indeed if teachers always enjoyed the endorsement of parents and students when they embark upon a tough course of action. Teachers, however, cannot count on basking in the warmth of all parents or all teenagers when they do the right thing.

What Talia and Julia Really Need Now

What these girls need is the last thing they want: somebody to take them seriously. Of course, they don't see that they have a problem. But what else would we call driving and getting high to alleviate a bleak mood (Julia) or to demonstrate loyalty no matter the risk (Talia). At the same time those concerns seamlessly open into other problems, such as doubts about self-worth and questions about the place of friendship. Yet as the teacher had learned from experience, and as we have said before, kids don't do something that doesn't make sense unless it makes sense, and they don't get caught unless they need to.

In this case, Mr. Salinas took the middle way: he did not walk away from what he viewed as a serious situation, and he did not escalate it beyond a defensible level. He approached the families to tell them what he knew and suspected, nothing more and nothing less. His information was valuable to the extent that his judgment was good and useful to the extent that the families had reason to trust him. Furthermore, without being heavy-handed, he gave these two teenagers a chance to take responsibility for their actions. He also gave them what amounts to an out: all he reported to their families was his perceptions, and the families were left to respond in their own way.

Some teenagers will react inspiringly to the invitation to be self-critical and candid. Talia certainly did. Some won't. For every Talia, there is a Julia.

Talia and her parents acted according to Mr. Salinas's fondest dreams. They used his call as the impetus for the family to take a close look at what was going on with Talia, and she seems to have used it as an opportunity to talk about some other intrinsically connected matters at the same time. They took advantage of this incident to make their relationships more honest, which almost certainly provided some uncomfortable moments for every one of them. All in all, they did not whitewash Mr. Salinas's report; rather, they allowed themselves to tolerate the truth without letting their anxiety get the better of them.

Talia herself was probably relieved that her parents heard from Mr. Salinas and that they had this conversation. Believe it or not, kids do not enjoy lying to their parents. Often they just don't know how to start the more truthful and difficult conversations. Also, many kids have parents who cannot tolerate (and therefore cannot be trusted with) the truth. (Being and acting honest is an acquired skill; lying takes less effort.) Fortunately, this was not the case with Talia's parents. This may have been something Talia didn't know about her parents until the crisis presented itself. Are we saying that she initiated such a crisis in order to test her parents? Possibly, though if so, probably not consciously. But it does seem clear that they have now built up a greater measure of trust than ever before. Who knows—that trust may be exactly what she needs to prevent her from making other, graver mistakes. There's an important lesson for parents here: even in the most strained circumstances, with openness and trust you can forge stronger family ties. Furthermore, those ties will mitigate the chances of future crises.

On the other hand, the reaction from Julia's family is the nightmare that probably disturbed Mr. Salinas's sleep the night before. Mr. Salinas put himself out on a limb for Julia and she and her family promptly sawed it off. Alas, this is an all-too-frequent reaction. But before a teacher can understand the angry reaction of her family, he must understand the development of a teenager from a slightly different vantage point—that of the parents.

Changing Relationships, Changing Families

When teenagers enter high school, their relationship with their parents has already changed momentously. Although that seems to be a universal experience in families, how and why is that so? To put it simply, teenagers need to exert more control over their lives, which means parents need to take a step back. Or, more accurately, *a step to the side*, where they can support but not control their kids' lives. This is a difficult transition for all parents, especially considering that most teenagers are not very articulate or graceful or conscious when it comes to these changes. Consequently, parents must search for a way to better communicate with and support their kids during adolescence.

How often do parents complain that their teenagers do not communicate with them anymore? When their kids are in high school, many parents grow discouraged because they feel they cannot catch up to their kids' lives. Simultaneously, though, they are also searching for a way to show their loyalty to, and their trust in, their kids. That is why many will deny having problems with their kids—or even deny the problems their kids encounter in their own lives. Denial is a defense against the prospect of their worst fantasies springing to life.

Enter, in this context of denial and resistance, somebody such as a Mr. Salinas on the other end of the phone. Without exactly knowing it, the conscientious teacher is strolling into a hurricane armed only with an umbrella. Obviously, Julia's mother does not want to see any problem with her daughter. That's why she distorts the teacher's words, deflects the information, and maligns the messenger of bad tidings. That's understandable: what parent wants to hear of a problem like this? And how many parents are equipped, emotionally and psychologically, to wrestle with the complications of their kids' lives? It is especially trying for parents who are struggling with their own issues (serious domestic troubles, according to Talia's testimony). The last thing they need, as they deal with their marital crisis, is a daughter in her own crisis.

Faced with alternative versions of reality—the teacher's and her daughter's—Julia's mother wants to prove to Julia how much she loves and supports her. What better way to sustain the illusion of a near-perfect kid and to demonstrate unconditional love than by unreservedly, and desperately, supporting Julia and her version of the story? As a practical consideration, too, what makes it easier for her to dismiss the call and the caller is that she has absolutely no connection to Mr. Salinas, which allows her to cast him in the role of unfair, mean-spirited authority figure. In her mind, she is no doubt doing what she thinks every good parent would do: coming to the defense of a slandered daughter. At this point, all Mr. Salinas can do—all that Julia's parent will allow him to do—is what anybody should do in a natural disaster: head for the nearest shelter.

Lesson Plans for Parents and Teachers

There are, in this one narrative of a quite un-extraordinary event, some important lessons for those who work with teenagers and for their parents, too. First, there is seldom a simple conversation between parents and teachers (and all those in positions of authority over your teenager). Everything can (and probably will) turn, without a moment's notice, symbolic and freighted (for both parent and teacher). Thus teacher and parent should go into these exchanges with a clear heart and with eyes and ears wide open, presuming nothing and hoping everything. Though it may seem self-evident, it must never be forgotten that teachers are talking about one of their hundred or more students this term, one out of the thousands they may have taught; parents, though, are talking about one of their own, someone they have nurtured from infancy.

Second, educators need to understand that if parents only ever hear from the school when their child gets in trouble, they are quickly going to lose faith in the school and the teachers. In other words, it is important to catch teenagers being good and to let parents know about a few of those moments, too. Parents find it much easier to hear difficult news from a teacher who recognizes the strengths and virtues of their teenager. It is easier for them to hear a hard message when they trust and respect the messenger, and when they believe they are collaborating with the school in the development of their children.

Teachers Are Not Innocent Bystanders

Why should Mr. Salinas, a teacher, choose to get involved? Some of his colleagues would say that this is none of his business—that policing the parking lot is not in the teacher's contract. Some teachers, perhaps many if not most teachers, would simply elect to look away and later justify their passivity. In fact, there are schools that will not encourage or even permit a teacher to initiate such interventions. We inhabit a cynically litigious world.

Still, sometimes a hard message, which a teacher like Mr. Salinas dares to carry home, may ultimately make all the difference in the life of that teenager and family. But he may have to wait a while to know for sure, or at least until he shakes off the lingering effects left behind by an argumentative parent. Then, later on, he might remind himself that taking a risk to reach out lies close to the reason he took up teaching in the first place.

Studies, Studies, and More Studies

Virtually every week of the year we read reports in journals and newspapers on drug use and teenagers. For instance, Columbia University's National Center on Addiction and Substance Abuse conducts annual surveys of teenagers' attitudes and practices. In the most recent polling of a thousand teenagers, they indicated (for the fourth year in a row) that drugs are the most important problem they face. "And the percentage of high school students who report that drugs are used, sold and kept at their schools continued to inch up, rising to 78 percent this year from 72 percent in 1996."[3]

This is the kind of quantitative information guaranteed to arouse the panicky attention of parents. Statistics like these, however, cry out to be placed in perspective. "Overall," the Columbia survey indicates, "41 percent of 17-year-olds said they have smoked marijuana, while 39 percent said they drank and 23 percent said they smoked in the previous 30 days."

Yes, it's important to grasp the gravity of the risk, and no one should be blasé for one second about the everyday availability of drugs and the toll exacted by them in families and the lives of young people. Still, if we look, for instance, at those survey numbers just quoted slightly differently, we see that 59 percent of 17-year-olds have *not* smoked marijuana and 61 percent did *not* drink and 77 percent did *not* smoke cigarettes in the last month.

What can we learn from such studies? For one thing, although the numbers seem alarming across the board, there nonetheless remains a very excellent chance your teenagers have not smoked or used drugs. For another, if your teenagers have done so, they are not automatically doomed to a life of failure and desperation. Which is another reason to remain vigilant— and calm—and sensible—and realistic—and hopeful. (The parent's best trick is juggling all those attitudes at the same time. But then, it isn't quite a trick.) But be pragmatic, too. Filter all the surveys and all the studies, and skeptically place such information in the context of your family and your teenager.

But Still, If You Do Get the Call . . .

To be honest, in the near term you won't be having a good day. You will be angry and disappointed and fearful—and you won't know for a while the object of your conflicting emotions. Are you angry, for example, at your child, or yourself, or the "other kid," or the teacher—or all of the above?

What to do? First, try to understand the motivation of your own "Mr. Salinas." In this story, one teacher took the high road, at considerable personal expense, when another teacher might simply have justified doing otherwise. Without incontrovertible proof, he might have elected to do nothing and spend a quiet night at home with his own family. He might have rationalized away any response at all. We can imagine somebody else in his set of circumstances saying to himself that this is no big deal; all kids experiment. Besides, it's a family problem, not his. He might even have used this incident to elevate his status to the level of being a really "cool" teacher who looked the other way. Or he might have decided to fight another time, when the cause was transparent. Instead, however, he struggled with himself, made the best determination he could as to his students' needs, then took the risk and dialed those phone numbers.

It is vital for parents to appreciate what a teacher in this kind of situation goes through, and what it means for the education and development of teenagers. It is the same chance any teacher takes when she contacts you with discouraging news. She does not do this because she is churlish or power crazed or harboring some irrational grudge against your teenager. And yes, it goes without saying that she herself is flawed and limited and far from a paragon of virtue—just like you and the authors of this book and everybody else you know. But she risks reaching out to you because she cares about the welfare of your child.

Even so, for you, as parents, this news can be impossibly difficult to handle. In one conversation your fears seem realized, your illusion of control and responsibility resolutely shattered. In such a moment it is not so easy to be gracious. All right. Fine. *Gracious*, when it comes to raising teenagers, is very nice work if you can get it, but not something to count on. Later on, when the adrenaline rush subsides, reflect on what the teacher did and the chance she took—it was not insignificant. At that point, you might want to initiate a follow-up conversation that begins, perhaps, "I've been going over what we talked about and maybe, you know . . . "

Here's another suggestion: familiarize yourself with your teenager's teachers in advance, if for no other reason than that they will be more ready to take a leap of faith along with you. If you do manage to do that, you just might get that dreaded phone call, which later on you will nonetheless mark as a wonderful turning point in the life of your teenager.

Will You Make "the Call"?

If you haven't pondered such a question, do so, because the opportunity will perhaps present itself. Like it or not, you yourself may have the chance to play "Mr. Salinas." Suppose you hear that your son's best friend, the one you find in his room every day after school, is smoking dope regularly? Or suppose you discover there is an unchaperoned party this weekend where, the rumor goes, alcohol will be served? Suppose your own teenager dates somebody who often seems to be remote and adrift, who calls at odd hours and wears a glazed expression and never engages in substantive conversation with you? You will need to act according to your own lights, of course, but ask yourself what you would value if you were placed in the other position? You should know and reach out to many other parents. Then you can mutually support each other—and your teenagers.

6

Race and Adolescence

Before we can leave our parents, they stuff our heads like the
suitcases which they jam-pack with homemade underwear.
—Maxine Hong Kingston, *The Woman Warrior*

I am an invisible man. . . . I am invisible, understand, simply because people refuse to see me. When they approach me they
see only my surroundings, themselves, or figments of their imagination—indeed, everything and anything except me.
—Ralph Ellison, *The Invisible Man*

There's No "I" in Team

– One –

Big game. Biggest game of the season. Tech versus Jefferson, playing for the
league championship. They had split their first two games, each team winning on the opposition's court, but this contest was taking place on a neu-
tral court at a local college gym that was packed to the rafters. Because the
history of the two schools included some vandalism and graffiti, as well as
a few inappropriate cheers, there was a little bit more than the usual security on hand. As a precaution, the league had asked the principals at the
two schools to meet with their teams to discuss sportsmanship before-
hand. So far, these measures seemed to be working. At their last game the

referees had called several technical fouls on both sides, but during this game no incident took place. Until, that is, the last five seconds.

That was when Tech's best player scored, was fouled, and went to the line with a chance to tie up the game by making a free throw. Just before he was handed the ball, Jefferson's best defender, Powell, called for a time-out. This is an age-old strategy called icing the player—making him feel the stress about the shot. The teams huddled up and both coaches talked strategy—what to do in the event of either a miss or a make—but probably few players could quite remember their explicit assignments.

As the teams positioned themselves around the key, the referee waited to hand over the ball to the Tech player. In the din made by the screaming crowd, Powell caught his opponent's eye and smiled at him. From a distance of a few feet, and while the referee's attention was elsewhere, he mouthed, "Your people are counting on you."

The Tech player, who was black, glared at Powell, who was white.

"You heard me, hotshot," said Powell as he clapped and exhorted his teammates to box out and get ready to rebound.

Then Powell noticed that directly across the key his teammate Shawn, who was also black, had witnessed the whole exchange, and even Powell could tell that Shawn looked as angry and upset as the Tech player. That was the first of several strange things that were about to happen to Powell. Right after the Tech player missed the shot and Jefferson rebounded and dribbled out the clock, Shawn came up to Powell, but not with the intention of celebrating the win. The gym was quaking and fans were pouring onto the court, but Shawn didn't seem to want any part of it.

"What's up with, 'Your people are counting on you'?"

"What?"

"You know damn well what I'm talking about. *Your people*—that's what I'm talking about."

"Hey, man, lighten up. We just won league."

"Lighten up? You crazy? Not with your racist bullshit."

Before Powell could respond, the crowd swallowed them both up and pulled them in opposite directions, and that was almost a good thing for Powell, because he was speechless.

– Two –

Shawn knocked on the coach's office door. It was just before third period, his only free period of the day. Coach was glad to see him. "Great game last night, Shawn." Truth was, of course, it wasn't one of his better games and both Shawn and the coach knew it.

"I was OK, but I can play better."

"Hey, important thing's we won."

"Yeah, you're right."

"You upset about the way you played? Because if you are, the main thing is we won as a team."

"I know, I just don't like the way we did it."

The coach looked confused. He took the opportunity to address what he thought was Shawn's disappointment in the way he played, and almost as if to reassure himself, said, "You know what they say, there's no *I* in team."

"Yeah, but there is an *I* in racism." That's when Shawn told Coach what he heard Powell say to the Tech free throw shooter. "For a second there, I heard Powell, and I wished the guy had made the shot."

– *Three* –

Coach tracked down Powell during lunch in the cafeteria. "Got a minute?"

Powell was basking in postgame glory with some friends. "Sure, Coach," he grinned, "I'd do anything for you and the team."

"That's exactly what I want to talk about. Let's go."

They found a quiet spot in an empty classroom, and the first thing Coach said was that Powell showed no class talking trash to the shooter. It was precisely the sort of provocation that the principal had warned them against, and the kind that Coach had inveighed against from the first day of practice. Coach was disappointed and angry, too. When Powell tried to defend himself, Coach cut him off. It was wrong, and what Powell had done was indefensible. Then Coach asked him exactly what was it he said in those last seconds.

"What's the difference? He missed, we won, end of story."

"Not quite. It matters to me what you said, and it matters to everybody on your team and at school, and it better matter to you, too. Here I am, the day after the biggest win in years, and all I'm thinking about is how angry I am with you."

"What is the big deal? First, Shawn calls me a racist and now you're giving me the third degree. Everybody talks trash."

"Maybe other teams, not ours. But—*your people are counting on you*—is that what you said?"

"Something like that . . . Yeah, that was it. Had to try to get inside the guy's head. I just couldn't stand there and hope he missed."

Coach was worked up, so he took a deep breath before he said: "Hey, Powell, in the ebb and flow of the game, things get said, I know that, but this is different. I can't believe you don't get how different that is, that it's a slur. *Your people* means there's something different and wrong about his race and that he represents them and that you're better than he is. When you say *your people* you make yourself out to be superior, you put the other race down."

"Man, everybody's so touchy about race around here. I'm no racist. You know it and so does everyone on the team. I didn't mean anything personal, even the Tech guy knows that."

"I doubt you're right about that, but I do know that your own teammates are taking it personally."

"You're right about that. Just because Shawn had a bad game, he doesn't have to take it out on me. We've been friends since sixth grade, and he knows I'm no racist. I've slept over at his house. We're doubling to the prom, at least we were planning to. I'm worried about him. He never used to be so serious about this stuff. He's really changed."

"If he has, it's a good thing. Besides, this isn't about Shawn, it's about Powell. State tourney starts next week. Whether you realize it or not, you need some time to yourself. Take the day off from practice and figure out why you need to apologize to Shawn and the team, and get back to me tomorrow during lunch."

"Apologize for what? Winning the game? This is unfair. Why are you doing this to me?"

"Because I care enough about you to be really pissed off at how stupid you're being."

"I thought you were color-blind, that you saw us as individuals."

"That's why I'm so angry with you, because that kid from Tech deserves your respect. And you disrespected every one of your teammates and me when you said that. That's enough for now. Work on this by yourself for a while."

Powell's Talk with Coach at the End of the Season

Two weeks after the final game, Coach met individually with his players. Especially for those players who would be returning, like Shawn and Powell, it was his way of

summing up the season and pointing out individual directions for improvement over
the summer. A lot has transpired over these two weeks, but then again that is an
eternity for a teenager, especially during a crisis of this magnitude.

—One more thing, Powell. How are things going between you and Shawn?

—About the same as between me and my girlfriend—rocky. Seems like nobody's going to let me ever forget that Tech game, and not because I scored
all those points.

—Glad to hear it, I guess, but what's that got to do with Marnie?

—Her reaction after the game was ten times worse than you or Shawn. It's
like she won't let me be myself. I can sort of see why people took offense,
but I didn't mean it that way. How come nobody has to be sensitive about
how I feel?

—I'm glad she won't let you forget it. What's with Shawn?

—Basketball, we'll be fine. We'll be in summer league and we'll be at the
same camp. Otherwise, we still have things to work out, and we're talking.
Man, it's hard work. Lots of the time we don't know what to say to each
other. It's crazy. Sometimes I want to scream at him. Other times I just
want to go back to the way things used to be.

—Why's that?

—He's making me look at myself, and it's hard. Now I see race everywhere,
and I don't like it. Not a lot of fun for me.

—You think it's fun for Shawn?

—Guess not, but I sure am learning things about him I never knew before,
like the kind of things kids say and do around school—or even more outside of school. It's like we almost live in two different worlds. What do you
think, Coach, you think you have to be the same race to be friends with
somebody? You ever see the cafeteria at lunch time? How everybody sits in
his own group? Never used to bother me before, but now I can't stop
thinking about it. But it's not like I do anything different about it.

—Sounds like you're already doing something different, by the way you're
thinking.

—Guess so. I'm pretty confused. Before the Tech game I wouldn't have said I
was racist.

—And now?

—Now, heck if I know. Shawn and Marnie both make me feel like I don't
know myself anymore, and I feel out of control in my own brain, like I
have to rehearse what to say to everybody.

—There's a world of difference between rehearsing everything you say and just being aware of what your words mean to others.

—You sound like Marnie

—Smart girlfriend. OK, but let me ask it another way. Is what you just said rehearsed?

—No. At least I don't think so. But I take that back. There is something I rehearsed before I came here today because it's true and I want to get it right. I shouldn't have talked trash to the Tech guy. I was out of line and I'll never do that again.

—That's a good start.

—Start to what?

—To being captain next year.

—Captain?

—Co-captain, with Shawn.

—You sure he's cool with that?

—Yes, in fact he thinks he's getting through to you, and I have to agree.

—I can't guarantee I won't screw up again.

—I'll take my chances. Twenty years of coaching, I'd say you're worth the risk.

Notes Home

Race Talk

There is hardly a more charged topic among teenagers than race and racism. These issues provoke conflict, even anger and misunderstanding. But they are indispensable for teenagers because questions about race are inextricably bound up with problems of their own identity formation. Feelings of alienation, the pursuit of justice, the mysteriousness of another's life experience—these are terms that characterize any dialogue around race. They are also terms that characterize any discussion of adolescent development. Teenagers are passionately invested in understanding and creating themselves, and they are drawn into the problems of living with others whose experience is foreign to their own, such as those of other racial and ethnic backgrounds. These discussions of race, then, for teenagers provide ways to search for available images of self in the world, images that are confirming or, in the case of racism, disconfirming. No wonder the pursuit of respect lies near the core of every teenager's identity. And no wonder, as well, that being treated with anything other than respect will guarantee a teenager's rage and disappointment.

On the surface, race is a straightforward subject, at least in intellectual terms. Most would agree that racism is wrong. Mutual head nodding, however, comes to an abrupt halt when we speak frankly to one another about issues of race, especially when we are speaking with someone of a different race. Why? Because suddenly the conversation turns personal and complex. We discover that our views and assumptions are not nearly as innocent and idealistic as we had imagined. This conversation is painful. The truth is, people do not learn about racism and prejudice in intellectual terms. Race, as some have observed, is always an issue of the heart.

In this story, Powell is shocked at the response to his words. When he does something he wrongly believes is appropriate in the name of winning a game, namely, saying something upsetting enough to rattle his opponent, he also rattles his friend, his teammates, his coach, his girlfriend, and eventually himself. He goes through many painful stages of self-recognition, all interconnected, all wrenching. Although this experience is hard, it is good. Imagine he had not said anything offensive. He would never have had the opportunity to search his own soul and to forge sounder, more honest relationships. Oddly, blundering and then responsibly facing the consequences can bring him closer to others, and to self-understanding, than if he had never made a mistake in the first place. This is education. If he were never challenged, he would have been complacent about himself and about the world at large. Allowed to go unchecked, his attitudes could have hardened. He was fortunate enough to be surrounded by adults and peers who forced him to confront his assumptions and belief systems, and he himself had enough integrity and strength to stay engaged throughout.

How Teenagers Grow Through Conflict

If two kids who don't know each other bump in the hall and one responds with a racial epithet, conflict is inevitable—and it is the sort of conflict that is not likely to produce much light for either party. In the absence of an ongoing relationship their responses will remain on the level of indignation, justification, intimidation, and rationalization. But Shawn and Powell have a personal connection, and their issue, if it ever made the news, would be headlined as follows: Racial Conflict Produces Understanding After Hard Conversation and Mutual Vulnerability.

Conflict in and of itself does not guarantee growth. We stand a better chance of growing when that clash is with someone who matters to us. So one lesson for adults to learn is that reducing strife for its own sake is not always the ideal goal; understanding is the goal, and that results from coming to terms with the reasons for strife, and strife is inevitable for teenagers. This is why it's misguided to inoculate teenagers from conflict with teachers, friends, coaches, and, most of all, parents. (See the Appendixes for how teenagers grow through conflict over the years, especially Appendix C, "What Are You Looking At? Being 16–17" and Appendix D, "Where Am I Going and Where Have I Been? Being 17–18.")

In conflict, teenagers unmask themselves, for better or worse. They shock themselves and those around them. They enter the arena of moral education and character development. When your daughter comes home from school and says that she can't stand her English teacher, that he doesn't understand her style, that he grades too hard, and that he won't give her a break, you have a wonderful opportunity not to do the wrong thing. Some wrong things you will consider include trying to transfer your daughter out of the class, observing that life is unfair, telling your daughter to stop whining, reminding her of how you deal with your unreasonable superior, reading her papers and underlining all the gems the teacher has ignored, and so on. Instead, the most useful intervention you can make is to stop what you're doing and ask your daughter questions that inspire her to look hard at both her role in the conflict and her assumptions about herself, her class, and her teacher. Does this mean that tomorrow she will return to class a thriving, happy child? No. Does this mean that her teacher is flawless? No. But it does mean that your daughter, as a result of her conversation with you and the questions you raised, will be better equipped to articulate the feelings that spilled out as anger expressed to you. And she will see conflict not as something to be avoided or as something that takes place outside of herself, but as a means to understand herself, helping her to live more fully and consciously in her world. Should you demand a parent–teacher conference? Maybe, maybe not. Until your daughter and you understand the roots of her anger and frustration, a conference might not be of much use.

As adults and parents, we must always remember, especially when the stakes are very high, that kids do not need or want ready-made solutions.

What they really need is the kind of guidance that's not felt as prescriptive. And this guidance is necessary all the time, from minor school discipline issues (such as tardiness) to the largest issues of social justice (like racism). Abdicating this responsibility for guidance can produce monumental consequences. In *Our Guys*, the nonfiction account of the infamous Glen Ridge rape of a retarded girl by a group of popular high school boys, Bernard Lefkowitz dramatizes the insidious ways that adults defended the boys and denied the truth. There is no starker portrait of adults who subvert the moral development of their own children by enabling them to skirt the shock, horror, and shame of what they did.

In the story in this chapter, for instance, Powell is guided sensitively by Coach, and seemingly by Shawn, too, so that he goes from professions of innocence to rationalization to minimization to responsibility to acceptance. Learning the truth about oneself is rarely a pleasant experience, and it's the adult's responsibility (and the parent's opportunity) to help the teenager see that his mistake, his misjudgment, is an aspect of growing up, not a confirmation of moral failing. In other words, Coach does three things: he holds steady the moral line (that was dumb and mean; we don't do that); he waits (he tells Powell to take the day off from practice and think about his actions); he calmly reaffirms his principles and his belief in Powell (he tells him that he is not an evil kid, that his actions were mean-spirited, but that Powell can learn from them and not let them happen again).

Powell is fortunate that no one rushed in to make everything OK for him or the team. He's lucky in that everybody compelled him to face up to himself and his deeds.

Shawn's Growth

In one sense, it seems easier to concentrate on Powell's metamorphosis than on Shawn's. After all, Powell begins a painful transformation and comes to a gradual self-recognition that is clearly significant. But Shawn has just as much at stake, if not more, and is equally traumatized but for different reasons and in different ways. He hears a racist remark; he feels betrayed by somebody he thought was a friend; he was robbed of the elation that should have accompanied victory. At a much deeper level, this occasion intensifies the already prevailing identity crisis of a teenager. And he is going through this crisis not simply as a teenager but as a black teenager.

Beverly Daniel Tatum, author of *"Why Are All the Black Kids Sitting Together in the Cafeteria?"* argues that "all adolescents look at themselves in new ways, but not all adolescents think about themselves in racial terms." Black kids do think of themselves in racial terms, as Tatum writes, "because that is how the rest of the world thinks of them."[1] What is so poignant and wrenching about this moment for Shawn is that Powell has dismissed him as a human being. He tells Shawn, in effect, that he is principally seen through the lens of a racial stereotype: "you people" and "your people." These code terms amount to a type of racial profiling. When someone is pulled over by the police for "driving while black," no one misses the racism, conscious or unconscious. But it doesn't make the experience any less painful or excusable if the racism is unconscious. It is one thing to be seen as black or brown or yellow or white by oneself or by others of one's race. It's another to be seen only as a racial type or category. "You people" means you are a *them*, an *other*, an *outsider*, a *not-me*. That's why the school's celebration of the victory is so hollow for Shawn: he has been excluded from the camaraderie of his teammates. It is no wonder that Shawn fleetingly hopes the opposing player will make the shot, since in this moment the two of them are united by being cast in the role of the other.

How does this incident furnish Shawn an opportunity for growth? He shows integrity and stands up for what he believes in by confronting Powell. He personalizes what was said. He realizes that if Powell can say something like that to the Tech player, he means the same thing about Shawn. It might have been possible at some other point in his life to imagine that Powell was not targeting him. "He's talking about that guy, not me—he's my friend, my teammate." But now that argument would fall flat. Why? Because Shawn, in middle to late adolescence, sees race as an integral part of his identity. If Shawn were six years old, he would not have heard that remark in these terms. At the same time, of course, Powell at a similar age would never have said it, either.

Is Shawn politicizing the conflict? Given that almost anything we do potentially has a political dimension, it would be foolish to dismiss that possibility. But it would probably not feel political to Shawn. It is much more emotional and personal for him. In one sense he is arguing for racial sensitivity, but the stakes are not abstract. His identity is at stake here—personally, intimately, immediately.

The core developmental question for Shawn is enormous and simple: Can he be seen as being all of who he is, or does he have to piece out his identity and reveal himself compartmentally, partially, and inauthenti-cally? On one level, Shawn, like every teenager, has learned to reveal him-self judiciously depending upon his surroundings and social context. He's one way at Thanksgiving dinner, another at the movies with his buddies, still another in class. What is painful for Shawn is the sense that he cannot be completely and wholly himself with his friends, which is a prime value for teenagers.

In one way, Shawn's identity crisis is an archetypal one. All teenagers are tempted to conceive of themselves as a minority of one who is misunder-stood, misjudged, and betrayed. That's only part of the story, to be sure. But what makes Shawn's struggle so complicated at this historical juncture is that his race is a contested value, and therefore his very identity is seen as dubious in the larger society. Consequently, when the black kids sit to-gether in the cafeteria, they are enacting, according to Tatum, a compli-cated and developmentally appropriate supportive strategy. They are identifying with one another and finding confirming positive images of their blackness, which the mixed world, and especially the white world, in-validates or ignores. (As one kid said, "It's a snowstorm out there. We hud-dle together for warmth.") Shawn's self-respect has been called into question. Even Powell, Shawn's friend, has no idea at first of the meaning of what he says. That gives Shawn a tremendous opportunity to define himself partly by confronting Powell. And to the credit of both Shawn and Powell, they are ready to learn and grow together. Their friendship is strong enough to weather this storm, and they may eventually become much better friends than either could have imagined. In fact, they may al-ready be better friends than they realize. Their staying involved and en-gaged with each other may show a deeper commitment to their friendship than they realized before. The word for this is *respect,* and every real friendship is predicated upon respect.

What else does Shawn gain from his engagement with Powell? He learns that people can change and that he can be the agent. He sees that he has the power to affect his world, which is an enormous discovery for anyone, especially an adolescent. He rediscovers both the burden and the beauty of his identity. He embraces race and integrates it as a part of his identity. He crosses what could have been a racial divide without making a single com-promise. Above and beyond all these considerations, though, Shawn goes a long way toward becoming an adult. That means that he has stayed vulner-able, and mutually vulnerable with Powell, and strong at the same time. He reaps the benefits of participating in the most essential conversation about race, respect, and identity.

Powell's Growth

Do we mean that Powell's growth is Shawn's responsibility? Absolutely not. Powell is fortunate, however, that Shawn is ready to hang in there with him. What does Powell go through and how does he change? In general, he faces his own demons and confronts for the first time in a personal way the notion of race, and he sees through to the assumptions of his presumed racelessness. He realizes that he is responsible for his unconscious racism and for the impact of the words he utters, that is, how they are heard by others. He gains a deeper curiosity about his own identity and history. He sees friendship in a whole different way—he'll value it even more. He will have a new respect for adults' wisdom. He will be more authentic. He will be less likely to see the world in either/or terms. He will see the gray areas, the ambiguities. He will see the world more clearly from a racial perspective. He is more likely to confront others on their racism or other biases. He will realize that growing up costs dearly. He will be different at home, too, and raise the issues there. Like Shawn, he has taken a step toward becoming a man. But at the same time he feels wistful, as if he has lost a kind of innocence. He harks back to a time when things were simpler with Shawn, and it is going to take a while until he understands that, far from losing his innocence, he has begun to discard his ignorance.

One pivotal incident in a teenager's life will give him the material for a lifetime of reflection. That's why each chapter of this field guide to teenagers could conceivably go to the length of a Russian novel. Each teenager's existence is infinitely rich, and richer for having had a life-changing ordeal. And each teenager is susceptible to—no, each teenager is seeking out—just such amazing transformations.

Athletics and Character Development

In *Raising Cain* Dan Kindlon and Michael Thompson write about a school with an impressive athletic history: "At the beginning of the last season, the football coach stood up and asked his players, 'What is my job as coach?' The boys said a number of things: to teach us skills, to motivate us, to make us work hard. When they had exhausted their suggestions, the coach said, 'Well, it is all of those things, but I'll tell you what my real job is. It is to love you. No matter what happens during the season, my job is to love you.'"[2] That coach has it exactly right, and so does the coach in this story. And so does any parent or any adult who works with kids and thinks that way.

Participating on a team can help teenagers become their best selves. For instance, in this story Coach is angry that Powell indulged in trash talking, and he explains what's wrong with that cheap tactic. And that lesson might be nearly as painful for Powell as his coming to terms with his racial insensitivity. But then again, a good coach makes these connections because he prizes the integrity of his students. In all respects, coaches, whether they are aware of their influence or take responsibility for that influence, play a huge role in the life of any committed athlete. The merging of the coach, school culture, teammates, and individual character is, ultimately, what determines the value of the sport for each participant. This is true whether the participation is in a team sport like basketball, soccer, volleyball, football, baseball, or water polo, or whether the participation is in a more individual sport like gymnastics, tennis, track, golf, or swimming.

Teenagers crave individuality, but they also yearn to be part of a larger group. While developing their individual identities, many want their identities augmented through a meaningful commitment to a group of their peers. This gives them a rest from the exhausting work of carving out an individual identity and a safe outlet for their passion in a manner that puts their self-consciousness to rest for a couple of hours every day—during practice or a game. Furthermore, playing on a team gives them a specific focus, for what's best for the team is always paramount. Probably the only other area of a high school student's life that is comparable to the intense interdependence of team sports is the performing arts. On stage, and in the countless rehearsals and hours leading up to performance, there develops the same sort of commitment and mutual vulnerability.

When everyone is working together, a team insists on, supports, and, most important, teaches teenagers better behaviors and better attitudes than they are able to maintain on their own. This cannot be overemphasized. Once a player has committed herself to her peers, she is capable of doing things that she would be unable to do on her own. In other words, she will not give up on herself so easily. This is because more people will be let down than just herself, and she would not know how to face them unless she gave it her best. Her best is defined largely by the coach. But a coach can also occasionally bring out and reinforce the worst in teenagers. The coach who believes winning is the only thing has players who live by that credo. In such a case, Powell's words to his opponent on the free throw line would be applauded, or tacitly accepted, rather than analyzed and criticized.

Here, Coach is continually holding the high ground while insisting to his players that they rise to that level with him. Furthermore, he stays out of the details. He simply points out the direction and keeps everyone honest with one another. He believes in them but maintains his distance.

Suppose the coach was high-minded but was naive about what was happening in front of him? In such a case Shawn still would have confronted Powell, but it is easy to imagine a coach rationalizing and minimizing Powell's words. "Are you sure? I doubt he'd say something like that. If he did say it, he probably just meant everybody from Tech. I'm sure he wasn't making a racial statement." The coach would in effect be asking Shawn to take one for the team. But it's one thing to efface yourself for the common good and another to deny your own integrity. If Shawn were to subscribe to the coach's dismissal of the incident, he would be left questioning what he heard and doubting himself, his coach, and his teammates.

Now imagine a coach who had zero tolerance for any sort of remark that smacked of racism. His tact may have been to throw Powell off the team, which would certainly have underscored his values in everyone's mind. There is also the distinct possibility that, deep down, Shawn would have resented the coach's coming to his rescue. Shawn would never have had the opportunity to work through this with Powell on his own, face-to-face. And worse, Powell would never have had the opportunity to work through this issue with his teammates.

What we have here is a coach who has uncompromising principles and who is wise enough to be realistic about teenagers. He invites each of the boys to grow up with and through one another. He asks them to become men who are capable of addressing and resolving their differences without resorting to threats or violence. He resists acting in an authoritarian and punitive manner. But he acts with tremendous authority because he believes in his players as human beings. And, most likely, he believes in them because he is the kind of coach who pays attention to his players and always keeps in the forefront their growth. He does not expect them to be men yet, but he does count on their becoming men through their experiences. He takes advantage of what Powell uttered and takes a leap of faith in each of them by believing in them at a time when they probably were unable or barely able to believe in themselves. In other words, he takes the best kind of calculated gamble possible. Powell and Shawn know that he is putting his faith in them, which means a great deal to each of them. Their coach's faith is what keeps them hanging in there with each other when they otherwise might have given up.

It is fundamental that parents know who is coaching their children, as well as what the coach and the school stand for. Athletics can be the site of health and growth and education, but only if that is explicitly intended. Listen carefully to the way adults and kids talk about what playing means to them. If you do not hear life-affirming values, neither will your kids.

Hate Groups, Race Supremacy, and Teenage Anxiety

It is hard for anyone, teenager or adult, to think clearly and talk rationally about race. In the current atmosphere of the national debate, trying to act rationally is like pausing to tie your shoe laces while running across a freeway. Even when we grasp that race is a culturally constructed concept, we still find it difficult to peel apart our feelings and our ideas, not to mention the feelings and ideas of others.

History's record of racial hate, ethnic intolerance, and religious warfare is staggering, but this last century seems exceptionally caustic. Rabid discourse is impossible to discount or avoid. People hate, and they often hate because of race, ethnicity, or religion. Skinheads, white-hooded mobs, and torched synagogues are only a few images of the horrific forces that have insinuated themselves into our lives. No race and no social class has the corner on vicious demagoguery. "White Devils" and "Aryan Brothers" are both spawned out of the same cesspool of muddled thinking.

Neither Shawn nor Powell seems likely to enlist in twisted causes, but the blandishments of hate can hold sway under certain circumstances, perhaps transitorily, for any number of vulnerable teenagers. The Littleton killers, Dylan Harris and Eric Klebold, are the most notorious exemplars of recent times, but they are hardly unique.

Hate groups of any stripe are indefensible, but it is useful to imagine why some kids, who are by no means given over to evil, may be drawn to extremist, dangerous causes. Hate groups offer a promise that may resonate grandiosely for them. To scapegoat the other for merely being the other provides some imaginary solace for those struggling with a shaky conception of self, for those living in a world of tough choices. What's more, there is a kind of glamor to being the seemingly brave outsider. There is also a deluded sense of security to having at the ready a totalizing, absolutizing answer to life's vexations and paradoxes. Some kids pursue these hate-filled chimeras of meaningfulness out of a mix of perverted idealism, exhaustion (it's tough to be honest and vulnerable, and it's a relief to hand over to a charismatic leader or even to an abstraction the burdens of consciousness), and ignorance. No wonder extremist groups, cults, and gangs recruit among the marginalized and downtrodden, and the young, who are tempted to project onto others their own inadequacies and failures.

How do we fight hate among teenagers? The same way we show that we love them: one kid at a time. One question and one brave stand at a time. This is precisely why adults—particularly parents—have their work cut out for them. Tolerance can only be taught by those wise enough to know that open-mindedness requires energy and commitment. It's not easy growing up in a world of complex social realities, of clashing values and variables. Therefore, education, along with enforcement of laws, is the way to resist hate. Will all kids see the light? Of course not. Somehow we have not yet learned from history how much we lose by subscribing to ideologies predicated upon the debasement of others. But as St. Paul recommends, better to light a candle than curse the darkness.

Growing Up in a Diverse Society

When Cornel West in Race Matters raises the problems of the racial divide, he asks, "Do we have the intelligence, humor, imagination, courage, tolerance, respect, and will to meet the challenge?" Of course, those are precisely the qualities that parents require daily in their relationships with their teenagers. The way we raise our teenagers, then, contributes to changing the cultural landscape. We model tolerance and respect in our everyday lives—in our friendships and social lives, in our confrontation with pressing problems, and in the way we tolerate the differences in our own teenagers. Through all the trials of growing up, somehow we need to convey to them that we respect them without question, even when we may not wholly understand or agree with what is going on in their lives. This is why respect is totally atheoretical. Respect is the air that we and our children breathe, the oxygen we share. Without it none of us can survive.

7

Eating Disorders

Much Madness is divinest Sense—
To a discerning Eye—

—EMILY DICKINSON, 435

HAMLET: Madam, how like you this play?
QUEEN: The lady doth protest too much, methinks.
HAMLET: O, but she'll keep her word.

Mirror, Mirror, on the Wall

Teanne and Phyllis couldn't honestly remember a time when they hadn't been best friends. Almost from the first minute they met each other, they shared many of the same interests—soccer, music, and student leadership. When they went to the movies, they hardly ever disagreed on what to see. Without planning it, they frequently wore the same color sweaters. They were both excellent students too, students who liked some good-natured competition with each other for the best grades in their shared classes. Even though there were three middle schools feeding the high school, and they both had other friends, Teanne and Phyllis's friendship grew stronger and stronger. In a racially diverse school such as this one, it might have been no big deal that one of them was African American and the other white. Yet when you looked around campus, you didn't see many kids crossing over that border.

Just recently, Teanne sensed a change in Phyllis, and she didn't like it. It all began when Phyllis went on a diet because she was sure she was getting fat and wanted to shed a couple of harmless pounds—nothing much, just a couple of pounds. She said the clothes she liked to wear were now being made in sizes too small for her. Teanne thought it was kind of silly because Phyllis looked just fine to her—and evidently to the boys who hung around her waiting for a moment's attention, which they sometimes received and sometimes did not. But who was Teanne to argue about what her friend ate? It wasn't her body, and she figured that Phyllis's weight and what was squirreled in her brown bag were her own concerns, right?

Gradually, though, Teanne grew uneasy about Phyllis's so-called diet, especially when her friend stayed on it way past a couple of pounds. If she was looking to dress in the best fashions, this wasn't the route to take. If she kept this up, pretty soon she'd be forced to shop in the kids' section. Teanne couldn't say for sure, but the dieting seemed to have been going on—since when? Since before Thanksgiving, and here it was late spring already. Where *did* the year go? In the meantime, Phyllis's food act and routine was wearing on her. How many times would they go over the nutritional contents on a package? How many times would they interrogate each other on the number of carbos in a juice drink? At every meal Phyllis would tabulate and discuss the demons called Calories. It was exhausting. It was boring. All their conversational topics these days went back to stories of Phyllis Eating or Phyllis Not Eating. Not only that, it was getting harder and harder to go out to eat with Phyllis because the list of foods she wouldn't eat (she said she couldn't stomach anything green anymore) was getting longer and longer. It was also frightening, not to mention crazy making. Why, one time Teanne presented her friend with an orange; she turned it around in her hand and studied it as if it were a moon rock.

"Something wrong with an orange, too?" said Teanne.

"You eat it. I don't want to take your lunch."

"What are you looking at? An orange doesn't come with a list of ingredients. It's mostly water."

"There's other stuff, but OK, I'll save it for a snack," Phyllis said.

"Right," said Teanne, guessing that the fruit would be thrown away or handed off to some unsuspecting grateful soul who sea-gulled around the girls' tables looking for scraps.

Then came a stunner: Phyllis mentioned in passing one day that she was through with soccer and wouldn't be playing next year. Through with soccer? Phyllis? She was a star goalie and the whole team looked to her for leadership. She said that she liked long-distance running better now. "Team games are OK, but I think I'm done with them. I want to compete against myself. That's the ultimate challenge." Then she invited Teanne to come to her favorite step aerobics class at the Y, five o'clock weekdays, where she worked out after her afternoon run around the lake.

One afternoon, a guest speaker appeared in their health class. Lily Patterson was the teacher, and Phyllis used to like her a lot. Once, after a good class on race and identity, they sat down for a solid heart-to-heart. She was probably the youngest teacher at the school, and she seemed to know things Phyllis thought she shouldn't have known—or should have forgotten by now. In any event, Phyllis had begun to regard her a little bit suspiciously of late: Call Me Lily (as she begged them on the first day) was kind of nosy, actually, and she asked her too many questions and too many follow-up questions (a phrase she was famous for, "Let me follow that up with another . . . "), and she made a point of crowding Phyllis on campus, especially in the cafeteria. *Who invited that woman into my life?* she sometimes asked herself when she was irritated. *Hey, follow this up, why don't you?: Why don't you have lunch in the faculty room where you're supposed to be anyway?*

At first Phyllis was relieved that there was a speaker; at least she wouldn't have to hear Call Me Lily's voice or huddle in small groups and share or be sensitive or anything. From the start, the speaker seemed bright, successful, fit, and outgoing. She was a self-proclaimed recovering anorexic, there to tell her story firsthand. She had gone to the other high school in town, and after famously losing a year to you-know-what had graduated not so long ago. Phyllis could almost remember seeing her somewhere, at a dance or maybe a game. Or maybe it was someone who looked like her or someone who used to look like her. Phyllis resented that she was forced to take this health class (she knew the material already, as did all the other kids, she figured), and here she felt she was being manipulated by the girl with the sad story. But class was only fifty minutes long, and as the speaker went on and on, Phyllis's attention wavered and she settled over her sketch pad on the desktop.

As for Teanne, she was listening to every single word. One day the speaker's father had told her that she could stand to lose a few pounds for her health and well-being, "Just a couple of pounds and you'll feel different about yourself." That's what the woman reported that he said. Her dad actually thought he was being affectionate when he called her his little "chubbette." In seemingly no time at all, everything was going downhill—she quickly shed those few disgusting chubbette pounds, but then she had a kind of vision: "I had the power to lose many more. And if losing a few pounds made you feel so good, then losing a few more could only make you feel better. And if I can lose these pounds, who knows what I can prove to myself that I can do." What was most frightening to Teanne was the speaker's saying that as she descended deeper and deeper into her condition, she withdrew more and more from her friends, from her normal social activities, and from everything she would have identified as her former life. "Anorexia," she said, "became my best friend."

Best friend. To Teanne, the phrase sounded like a kind of accusation. By the time the speaker left the room, Teanne was shaking a little. She sounded so much like Phyllis that it was freaky. At one point in the talk, Teanne realized that she had been staring at the speaker without ever taking her eyes off her. Then she turned to the side. Phyllis was doodling on her pad with a red felt pen, and there were dozens of stick figures marching down the page in strict column formation.

Teanne resolved right then and there to have a talk with Phyllis soon, and the opportunity presented itself when they had a free period.

"T-girl, what did you get on that hard quiz?"

"What did *you* get?"

Teanne told her. Each girl got the same score.

"That's not fair," said Phyllis, facetiously, faking a pout, something she was good at. "We have divided up the school day. You're supposed to be weak in math and strong in science. I'm the Quadratics Queen, or did you conveniently forget, once again?" They began walking down the hallway to the library.

"Right," Teanne said, in a tone that failed to convey the lightness she wished she could feign. "Hey, I wanted to ask you. You know, the health speaker?"

"Man, I know what you mean. *Oprah*-lite. Wasn't that gross?"

Teanne didn't know exactly what Phyllis thought was gross, but she couldn't get the question out fast enough, and the moment passed.

"Plus," Phyllis said, and she came to a full stop, as if for emphasis. "Plus, she was so full of herself. But you know what the absolute sorriest worst part was?" She waited for all of a second for a response that did not come. "My opinion? The girl could still stand to lose a few pounds!"

"What are you talking about? That's the whole point. I respected her showing up and talking to us. She seemed perfectly normal to me. Little too normal, actually."

"Excuse me. But she was pathetic."

Teanne then said something that she might not have if she had thought about it some more. But the words just tumbled out: "You know, she kind of reminded me of you."

Phyllis was sneering in the way she often sneered when sizing up a soccer opponent taking a penalty kick. "So that's what you think, that I'm some sort of weirdo-anorexic? That I'm like that girl?"

"Liss, you've lost so much weight in the last couple of months. I'm starting to get scared."

"Get out of here. I'm fine. C'mon, don't turn on me now. I'm fine."

"Turn on you! I'm worried about you, Liss."

"I have never felt better, thank you very much."

"Could have fooled me."

"This your idea of being my friend?" Phyllis was whispering and shaking her head.

"That's exactly what friends are for. Listen, just start eating a little bit more and I'll stop bugging you."

"I've never seen things so clearly. I can almost see through people these days." At that very moment, she felt that she was seeing right through Teanne, in fact. "I'll bet you and Call Me Lily probably arranged for that speaker."

Teanne was now convinced. "You see things clearly? Do you see how you've got me worried sick?"

"What I eat, what I don't eat, that's my business. That means it isn't your business. In fact, I eat better than most people—and definitely better than you. You've changed a lot lately, haven't you? You should go visit the counselor or something. I've got to go now. Don't worry, no need to put a narc on me, I won't be sticking my head in the toilet bowl today."

"Liss, come on, don't. Don't walk away like that, would you," she said, but she was talking to herself.

Phyllis and the School Counselor

Phyllis passes the open office door of the school counselor and pauses because the woman looks very familiar. She is working head down at her desk. Then

Phyllis remembers. She was in aerobics class yesterday. Phyllis peeks around the door and says:

—Get a good workout at the Y?

—Excuse me?

—I was at class, too. Isn't she great, the teacher?

—Oh, now I remember you. Front row, blue leotard, white Reeboks. Yes, that's a great class. Do you go often?

—Every day. So what do you do here? Do kids really just come in and spill their guts?

—I stay pretty busy if that's what you mean.

—I bet. There are a lot of crazy kids in this place.

—Not necessarily crazy. You might be surprised. They just need somebody to talk to.

—Don't they have friends or anything?

—Sometimes friends are what they need to talk about.

—Tell me about it.

—So, is there anything I can do for you today?

—I'm fine. I just recognized you, from class.

—What did you say your name was?

—I didn't.

—My name's Sasha.

—Mine's Phyllis, but there is nothing bothering me really.

—Good.

—Actually, it's my stupid friend Teanne. Well, she's not stupid, but we had this awful fight today, and I'm not sure what to do.

—What did you fight about?

—Nothing. I mean it was stupid. I know she was trying to be helpful, but she said some really mean things to me.

—What kinds of things?

—It doesn't matter. It's just that we've never fought like that before. We've been best friends since middle school and I don't want to lose her now.

—Sounds to me like what was said must have mattered a little.

—It's nothing. We had this stupid speaker in health class today—an anorexic woman. She talked and answered questions for the whole period. Not that I was listening too close. It was boring, but it was no big deal. But later Teanne was all over me, basically telling me that I'm an anorexic. And I couldn't get her to stop.

Eating Disorders 109

—Until?

—Until what?

—You couldn't get her to stop until what?

—I had to walk away from her. She's never done that to me and I've never done that to her. But there was no way to get her to stop.

—What she was saying really bothered you. How come?

—I think she's jealous of me. She's gaining weight. She's never acted that way before.

—So, do *you* think you're anorexic?

—How would I know? Of course not. I don't know.

—Which answer you going with?

—One thing, I'm nothing like that speaker. She was disgusting. Hey, I was talking about my friend, Teanne.

—That's what you said. You want to sit down, Phyllis?

—Will you be at class tonight?

—I don't know for sure, but I'll be here all day tomorrow.

—Good.

Notes Home

Anorexia—Whatever Else It May Be— Is Also a Thought Disorder

Fortunately—or perhaps the word is *unfortunately*—anorexia and other eating disorders are no longer the dirty dark secret nobody ever talks about. Over the last few years, most of us have become conversant in the vocabulary of bingeing and purging, distorted body image, grueling exercise, and obsessions with perfection. We know that girls in their mid to late teens are the usual victims, often athletes and other ambitious and talented girls, and the topic is a staple of tell-all pop culture as well as serious research. (Approximately 90 percent of anorexics are girls, but boys are making inroads in recent years.) And yet, even after so much emphasis, eating disorders remain as baffling as they are tenacious. Their most obvious effects can be seen in the girl's ravaged body and scarred psyche, but the origins are more difficult to understand. No wonder we stumble about, stuttering to make sense. The stakes are sky-high; that much we know. In the extreme, anorexia claims lives. What makes anorexia particularly insidious is the way it devours its victim's mind and soul and imagination. When we speak to children suffering from anorexia, we almost wonder who's listening. Here's who: the disease itself.

Early stumbling blocks to recognizing anorexia are family resistance and denial along with peer envy. Many anorexics report that at the height of their illness they were being complimented at home and by their friends on their attractive appearance. In the initial stages, observers can easily be deceived. The girl conveys strength and determination. She seems to be taking responsibility for her health and well-being, watching what she eats and working out with a sense of commitment. It's certainly good to pay attention to nutrition and to exercise. But that's not the anorexic's project, which becomes evident when this new outlook turns into a dark, secretive quest.

A mother and father can feel terrified watching their daughter fiddling with her food at the dinner table, telling them lies about what she supposedly enjoyed for lunch. Such insight is devastating. Pragmatically, it is difficult to keep track of gradual changes in eating behaviors and weight loss when you see your daughter day in and day out—especially because most anorexics are pretty clever about hiding their weight loss by wearing baggy clothes and sweats.

One thing you can count on: your child will probably not walk into the kitchen one morning and announce to you that she is an anorexic. It is not unusual, then, for parents to "hear" about the problem from one of their daughter's friends, a teacher, or a neighbor and—with guidance, support, and counsel—"see" it clear-eyed for the first time. More likely than not, someone outside the family will bring the problem to their attention, and will offer help and support. However you find out, be glad it is sooner rather than later. Then get to work. It takes bravery and unstinting love for parents not to let disappointment and anger misdirect their energies. You may feel you're working without the cooperation of the victim, and you may very well be right. Nonetheless, you have no alternative. There isn't a single moment to lose.

Reverberations Throughout the Social Web

Teenage peer pressure is a popular journalistic theme. According to the caricature, kids are the helpless, hapless pawns of their peers, lemmings pursuing one another to the point of self-annihilation. In the case of Phyllis and Teanne, though, one teenager may very well have saved the life of another. Certainly, that seems to be Teanne's hope. Though seldom highlighted, such lonely altruism is far from unusual among teenagers.

With Teanne's resolute action in mind, it's important to note that for every anorexic there are numerous others affected by the experience. Anorexics draw others into their orbit, and in this way they exert an authority they never thought they had over an expanded world of influence. Nonetheless, once a teenager has an insight about a friend and a dangerous situation—as Teanne has about Phyllis's anorexia—the reverberations immediately begin to be felt throughout the social web of both girls and then beyond it. Even if Teanne plans on saying nothing to anybody else for the moment, others will inevitably become involved. Teenagers recognize when something is amiss between best friends like Teanne and Phyllis and, in all sincerity, they inquire. It will be tough for Teanne, especially after being rudely rebuffed by her best friend, not to accept the support these friends will offer. But even if she does refuse, these other friends will pay closer attention and soon figure out for themselves what is at play. Either way, once they get a sense of the true story, their concern will prompt a response.

Many adults may be astonished to learn that teenagers are quick to realize that they are in over their heads, when friends are perceived to be in danger. They seek the counsel of the nearest trusted adult—coach, teacher, employer, even parents. Therefore, it is just a matter of time before others will talk with Phyllis about her eating habits and approach Phyllis's parents with their concerns. As a consequence, Phyllis's ground is on the verge of being jolted. Her private obsessions about food are about to be public topics of no small urgency. (Already it seems more than likely, for example, that the health teacher Phyllis says she scorns has zeroed in on her.) For Phyllis all this concern will not seem to be well-intentioned support; it will feel like there are pathetic meddlers intruding upon her life.

Oddly, for all the legitimate emphasis upon the anorexic's pain and suffering, few pay attention to the friend who is usually struggling simultaneously, right alongside. In this context, it's important to see that Teanne has grappled with the conflicting standards of being both true to herself and being a best friend: trust your friend absolutely, goes the convention, but also risk everything to do the right thing—even risk your friendship if necessary. Teanne has endured (and continues to endure) her own trial. In deciding to confront Phyllis, Teanne has had to struggle with her mixed feelings of loyalty and fear, and her feelings of guilt no matter what she does. She's going to need her own support and care now, and she is not going to get it from the source she could have always counted on in the past, namely, Phyllis.

As adults get involved in the drama of Phyllis's anorexia, they need to remember Teanne. In an act of selfless courage and unconditional love Teanne has risked the most important friendship in her life. She will be hurting deeply for having done the right thing and alienating her best friend, at least in the short run.

Acknowledgment Is Gradual

Nobody who suffers from anorexia recognizes the condition from the outset. Quite the contrary. That is why at first Phyllis can recognize the isolated facts (clothes are loose, parents are batty, friends are worried) while simultaneously denying the big picture (who me, anorexic?). As a result, it takes a number of confrontations (like Teanne's), candid self-reflection, and a substantial passage of time before an anorexic will acknowledge her own condition.

But this is the insidious part: after self-recognition it takes the anorexic even longer to admit the problem to someone else and still longer to seek treatment. At first the anorexic will try to solve the problem herself: she might entertain a variety of rationalizations and adopt minimal behavior modifications. She might delude herself into thinking that as long as she eats breakfast every day she isn't—technically or really—anorexic. Or that if she buys the school lunch she isn't anorexic. At the same time she manages to ignore the fact that these might be the only times she eats all day and that she works out for hours each day. She also "forgets about" the days she missed that meal for some perfectly understandable reason—as when she overslept or had to take a makeup test and passed on lunch. As time goes on, though, more and more of these pseudolegitimate occasions occur.

For all these reasons, compassionate confrontations and accurate assessment are necessary. For parents, one crucial step can be consulting a physician. Explain your concerns and set up a physical for your teenager. (Not all physicians may be comfortable, or conversant, with eating disorders, but if yours is not, she will provide an appropriate referral.) If her assessment confirms your suspicions, you will soon be mapping out a treatment strategy in collaboration with her, your daughter, and the rest of the family.

Finally, when reality can be denied no longer, the anorexic will ask for, or allow herself to receive, help. But realize that anorexia is powerful and will be doing its best to get your daughter to undo all the help, even while she is accepting help. In the beginning, it's distressing to note, anorexia usually has the upper hand.

What Is Anorexia?

Anorexia is a progressive disease. Nobody wakes up one day to discover herself in the throes of full-blown anorexia. It usually begins with concern—real or imagined—over excessive weight. This perception leads to decisions: to go on a diet and/or to practice a taxing exercise regime. But somewhere during these efforts to lose a few pounds the anorexia gains force. It is an intrepid enemy. The victim comes to feel the pleasure of losing some weight and taking control of her life. At the same time, her self-perception is distorted, and therefore there is always more weight to lose and more victories over the body to be won. These feelings become intoxicating and the person wants and needs more of them. Thus her efforts switch from losing the weight to having more and more of these positive feelings associated with the power to lose the weight. Once this switch takes place, anorexia, as a thought disorder, has a forceful grip on its victim.

At the risk of oversimplifying such a complex subject, there are two principal conceptualizations of anorexia. One is the intrapersonal version; that is, anorexia is a disease that strikes from within, and its roots are located in the history of the victim's relationships to family, friends, and self. This understanding, rooted in a psychodynamic thinking, affords us a full, subtle view of anorexia. However, treatment inevitably pits the self against another part of the self, the part of the self from which anorexia emanates. For the adolescent, a probable consequence of this internal struggle is that treatment becomes a battle that the self can afford to neither win nor lose. She doesn't want to be sick and certainly doesn't want to die, but she also doesn't want a life without passion and meaning either, which are the "rewards" anorexia showers upon her life.

A second way to view anorexia is provided by interpersonal, social, and narrative psychologists. Michael White and David Epston in *Narrative*

Means to Therapeutic Ends argue that anorexia is an external, pernicious entity eroding the psychic integrity, as well as the body, of the victim. On the surface, this perspective might indeed seem odd, but it points toward an often life-saving treatment and strategy. Here the approach consists of framing the condition this way: the beleaguered anorexic self is a victim pitted against an intruder that is the disease.

Teenagers detect a kind of brutal elegance in this conceptualization of their disease. They are now involved in a black-and-white battle against an identified and thus demystified adversary, which is certainly "not me." She is now a rebel with a cause, and the energy she formerly invested in counting calories now goes into a battle for her own survival. The victim thus gains distance and thinks critically about the condition that she once upon a time considered her best friend.

Having made this shift in perspective, the anorexic is free to think about cultural pressures applied to women with regard to health, youth, and fitness; media images of women; the unfinished business within her family (all families, no matter how stable, have issues to resolve or at least address); the difficulty in negotiating the trials and tribulations of adolescence. But the real advantage of this alternative vision of anorexia is that it furnishes the victim, and all who associate with her, with the freedom to act and to be, all the while retaining the sense of self-efficacy, power, and passion that she felt when she was being romanced by her relationship with anorexia.

The Ambiguous Path Ahead

There is no one event, no matter how upsetting, no one comment, no matter how insensitive or provocative, that transforms someone into an anorexic. At the same time anorexia does not occur in a vacuum either. Family, social expectations, school—all may be, and usually are, implicated. Fixations on beauty (and all of its mythology), remarks about body and self-image, reinforced and endorsed behaviors of self-denial, self-renunciation, reduced expectations and hopes, and dashed dreams—so many factors may conceivably conspire to propel someone into anorexia. It is important to understand this metamorphosis because the corollary is just as true: there is no formula for releasing a loved one from the grip of anorexia.

As the developmental psychologist Robert Kegan writes in *The Evolving Self*, it takes a "special wisdom" to parent a teenager, and wisdom of a very high order to parent an anorexic teenager. As a parent, it's terribly easy for you to feel crazy, out of your depth, guilty, and helpless before anorexia. That's natural, probably inevitable, given the nature of anorexia. Small wonder that anorexia and anorexics are so perplexing to treat—and to parent. Anorexia is an *it* that is attempting to become your daughter.

It is not unusual for parents to feel a sense of helplessness when confronted by what they believe to be self-destructive behaviors in their teenage children. For example, you may endure the distress of seeing your teenager become romantically attached to someone who is without a doubt the wrong person. What is there to do? If you submit to the temptation to panic and mount a campaign to trash the relationship and crush the object of that love, can there be any question as to what will happen? Usually, that will only drive your teenager more deeply and more desperately into that bad relationship. So how do you respond?

The key is that your teenager needs to learn what is wrong with the relationship—and learning such hard truths at this delicate and tense stage is, at the very least, problematic. The place for a parent to begin is the frank and honest acknowledgment that this *is* love, and that love and relationship are profound and important and rare. With subtle and cautious guidance, as well as boundary setting, you can hope to make clear to your teenager over time (and it won't happen today and probably not tomorrow) that love is not an absolute good, however, no matter what all the songs may claim, and that there are loves that are plainly bad for us. Although intimacy with another person can be beautiful, it can also be painful, unwise, and destructive. And don't forget, too, that the very danger and risk of a relationship others see as a bad one (and that teenagers themselves see as a risky one) is itself a kind of turn-on. If you think, however, that saying all this in so many words is going to turn the tide instantly in your favor, you would be very wrong. Once you have determined that your teenager's health and safety are not at risk, what is going to work to her benefit, and therefore to yours, is your unconditional respect for your teenager's feelings of love and passion, even if, in your judgment, they are misdirected, undeserved, or unearned.

The starting place for the confrontation of anorexia is strikingly and perhaps even bizarrely similar. In the case of a bad relationship, we may take refuge in the knowledge that this is merely a phase he or she will get over in time. Anorexia affords us no such leisure. We know that complacency can kill. So acknowledge both to yourself and to your child the force and the power and the thrill of the anorexia. Your teenager is under a kind of self-induced spell, but unfortunately, unlike hypnosis, you cannot clap your hands and make the clouds in their eyes dissipate. That is, you can't blame her for submitting to the allure of the disease, though you can expect her to fight back for her life. Still, you can't infuse your teenager with the plasma of your own wisdom. What's more, you can't follow her into the bathroom all the time, can't accompany her to school, can't force her to consume the carbohydrates and proteins that she needs, can't make her feel the pain of your tears and cries. Even trying to do that is futile—and this is a potentially tragic paradox—since she feels very healthy and full of self-esteem in the blossoming of anorexia. As she sees it, all the pamphlets you are shoving at her and all the documentaries have absolutely nothing whatsoever to do with her own personal experience. As someone once said, "Anorexics manage not to eat their cake and have it too."

It Takes a Team to Fight Anorexia

Like other eating disorders, anorexia nervosa is not solely a psychological condition, medical problem, family illness, social evil, or product of brain chemistry. To one degree or another, it is all of the above, and that's why all your emotional and mental resources will be taxed, if not drained. Don't underestimate your foe. And don't be distracted. For instance, school or sports may suddenly strike you as the villain, applying so many pressures and stresses on your teenager's life that she breaks down and resorts to anorexic behavior in order to assert her self-control and her power over herself. Even if there is an element of truth in that insight, school will likely be a lifeline for your teenager and you.

After anorexia has consolidated its hold on a teenager, it takes a group of people working together closely to help her break free. In the ideal situation everyone works together and everyone has a role to play, for instance:

1. A physician who strictly monitors weight and other health matters. She is the hard-liner, the one who probably sets a weight limit—which, if it is not met, is her ticket to automatic hospitalization.
2. A counselor who talks with the teenager about the other developmental issues in her life that are not being tended to because of the anorexia, such as sexuality, autonomy, sibling rivalry, and self-definition.

3. Parents who are supportive of their teenager and who, following the directions of the physician, never question their daughter about her food intake or beg her to eat a burrito for dinner.
4. Friends who see through the fog of anorexia and stay in touch and connected with their friend who is suffering from anorexia.
5. Siblings who treat her just as they have always treated her.
6. Teachers, coaches, and employers who are empathetic but maintain unambiguous (though probably modified) performance expectations.
7. Others who have dealt firsthand with anorexia, especially former anorexics and the parents and friends of former anorexics.

Mirror, Mirror

More so than adults, teenagers hate criticism, especially when it is on the mark. In fact, when the issues are sensitive and close to home, most teenagers can't quite hear you even when they assert that your honest opinion is exactly what they want. That is why, no matter how well Teanne picked her moment, it was practically a given that Phyllis would reject her.

As teenagers mature physically, socially, and emotionally, they also mature cognitively. In fact, the way they think actually changes. This is what Jean Piaget, one of the leading theoreticians of cognitive development, termed the shift from concrete thinking to abstract thinking, and this adjustment takes several years. Abstract thinking, which overall is a wonderful and essential human development, also ushers in self-consciousness, which for adolescents is a daily trial of gazing into foggy, cracked, and prismatic mirrors. No matter how hard they try, they cannot escape. Sure, they try mightily to live in the moment, but even then one part of them is watching, another evaluating, another acting. The development of self-consciousness is liberating in the long term, but in the short term it is nothing less than exhausting. Consequently, if you say something poignant or critical to teenagers, they go to their room or for a drive or for a bike ride (somewhere by themselves, any elsewhere will do) and think about what you said.

It's simply a fact of life that most teenagers—and not just those affected by eating disorders—are defensive with their parents during the height of their adolescence. Such defensiveness is not to be feared. It does, however, mean creatively altering your communication strategies. Simply put, that twenty-minute conversation you have in mind is better off being split into four five-minute conversations with at least a day between sessions. Why? This is how much time most parents have before their teenager's natural (by adolescent standards) defensiveness (or self-protectiveness) kicks in. So rather than beat your head against the wall, stop yourself just shy of making contact.

In this same vein, understand that teenagers' hypervigilant self-consciousness is simultaneously getting the better of them, even when they are attentively listening to what you have to say. This means that it will look very much like they are not paying attention. But count on your teenagers' hearing everything you say.

You Will Need the Whole Armamentarium of Your Resources

Liberating a loved one from the grip of anorexia requires the following:

Time: Anorexia will not go away overnight. Don't count on a miracle, in other words. It is a resilient, inventive, protean, complex thought disorder. Be satisfied with a progress that consists of two steps forward, one step backward. *Satisfied?* Be elated.

Patience: Not only will treatment require lots of physical and mental energy, along with the full investment of your attention, it will also force you to face down your fears. It will try to break your spirit by making you feel despairing and powerless. Savor the tiny victories because they will give you the confidence to keep you moving forward.

Courage: In this battle you will have to face your own behaviors and attitudes, ways of being and acting that may have unintentionally contributed, you now dread to contemplate, to the anorexia. Be brave and avoid the guilt. You did not say or do the one thing to turn your child into an anorexic; you are indeed influential, but no one is that important. Your conceivable guilt—even your conceivable responsibility—is not at the center of this drama. It's your daughter's crisis. So simply do your best to change your behaviors and attitudes. Doing so counterbalances the sense of powerlessness, and, besides, it is never too late to introduce constructive change into the family dynamic.

Acceptance: Do not get attached to the outcome of each treatment stage; instead, accept each and every day for what it brings, and each and every newly revealed aspect of your child, and her ordeal. You will likely be shocked, impressed, and proud. Do the same for yourself. Again, this defeats the sense of powerlessness.

Perseverance: Never, never let yourself give up. Like any other foe, anorexia is toughest when it is about to be defeated.

Love: Above all else, your children must never lose sight of your deep, ongoing, and unconditional love. They need to feel that love, totally and relentlessly. They need to feel it twenty-four hours a day. Remind them of how much you love them, especially when it appears that they aren't taking it in—or when they don't necessarily like the way it's being served up.

8

Learning Abilities and Learning Disabilities

Thus while one may be horrified by the ravages of developmental disorder or disease, one may sometimes see them as creative too—for if they destroy particular paths, particular ways of doing things, they may force the nervous system into making other paths and ways, force on it an unexpected growth and evolution.

—OLIVER SACKS, *AN ANTHROPOLOGIST ON MARS*

Again I saw that under the sun the race is not to the swift, nor the battle to the strong, nor bread to the wise, nor riches to the intelligent, nor favor to the skillful; but time and chance happen to them all.

—ECCLESIASTES 9:11

What's Up with Russell?

Russell, Russell, Russell.

For a long time I just couldn't figure out what was going on with Russell.

I first taught him when he was a ninth grader. Nothing sensational, the kind of teenager who hangs in there. Isn't it just about impossible for a teacher not to like a kid who perseveres even if the results don't exactly seem to match the effort? But I also felt a little bit sad for Russell because it was apparent to me that he would never truly shine academically, despite his commitment. Fortunately, though, he was a gifted musician who mastered one instrument after another—guitar, piano, violin, trumpet, tenor sax—the way some special athletes seamlessly star in one sport after another, season after season, or the way some kids just pick up one language after another. The jazz band, the symphony orchestra, the spring concert—if there was music playing anywhere on campus, you could count on Russell's being at the heart of it.

In the second semester of his junior year, Russell was once again in my class. The problem was that he had become a very different kid from the one I recalled, and I didn't like the change. Although most teenagers undergo profound changes between freshman and junior year, seldom do they shift so radically. Somewhere his dedication had been replaced by a huge chip on his shoulder. It was difficult to get him to make eye contact, let alone have a conversation. He was full of excuses and edgy questions. He had regressed to the combative level of about a seventh grader. *Why do we need to learn this? We'll never have to use it. How come you get to decide what we need to learn? None of this will ever help me get a job.* Whenever I tried to answer those concerns, I could tell he was close to singing, "Boring."

Finally, I had had enough. After class one day I called him aside and told him to stop by after school. I could tell he was surprised. Then I could see him begin the search for excuses as to why he couldn't show. I cut him off. "I'll see you at 3:15." I then picked up my things and headed for the door.

Later, as I waited in my room and the clock approached 3:30, I was having my doubts. Would he dare not show?

"Hey, Ms. Tolferson," he said, sauntering in. "Sorry I'm late."

I thought about lighting him up but thought better of it and just thanked him for coming. Even if he was late.

"Sure. What's up?"

"*What's up?* That's exactly what I want to know, Russell. You were in my class as a freshman and you worked hard and seemed to take pride in your work. But now, well, let's just say I detect a dramatic change in your attitude. So, why don't you tell me what's up?"

"This is so flat. I'm still the same Russell, maybe it's you that's changed."

I was afraid of this and I instantly regretted calling the conference, though something compelled me to go forward: "OK, let me make myself a little clearer for you. We've had six homework assignments and you've already missed three." I just happened to have my grade book from two years ago in the desk and I showed it to him: "And look, all freshman year you only missed two assignments. So I ask you again, what's going on?"

"Maybe I'm just getting smarter. Maybe I've caught on that this school stuff is way overrated. I mean what good will it ever do me to finish all these assignments of yours? Or all these silly little exercises you come up with. I'm beyond all that stuff."

I held up my hand. "Wait a second, where did all this come from? Do you actually believe what you're saying? Besides, even if it were true, and I'm not saying that it is, it is not an excuse for how you have been behaving in my class."

"You just don't get it!"

I felt as if I had been slapped. What had happened to the Russell I once knew?

"School is a make-believe world. I want to be a part of the real world. I don't need most of this stuff to get a job and make money. I don't need any of it! Besides, I'm a musician, so all I have to know how to do is play my music. You and I both know how good I am. That's my future, not academics."

"Russell, you sound like you're trying to convince yourself. That isn't you at all. You're smarter than that." I said it, and I hoped I still meant it, but I myself was getting a little doubtful.

"Forget it, why don't you? You'll never understand, anyway." And with that parting shot, he was up and out the door before I could find the words to stop him. Maybe I didn't want to stop him. Maybe I wasn't sure I knew what to say. I did know that I was dazed. What had just transpired? After I sat with myself for a while, I determined I had to do something to find out.

I went to the faculty room and called Russell's mother. I remembered her as a caring parent when we had met at back-to-school night during his freshman year. Without telling her the details of what had happened today I explained that Russell didn't seem like himself these days. I asked if she knew of anything outside of school that could be distracting him.

She didn't answer right away, and I was afraid I had come on a little too strong. In the meantime I kept listening to the white noise filling up the telephone line, and I waited and waited, hoping I hadn't ruined my relationship with her, too. Finally, however, I was relieved to hear her speak. Right away I could tell it wasn't easy for her to say what she wanted to say.

"Well, I promised him I wouldn't tell anybody, but I can't hold back any-more. He needs help. It just doesn't seem fair to him or his teachers—be-lieve it or not, he really likes you, Ms. Tolferson. You were his favorite teacher freshman year. Last year his grades started to slip and neither he nor I could understand why. He was working so hard, sometimes five hours a night, weeks on end. But nothing seemed to do the trick. His grades just kept slipping, and it was enough to break my heart seeing him struggle like that. We found a tutor, but that didn't help either. Eventually I began to suspect some sort of learning disability. I've been reading about that in the papers and in some magazines, but Russell—you can imagine, he didn't want to hear anything about it at first, said he wasn't stupid and said he wasn't sick. I don't know how I talked him into it, but somehow he agreed to get tested—I had to pull out all the stops. And I'm glad I did, be-cause now we know what kind of problem he's been dealing with all along." She told me what the diagnosis was, a condition that a fair number of kids these days endure and battle, some with more success than others. "Nobody at school knows."

This was a new one for me. Why in the world would she keep this a se-cret?

"That's my Russell. He's very proud. Plus, that's the way he wants it—and that was our agreement if he got tested. At first, he just worked harder, but this year he just seems to have given up on himself. It's just the two of us at home and I'm not sure what to do, or if there is anything I can do. Should I just let school slide and help him do what he can do so well, the music?"

"But what about his music? He's incredible. How does he read music?"

"That's interesting. Last year, after he heard an interview with Pavarotti, he said something to me. You know, Russell likes all types of music. Music is music he says, classical, hip-hop, pop, rap, rock, alternative, jazz, Latin, whatever, if it's music it's good. Anyway, that's when he said to me, big smile on his face, happiest I've seen him in a long time, 'You know, Mom, one day they'll all say Pavarotti, Duke Ellington, Erroll Garner, and your son, Russell, all had something in common, besides musical genius, of course—we all played by ear.' And that, Ms. Tolferson, was the first I ever heard. All those summer music camps and music composition courses we save up for . . . How could I know how to help him? He kept it from me all along."

Notes Home

Teenagers Learn That Life Isn't Fair

Teenagers are thoroughgoingly idealistic, so one of the most difficult truths for them to confront is that life isn't fair. At first glance, learning disabilities and learning differences confirm this realization. A teenager facing this recognition is in for a tough ordeal. Like it or not, he cannot make a learning disability go away—it's a part of him as surely as eye color. There's no quick fix to how the brain takes in and processes information.

Teenagers are idealistic in all senses of the term, too. They are prone to be idealistic in their politics, in their relationships, and in their aspirations. They also have an ideal of physical beauty, for instance, or of success. And for them, as well as for adults in our consumerist society, these images have magnetic pull. Adolescence is the time, though, that reality begins to hit home. Most teenagers begin to get their first inkling that no matter how much they want to, they probably won't play point guard for Duke, sing at Carnegie Hall, or star in a movie. Do they trust this intuition? Depends. There's a fine line between accepting one's limitations and allowing oneself to settle for less than one's total effort, between living in the clouds and giving in too soon simply because achievement comes at too high a price.

Who Wired My Brain and Whose Body Is This?

There is a poignant and crucial time during adolescence, when teenagers believe that their very bodies and brains don't show any signs of cooperating, don't demonstrate a willingness to line up at all with the desires that burn within them. They obsessively examine themselves before omnipresent real and imaginary mirrors. Their hair color, their foot speed, their voice range, their chances of being elected class president, their inability to find a boyfriend or girlfriend—they scrutinize everything. And sometimes just about everything seems off. Depending on the degree of disappointment, this is the moment that may push them to the brink of despair, when they are at tremendous risk. No wonder some teenagers are tempted, in a sense, to *revise* themselves, their bodies, their images: to take steroids, for example, or to sleep around, join a gang, or work out to the point of injury and beyond. It is also the time when they might cut themselves, get a tattoo, or pierce their nose. When adults think back on high school and cringe, they probably do so remembering the pain they felt facing up to their limitations and, more likely, their denial of such limitations.

Coming to terms with learning disabilities falls into this category. It is one thing for a person of moderate height to be stifled in attempts to play center on the basketball team. It is a stranger, somehow crueler thing to be stifled in the ability to think, read, spell, remember, pay attention, or sit still. Such an individual's mind and body seem to be bent on sabotage from within. Teenagers facing this reality are in for a tough ordeal when they deny its existence, which is what they will be strongly tempted to do. Of course, they can play a game with themselves by keeping the information away from teachers, and in that way they believe they can sustain, for a while longer anyway, that previous inviolate, impregnable image of themselves.

Now let's take a step back. Having a learning disability is significant, no matter the extent or degree. Immediately upon being diagnosed, these teenagers (who have likely been working harder than their peers, almost invariably for lower grades) usually feel two waves of emotion wash over them. First, there is a sense of relief: the diagnosis officially, objectively confirms their subjective experience. As Edward Hallowell, author of *Driven to Distraction*, writes of his being diagnosed with ADD: "It was one of the great 'Aha' experiences of my life. Suddenly so many seemingly disparate parts of my personality made sense."[1] Second, there is a sense of futility, that there is no way out of their dilemma. Unfortunately, if we're not careful, their learning often stops at this point.

Russell used to work hard as a student but he gave up when he was diagnosed, rationalizing his surrender and his apathy. The primary target of his aggression became his teacher, but he also took aim at the purpose of education and its applicability to his life. Simultaneously, he covertly attacked himself for being flawed and was fearful about being exposed as such. Yet as long as he remained transfixed by fear of exposure, he could never confront the diagnosis. This may explain why he instigated conflict with Ms. Tolferson, perhaps unconsciously attempting to draw her into his problem so that she would help him face up to it. Of course, he dismissed the relevance of her class, but he did so by contrasting the classroom with the arena in which he flourished, music, which seemed reasonable to him.

He asserted himself and his strengths when he felt besieged. He sensed the precariousness of his self-esteem, yes, but he also affirmed it at the same time. During the phase of denial and combat with the frustrating realities of school and self-limitations, a teenager's self-esteem can be eroded. And the character trait that can help him face his problem, healthy self-esteem, is the aspect of himself insidiously assailed by the problem itself.

The Circularity of Self-Esteem

Let's take a long look at that elusive and controversial term, self-esteem. A concept that flowered in the 1980s and whose earliest advocates were often criticized for uncritically embracing the assumptions of the so-called me-first era, self-esteem in the nineteenth century was excoriated as a character flaw akin to arrogance. (Henry James refers to the "sin" of self-esteem staining the protagonist of one of his major novels.) Nowadays, however, there are hundreds of thousands of Web sites dedicated to self-esteem and related notions, along with countless programs in schools and organizations. The value of self-esteem seems evident. At the same time, psychological research is beginning to cast a jaundiced eye; to quote the headline of an article in the *New York Times*, "Self-Image Is Suffering from Lack of Esteem."[2]

Nonetheless, for good reason most of us retain the commonsense view that self-esteem is vital to healthy adolescence—even scholarly debunkers will grant that living without it is not exactly a pleasant prospect and that those devoid of self-esteem stand at greater risk to harm or subvert themselves. They are also less likely to respond to the promise and challenge of their lives. In the real world, the term pops up continually in parent–teacher conferences and during parent gatherings. Parents of teenagers troubled by learning problems are disquieted when they observe evidence of their children's plunging self-esteem. So how is self-esteem defined and, more to the point, is it possible to promote self-esteem in a teenager?

Much like self-motivation, self-esteem cannot be instilled from without, though it can be undercut from without—and for related reasons. Self-esteem is both a process and a product, a mode of being, a confident but realistic sense of self that opens up avenues of engagement with the world.

That explains why any teenager who intends to garner self-esteem will be thwarted: self-esteem is not an object available for possession. Defining and developing self-esteem is as complicated as defining a *self* and explaining how it develops. Many are troubled by the notion of promoting self-esteem as the goal of education, asking, What is the purpose of a goal that is by definition amorphous if not unattainable? Beyond that, self-esteem seems at best awkwardly tethered to achievement, and as a consequence it chances deluding teenagers into subscribing to grandiose convictions of competence and power. What is interesting, though, is that teenagers who believe they are competent usually stand a better chance of acting competently.

The problem when contemplating self-esteem is that we invariably link it to accomplishment, as if accomplishment flowed from self-esteem or even the opposite, as if self-esteem flowed from accomplishment. But which is the cause and which the effect? If we have high self-esteem do we accomplish more? Or do we accomplish more because we have high self-esteem? In the real world, is that a distinction without a difference? But these are not the right questions; there is no necessary causal relationship between self-esteem and accomplishment. Self-esteem does not proceed from accomplishment; if anything seems true, it is that self-esteem is what allows someone to appreciate her accomplishment. As has often been noted by researchers, gang members, for instance, score very high on self-esteem scales, as do anorexics. Great artists, however, may very well wallow in low self-esteem (as their biographies often sadly dramatize). It is even possible to imagine those possessing profound self-esteem who accomplish little in terms of conventional success, like monks and philosophers and poets. And many of us are familiar with people who have ten pages of awards listed on their résumés who doubt themselves at every turn. One person sets low standards and feels great, whereas another feels terrible because his or her standards are set too high. What does all this mean for parenting and teaching teenagers?

Self-esteem programs that encourage teenagers to feel good about themselves as an end in itself can often strike their intended beneficiaries as being disingenuous and counterproductive, if not hypocritical. Parents and adults who praise teenagers at every turn whether they deserve it or not foster more problems than they solve. For authentic self-esteem has nothing to do with self-aggrandizement. Flattery is the flip side of abuse. Ironically, promoting self-esteem as an end in itself may very well lead kids to be more dependent on external approval and less likely to develop a genuine belief in themselves and their worth. Yet without self-esteem, it should be stressed, teenagers are at great risk because the self that they might endanger is regarded by themselves as having no value anyway. And with self-esteem, teenagers not only avoid peril but also pursue enrichment, expansion, and confirmation of the value of their lives.

Authentic self-esteem is a byproduct of one's total and effective relation to one's world. For all of us, not only teenagers and not only teenagers like Russell afflicted with serious learning challenges, self-esteem grows in and across the following three overlapping fields:

Relationships: We all need to have people around us who care about us—people we care about as well. Furthermore, we need to have influence on these relationships. For teenagers these relationships include peers, teachers, and parents. Teenagers need to feel their influence in all of these different relationships, however. Although not commonly understood, it is simply not enough for teenagers to feel connection with peers, for instance, if they don't also feel connection with adults, and vice versa. If a relational imbalance exists in their lives, that is, if they can only relate to a parent, for instance, and not a teacher or a peer, they will struggle with their self-esteem.

Activities with successful outcomes: Through our own efforts and work we need to influence those outcomes we value, and we need to experience success that accompanies some kind of recognition, including self-recognition. For teenagers, this may run the gamut—grades, elections, athletics, performance, art, community service, and so on. The key is that whatever the arena, it must be perceived by them (though, interestingly, not necessarily by others) as significant and as one in which success proceeds from personal investment, work, and commitment. If, for example, sterling grades or sports awards come effortlessly, they may conceivably make no appreciable contribution to a teenager's self-esteem.

Integrity: Integrity is not merely asserting a moral dogma or insisting on an abstract principle. This is not to imply that integrity is not at its core a moral enterprise, because it is. Teenagers' true engagement with problems is intensely moral, contrary to the prevailing assumptions of teenagers as being self-centered and unprincipled. In fact, with teenagers, though not so obviously, personal integrity is just as important a component of self-esteem as relationships and successful activities. Teenagers routinely make stunningly honest statements about themselves: *I don't know what I believe. I don't know if I want to be the person my friends want me to be. I don't know if I like who I am when I'm around my friends.* This is the ordeal of integrity: struggling to align behaviors and beliefs. And for most teenagers, it is a quasiviolent internal struggle. (Of course, adults recognize this phenomenon all too well, for they too in their personal and professional lives continually strive to live the values they believe they hold.)

In sum, then, self-esteem is an intensely active and ongoing engagement with the forces of the world and the self, not some fixture in a one-dimensional personality. In Russell's case, his self-esteem has been damaged, as often happens after the diagnosis of a learning disability.

But what if Russell's mother saw his problem as only one of self-esteem? She would do all she could to make him feel better. She might buy him a piano or a car, if she could afford it, or she might remind him how much she loves him or how talented he is in other areas. In addition, she might go along with his view that college isn't for everyone, and she might do what she could to remove him from the class and lighten his academic load. All of these strategies may assuage Russell's pain, but they will not increase his self-esteem. If she directly addresses the issues that impinge on his self-esteem, however, his self-esteem will be bolstered.

Specifically, Russell feels abject humiliation, which gives his mom a chance to help him deal with the facts of brain chemistry and learning styles and his individual learning disability. Russell wants to cover up the truth by keeping his teachers out of the loop. But his mom can lead him to understand that teachers can be his allies only if they know what his challenges are. In letting his school know of his disability, she is going to help him redefine what intelligence is and how he thinks in his own way. She will, in other words, give him all the material he needs for authentic self-esteem, even though she cannot give him self-esteem. That is his work alone: revisioning himself and revisioning success.

The Nonexistent Pleasures of Self-Sabotage

What does Russell need? He needs honesty and support. He needs to know that the deck is stacked against him: conventional expectations and methods of student evaluation will be onerous when applied to him. The truth is that he will have to work much harder than his peers to achieve the same—or sometimes lesser—results. This is a harsh truth, but if we pretend otherwise or gloss over the disappointment, we may exacerbate the pain that will come from low grades and ruined relationships with family, friends, and teachers.

But the story doesn't end on this sad note. Russell also needs to know that the disparity between himself and others is not some fatal flaw. His learning disability need not overshadow the whole of his life, or even the next stage of his life. That is, if he accepts the unfairness and commits himself to the extra effort inside and outside of the classroom he will grow enormously— not only as a student but also as a human being. In a curious way, he may acquire more out of his high school education than his peers as a result of his struggles. His efforts may finally achieve fruition when he enters the working or professional world, when his perseverance, his self-discipline, and his thoroughness may be amply rewarded. This is another truth he must understand—success beyond the classroom has more to do with how he has gone about doing his work instead of grades attained. People with learning disabilities may flourish in the working or professional worlds, where learning disabilities, while not quite disappearing, fade into the background. Once outside of school, he can take greater advantage of his strengths as well as his coping and compensating abilities. People who do this often say they eventually succeed because of their training in working hard and because of their exercise in defeating self-doubts, all of which a learning disability programmatically invites them to do.

A learning disability insists that the teenager confront his exceptionality. We are all different and bring unique strengths and unique limitations to the classroom. Every student learns differently. By now all of us are aware that individual people process information in vastly different ways. Additionally, through the work of researchers like Howard Gardner, Robert Sternberg, and Daniel Goleman, we have come to recognize and understand theories of multiple intelligences, including emotional intelligence. For instance, Gardner delineates six different kinds of intelligence: linguistic, musical, logical-mathematical, spatial, bodily-kinesthetic, and personal (both intrapersonal and interpersonal). This variety of strengths makes intuitive sense. We are familiar with how teenagers shine in their particular arenas, whether it is the stage, the field, the band, the art room, the peer advising group, the student government. Within the theory of multiple intelligences this is explained nicely: people excel in the area of their dominant and most natural intelligence. However, schools are usually not congenial to all of the various intelligences. That is, traditional academic subjects depend on just one or two of the intelligences. Unfortunately, this leaves a lot of intelligences and many intelligent people out of the equation. As parents and educators, we can always improve the way we highlight these various intelligences as they surface in a teenager. As a practical matter at home, encourage your teenager to pursue his interests and to build on his strengths.

Does Your Teenager Have a Learning Disability?

Have you detected over time a maddening pattern of disappointment, bafflement, and inconsistency? Are your teenagers or you feeling increasingly frustrated in school for reasons you cannot pin down? Are their grades and conduct slipping suddenly, despite their efforts to improve? Do you receive reports of erratic behavior, boredom, malaise, fatigue, rage? Can you sense the unreliability of their memory, or their inability to sustain concentration or control a pen or spell? At bottom, do you have a hunch that something more or something other than normal teenage development is accountable?

Any of these attitudes or behaviors may point to serious concerns. Your children may be suffering from undiagnosed medical conditions (like migraines, impaired hearing or vision, hormonal imbalances, eating or sleeping disorders), socialization difficulties (such as bullies, excessive partying, alienation), or family traumas. Of course, some teenagers may simply be, for some reason, uninterested in school or unmotivated. But even those factors may indicate underlying problems, including learning disabilities. And this is why families need to address the totality of their children's lives.

Consult your physician to rule out health considerations. Speak frankly to your children, and their peers, about their social life at school. Acknowledge any complications at home. In addition, reach out to teachers and administrators for information. Ask them if they notice anything unusual or disconcerting about how your teenager learns or performs. If they voice a suspicion that your children may have learning problems, or if you cannot locate other sources for their difficulties, you should consider a clinical learning assessment. The school or your physician can provide you reputable references.

In some circles learning disability carries a social stigma (Russell certainly suffered from this), but this must not deter you—the stakes are too high. After all, you love your children and you want them to treat themselves (and to be treated by others) fairly and sensitively. As one teacher put it, "We can't all be taught the same way because we all don't learn the same way." The results of a learning assessment can be a powerful tool for kids to use in reclaiming their lives. They come to learn how their brains are wired and how to maximize their efforts. That is, you are not exclusively tracking deficits; you are also identifying variations, idiosyncrasies, and hidden strengths.

In assessing your teenagers, professional clinicians interview and test for attention, memory, compulsivity, cognition, organizational styles, performance anxiety, and adaptability. They consider neuropsychological determinants, sensory powers, and physical skills. (An initial consultation may take up to three hours, often broken into two sessions.) Much of the clinician's work is stunning in its apparently mundane simplicity. For instance, one useful exercise might be to ask a teenager to bring her backpack to a meeting—and she might be led to understand how she organizes her binder, as well as her personal life, and to see how to increase the order of her daily existence. There are as many ways to organize a backpack as their are teenagers' backpacks; that is why the clinician's job is not to judge behavior but to understand your teenager's disposition and to suggest, when appropriate, helpful adjustments.

Not every teenager diagnosed with, for example, attention deficit disorder, hyperactivity, or dyslexia is destined for special education programs or drug interventions. Some children, to be sure, do require, and benefit, from learning outside the mainstream or from psychopharmacology. More often, though, teenagers so diagnosed markedly improve their lives by enacting (with the cooperation of the school) bypass strategies, such as moving to the front of the room, audio-taping classes, taking tests untimed, or employing visualization techniques in class. These are the issues that will be addressed in the written report you receive after the assessment, a document that you will go over in detail with the school and with your teenager.

Having a Real Learning Disability in a Talk Show World Where Everybody Seems to Have One

Before we leave this subject, a word about terminology. It is easy to make light of what seems the sometimes euphemistic, woolly language employed with regard to students who are "special" in one way or another, that is, who have legitimate exceptional needs. Yes, there may be the rare, unethical, unscrupulous testing going on, there may be dubious tendencies in our society to victimize some and give others an unworthy out from personal responsibility, and perhaps some families may be able to buy excuses for a child's laziness or at least an untimed SAT.

However, neurological impairments do rob some children of an equal chance to succeed in school. Whether we can finally serve them in our schools is one issue; whether we should try is quite another. "Handicapped," "dysfunctional," "challenged"—we struggle to find a way to talk about who these students are and what these students need. The last thing a teenager who is diagnosed with dyslexia or attention deficit syndrome needs is to be stigmatized with a label that may never be erased from his transcripted history. Schools have made tremendous strides in recent years in the area of dealing with such children, but it is the rare school whose resources are not strained as a result. When a student requires extra time (or even unlimited time) to take a test—and some educators are beginning to decry this concession to their differences on the grounds that these students must sooner or later learn how to cope within the strictures of the real world—the ramifications are deeply and widely felt. Again, over time we will work out these challenging complications, these competing agendas, but for now we should do what we can to reduce our dependence on simplistic labels—"LD students," "dyslexics," "ADDs." Mel Levine, M.D., is the leading proponent of a phenomenological and humanistic approach to these children, and the leading voice in the discussion of (to cite the title of his major work) *Developmental Variation and Learning Disorders.* In his words, "These children are simply too complex to be characterized by simplistic labels, tidy systems of subtyping, or statistically generated syndromes."

For at the deepest level, what these teenagers help us focus on is the most important activity of education. We want our children to learn how they learn, however they learn. To take it even further, isn't that the most traditional, classical charge of education? It was Socrates who placed at the center of the search for knowledge this principle: Know thyself.

Don't Let Your Teenager's Natural and Inevitable Struggle for Identity Turn into a Power Struggle

As teenagers grow into adults, they undertake the development of a personal identity, which at home can feel like an extreme demand for independence. In the negotiations that occur around independence and dependence, freedom and responsibility, be careful not to let academics become a power struggle between you and your teenager. When parents are too involved in academics, teenagers might assert their independence by doing poorly in school. Therefore, your job is to make sure that independence negotiations don't infringe on learning. And you will always know when negotiations falter as you struggle over ideas of control instead of ideas of well-being. For instance, you can insist that they be responsible for doing their homework. But if you insist that they start cracking the books the minute they walk in the door, you have crossed the line into overcontrol. Let them choose the time to do their work. After all, they are learning to know themselves.

Such parental equanimity and farsightedness is much more difficult to maintain in the case of a teenager with a learning disability, but it is applicable nonetheless. You must always be wary of crossing the line between being the necessarily helpful parent and the unnecessarily intrusive parent. (Don't worry, your kids will keep you posted as you approach the latter state. Unfortunately, however, they don't always let you know when you are the former.)

Demystification

In *Educational Care*, a book aimed at younger children but with more than enough insight pertaining to adolescents, Mel Levine writes about the importance of "demystification" for kids and parents alike. What Levine has to say about demystification with regard to learning disabilities applies not only to students in that predicament but also to any teenager feeling weighed down and beleaguered and exceptional (which includes most teenagers a fair amount of the time). He writes:

We cannot emphasize enough the importance of children understanding themselves. When they are unable to perceive the causal relationship between their specific weaknesses and the problems they are experiencing when they attend school, they tend to fantasize about themselves. Unfortunately, their fantasies are most often far worse than the realities. They may believe they are retarded, crazy, or just born to lose. Such attributions promote fatalistic feelings and a strong belief that effort does no good in school. In addition, when children feel pervasively defective, they are likely to suffer a serious loss of motivation.

Demystification is a process which provides children with more accurate personal insight. *Through open discussions with adults who are working with them, they put borders around their deficits and come to recognize that like everyone else they have strengths and weaknesses.* Very importantly they learn the vocabulary of their problems. (our italics)

Levine breaks down the steps for achieving demystification: (1) a discussion of the reality that all people "have parts of their minds that need to be worked on"; (2) a discussion of strengths and competencies; (3) a discussion of weakness—"explained in plain language"; (4) the "induction of optimism"—"each child should be helped to see real possibilities in the future for his or her kind of mind"; and (5) the formation of alliances with adults, and the reassurance that "everyone needs help in life, that no one can be completely independent."[3]

When you and your child's school work together on demystifying your child's condition, and when all of you devise a strategy and an approach to address the long-term needs of your child, then the guilt and shame will be lifted from your child's shoulders. The teenager in this predicament needs to hear over and over that there are "different kinds of minds, different strengths and weaknesses, different interests and specialties. Such variations should be legitimized in the eyes of students, so they need not feel ashamed of the way they are." Of course, this is ongoing and along the way you will confront all the issues, some of them painful. "Managing these complex problems can be confusing and lonely for a parent. Mothers and fathers shouldn't have to confront the challenges in isolation. Nor should their children!"[4]

Finally, and this is the key for all of us, there is no imaginable issue pertaining to growing up that does not entail demystification.

When Everybody Has a Stake in Russell (Including Russell)

Before we conclude, let's return to Ms. Tolferson. When a teacher calls home under these circumstances she never knows what to expect. In Russell's case his mom was open to the inquiry, but she needed prompting to discuss his problem. She could have conceivably shrugged her shoulders, however, and honored the agreement to keep the silence she made with her son.

No matter what Ms. Tolferson does with the information she received from Russell's mom, her relationship with Russell (and his mom) has undergone a revolution. Mystified before, she now knows what informs his attitudinal shift. Whether or not Ms. Tolferson will or even can work with the mother, or, for that matter, with her colleagues, is an altogether different question. It also remains to be seen if she, or they, can effect in the short or long term any positive change in Russell. Nonetheless, now that the parent has taken a leap of faith—faith in the teacher, yes, but faith ultimately in her son too—there are, at the very least, possibilities to pursue, entries, where all the doors seemed closed before. Not that this will be an easy moment for any of the parties involved. Russell and his mother could have some very unpleasant conversations on the immediate horizon; he could feel betrayed and she could feel frustrated. He may even shut down or lash out. Russell could feel angry with Ms. Tolferson and violated by her as well, since she has intruded into his personal life and has compelled him to acknowledge (in what amounts for him to a public way) the realities he wished to have deferred.

This is the moment when teenagers count on adults' being caring, strong, clear, and supportive. If adults keep Russell's ultimate good uppermost in their minds, they can sustain the fury and the denial. But it won't be easy.

Russell's Conversation with the College Counselor

This conversation takes place much, much later—in fact, a year-and-a-half later, in April, during his senior year, after college acceptance letters have been received.

—So Russell, congratulations.

—Man, I can't believe I got in. Hey, I can't believe I applied!

—The phrase *by the skin of your teeth* does come to mind. Things have changed for you.

—Tell me about it. My music's never been better. It's not just in my head anymore: I can even write music other people can play. My mom and Ms. Tolferson—they've been incredible. And to think a couple of years ago, I thought they were conspiring to make my life a living hell. Which of course is what I was doing to them. When I look back, I know together they made me face up to who I am and how my brain works. They got me the support I needed—the support I didn't know I needed.

—So you owe it all to them.

—Hell no. I'm the one busted my tail. You think working with a tutor is easy? It isn't. It took me a long, long time to stop feeling sorry for myself, too. I mean, everything took effort, planning, planning on planning, setting up meetings, meetings to set up meetings. Worst of all was trying to explain things to everybody around me. I could tell you things, man.

—Ms. Tolferson went out on a limb for you. Maybe I shouldn't tell you this, but she wrote the best letter of recommendation I have ever read. She didn't pull any punches, either. She just told the truth.

—Yeah, she gave my mom a copy. I put it in my scrap book, alongside all my music awards.

—It's not over yet, Russell.

—Of course, it's not over yet. Now, it's all a matter of hard work. Before, I felt stupid. I was like an instrument I just couldn't figure out how to play.

9

Freedom and Responsibility

....

In America, the young are always ready to give to those who are older the full benefit of their inexperience.

—Oscar Wilde

. . . and I was somehow very small and lost and lonely like a child astray in the snow. And anything that happened to me afterwards, I never felt the same about again.

—Frank O'Connor, "Guests of the Nation"

Party at Franny's!

"So her folks won't be home?"

"For real?"

"Saturday?"

"Her parents are leaving in the morning, and they're not coming back till Sunday, late."

Melinda was on the bus with her teammates, heading home from the volleyball game on Wednesday night, when she heard everybody talking about Franny's party. Until now Melinda had assumed it was going to be just herself and a couple of good friends. That was the extent of the planning she was aware of. That and Franny said she was going to see if she could sneak a bottle from the liquor cabinet.

"Franny's house?"

"Franny's really changed lately."

"She sure has. I hardly ever see her at a party. Never figured her for having her own."

"Yeah, some of us might spend the night."

"Home alone for the weekend. They're not even having anyone stay with her or anything."

"Some guys I know say they're going to drop by."

"This'll be good."

The mood on the bus was jubilant after a big win, and the coaches who were sitting up front were too far away to catch what the students were saying. Meanwhile, Melinda kept wondering if she was hearing what she was hearing. This wasn't at all what Franny and she had talked about.

That's the exact moment somebody called out Melinda's name and asked her if she was going to Franny's on Saturday. She shrugged and for some reason looked at her wrist, where there was no watch. Then she calculated that in about seventy-two hours, she was supposed to be at Franny's house. Which gave her a very funny feeling. Did Franny know what was going on, or was Melinda the one who was in the dark?

Back at school in the early dark of a fall evening they unloaded the bus. One by one the kids were picked up by parents or drove off in their own cars. Melinda lingered until she was the last girl to leave. She couldn't tell what was keeping her at school.

By the time she had walked all the way home, though, she decided she would call Franny and tell her what she had heard on the bus. But something kept holding her back. Maybe Franny knew what she was doing. And even more upsetting, maybe Franny didn't want Melinda to know what she was planning. Maybe Franny was leaving her behind. Maybe she really was changing.

She picked up the phone a dozen times and put it back down each time, until finally she dialed the number. Right off Melinda filled in Franny with details about the game, about how she finally got to play today, only because the score was so lopsided. She also couldn't resist adding it was about time. After all, she had been on the team for three years. Franny promised she was going to come to the next home game, but to tell the truth, sports hardly interested her. Unless you counted pro wrestling, which was pretty funny.

"On the way back some girls were talking about you on the bus."

"What'd they say?"

"They were talking about your party Saturday night."

Franny fell silent.

"They're all planning on coming over. Gillian. Cass. Toya. Jeanie."

"Gillian? I didn't invite her, but she is a friend of Maura's and maybe she told her. I don't even know the other girls."

"Who *did* you invite?"

"You and Maura and Cynthia. And Billie, I think, but she was still going to check. You sure about Gillian? I don't even know the girl all that well. But I guess it's OK; one more is no biggie."

"How about ten more, thirty more?"

"You're coming off the top rope, Melinda. What are you crazy, thirty more?"

"Somebody said some guys are going to show up."

"No way, I never invited any boys."

"Franny, I heard them. They know your parents are out of town. Everybody's talking like it's an open party."

"It's my house."

"What are you going to do, bar the door?"

"This is getting out of control."

"What are we going to do?"

"My parents'll kill me."

"Maybe, but not soon enough to help, Franny."

Franny's Conversation with the School Nurse

Franny asked to leave class the first period after lunch on Thursday, saying she had an upset stomach. The school nurse, Mrs. Karin Branden, took her temperature and said it was normal.

—Did you eat anything today?

—No.

—Maybe that's it. Why don't you lie down and rest. I'll get you some fruit and crackers. If you don't feel better soon, I'll call home.

—I don't expect to feel any better anytime soon.

—What's wrong, Franny?

—I feel shitty. You sure I don't have appendicitis?

—Something's troubling you.

—You don't want to know.

—Try me.

—I seem to be having a big party on Saturday night.

—What's the occasion?

—I have no idea. I mean, I was only going to have a few good friends over, but now it seems like it's out of hand. These people I don't really know keep coming up to me, asking for directions, and they're saying what can they bring. This is out of control.

—What do you tell them?

—That's the worst part. I don't say anything. It's like a bad dream.

—Do your parents know?

—What can I tell them? I already promised them I wasn't going to have anybody over. They're going off for their anniversary, and they're going to be a couple of hours away. Think they'd mind if I joined them?

—OK, Franny, let's analyze what's going on.

—I don't have time to analyze anything. I have to do something quick. I wish it was next week.

—What do you want to do about the party, Franny?

—Why did my parents all of a sudden decide to celebrate their stupid anniversary?

—Earth to Franny. Do you want to stop the party?

—I can't tell my parents. I can't tell people not to come over.

—Why not? Either way, your problem is solved.

—It's not that easy.

—Why not? Who are you going to disappoint?

—Everybody, that's who. The only way out is to pull off the party without a hitch. Which is impossible. So there is no way out.

—What about you? If you don't have the party, you think you're going to be humiliated. If you have the party, you'll disappoint yourself by lying to your parents. If you don't cancel the party, you'll disappoint yourself by letting your friends push you around—who, by the way, I suspect aren't really your friends. Seems like you're trying to take care of everyone else but yourself. So what about you, Franny?

—Never thought of it that way.

—Maybe it's time you did.

—You sound like Melinda.

Notes Home

The Metaphysics of the Party

Remember the first birthday party? A decorated cake, the grandparents in attendance, icing all over your child's hands. You have dozens of snapshots of their beaming faces and bright eyes. Remember the fifth? Streamers, making a wish, blowing out the candles, the pleased look on everybody's face, the presents. The tenth? Now, we're much more grown up. Invitations are mailed out. Wishes are made much more seriously, the presents seem more personal and meaningful. The video camera documents everything. Maybe there is a piñata, maybe a gathering at a park, where friends show up to join the celebration and play organized games. Then number thirteen. We're a teenager now. Things are certainly different. The opposite sex may well be invited. Will there be music or dancing? Should it be a sleepover? Parents are close by, in the next room, usually with other parents.

Why do things become so much more complicated with regard to parties by the time your children enter high school? What happened?

Well, to risk stating the obvious, adolescence is what happened. And now you will find yourself, if you are not vigilant, out of the loop. Which is precisely where most teenagers don't mind placing their parents for the time being. As far as your teenager is concerned, the one ironclad rule for a party is that you not be there.

Once your children are fifteen, sixteen, or seventeen, parties become supercharged events. What are teenagers looking for in a party? Meaning. Relationships. Fun. Friendship. Risk. A floating opera. New adventures. Relaxation. Camaraderie. An adult-free zone. Randomized predictability. Sex is in the air, music is in the air, talk is in the air, letting go is in the air, and so is finding oneself. Are teenage parties universally sites of debauchery? Only in some Hollywood fantasy. Are your teenagers necessarily planning on crossing the lines with regard to sex or alcohol or drugs? Possibly. Will they always flirt with catastrophe? No. Then again, sometimes they may. (See Appendix B, "Who Am I? Being 15–16.")

If you think of a party in almost metaphysical terms, which is how your children think of it, you might be able to forge a few more sensible guidelines in collaboration with them. At the deepest levels, a party suggests worlds of intense exploration. Trying on adulthood. Testing the limits. Enjoying the fantasies of limitless possibilities. The joy of playing new roles, trying out new identities. Party animal. Hunk. Heartthrob. Pied piper. Follower. Sidekick. Player. Organizer. Princess. Helper. Clown.

Your job as parents is to influence this searching, not short-circuit it. After all, your ultimate goal is to help your teenagers grow into reflective, responsible adults, and they cannot do that without experience being away from you. When it comes to parties, the problem is that your searching teenagers will inevitably take all sorts of paths, some routes better than others. In fact, they can take the wrong path without your knowing it. But the right path does not always announce itself, and sometimes teenagers do not know it's the right path until they have been diverted. Thus when they are going off to a party they are also going off in search of themselves. Frighteningly for parents, you are not able to witness this leg of the journey.

The Party, the Gamble, and the Internal Life of a Teenager

Franny has sound reason to believe that a party will end in disaster. After all, most teenagers know the scenario from legend if not from firsthand experience. The host's ten best friends invite their ten best friends, who invite people they met from another school at another party. The next thing you know, somebody's house is trashed in record time, jewelry gets stolen, TVs and VCRs are missing, black-and-whites with flashing lights arrive on the scene, the parents' weekend is canceled, and the family trust gets destroyed. The scene sends shivers down everybody's spine.

But here's the funny (and dangerous) part. If by some miraculous twist of fate somebody can pull off a party without incurring too much damage or adverse publicity, then what a bonanza awaits her. There are the enormous gains of a significant increase in her social standing—achievements not to be glossed over when considering the perceived mundane realities of most teenagers' lives. And these are exactly the kinds of gains that somebody like Franny, who has been typecast already as someone on the fringe, might yearn for. And it's often the one on the fringe who will take the greatest risks—because she has the most to gain.

Franny wishes she could delete the party from everyone's short-term memory so that she wouldn't have to deal with it. On another level and at the same time, though, she is reveling in the attention. Nobody at school would have counted on her throwing a party—including herself. But now that she has been cast in a new role (bad girl, party giver), she is seeing a new Franny in everybody else's eyes. In other words, she is fascinating herself: what a drama is taking place around her. And as much as she is frightened by what is going on, she relishes the attention. As she contemplates her seeming powerlessness to affect her world, she exaggerates her self-importance; after all, everybody is coming up to Franny, and they are organizing their Saturday night around her. And it is that self-consciousness that propels her to initiate a dialogue with Karin.

But Franny gets more than she bargains for. In conversations with Karin, she catches a glimmer of the truth that she needs to get in touch with her deeper problems, such as insecurity about associating with the more popular kids. When Karin points out that Franny seems more concerned about others than about herself, she strikes a chord. It is also significant that even before she was swept up by the party panic, however, she took the first bite of the apple: in defiance of her parents' guidelines for the weekend, she was already planning a party with Melinda and a few friends, and she was flirting with the idea of drinking. This decision may contribute to her current paralysis. She had begun to flout her parents' wishes—which makes it conceivable that she can go to the next stage. And once the inconceivable becomes conceivable, then the improbable is inevitable.

Crises of Conscience

It would be difficult to overestimate the significance of friends and friendship in the life of teenagers. Their commitment to friends is virtually religious in its depth and intensity. In these close relationships, teenagers' own well-being is extended to that of their friends. When their friends are happy, they are happy. When their friends are depressed, so are they. This is love, and it keeps them on the phone for hours late at night. The telephone is a sacred instrument of connection. When Melinda senses that her friend is at risk, she strives to save her from ruin by insisting that Franny see things as they are. At first neither friend conceives of a way out, except to hope that her parents don't find out and that they don't get into trouble. But Melinda conveys her doubt and concern, which is another form of peer pressure. Her comments gave Franny a stomachache and an excuse to see Karin.

For an adult, Franny poses a different kind of crisis. Most adults who work with teenagers respect and understand the trust that develops from an imminent crisis. And they have learned from experience that this trust is a burden. It's important here for the nurse to understand what sort of help Franny really needs—and what sort she doesn't. Yes, Franny is struggling and, yes, she is trusting an adult. But she is insisting implicitly that the party is her problem.

Ideally, in ambiguous situations like this one adults help teenagers decide and act on the right course of action themselves; that is, adults do not *act for* them. This is particularly true when it is hard to know what the right thing is and when teenagers doubt they can do it. In this story the challenges are multiple and interrelated: how to get Franny out of hosting the party, how to save face in front of friends, and how to help Franny take responsibility for herself in resolving these issues. Is there a way that will take Franny out of this predicament and allow her to be proud of herself for making the right decision? For teenagers, such mediations are part of their daily existence. In other words, the party is ultimately irrelevant for Franny. She could have stopped those kids from coming to her house if that were the sole issue. She knows, perhaps unconsciously, there are more urgent considerations, and that's what led her to talk to Karin in the first place.

The Easy Way Out and Why It Isn't Easy and Why It Isn't a Way Out

Karin does have a couple of straightforward options. She can tell Franny there is nothing she can do, as the party is an out-of-school activity and therefore none of her business. Or she can call Franny's parents and inform them what is going on. She could find support within herself, and among her colleagues, for either choice. But now let's take a look at both of these options from Franny's perspective.

Karin's first option—doing nothing—abandons Franny and constitutes a renunciation of that trust placed in her. What will Franny gain or learn from this option? Nothing good, for sure. Perhaps she'll conclude that it isn't worth consulting with or trusting the adults around her. Or maybe she'll come to believe that she must handle everything herself. Or maybe she'll simply conclude that it isn't worth letting anybody get too close. Or maybe she'll conclude that adults are even more hypocritical and legalistic than she thought.

Karin's second option—she will take care of everything—infantilizes Franny and denies her the opportunity to take responsibility for herself in a difficult situation. What will she gain or learn from this option? Again, nothing good. Maybe she'll grow resentful for being treated like a little kid and act in some inappropriate manner to prove she isn't a little kid. Or maybe she'll think that adults can't be trusted with anything, that they're all the same. Clearly, neither of these options will further the learning or growth of anyone involved, even though they appear to resolve the problem neatly in the short run.

The Intervention

Intervention is often viewed as a big deal, a life-and-death drama. Family and friends gather to confront loved ones on their drinking habits. Or colleagues assemble in an appropriately somber guise to insist that peers seek treatment for, say, their mood swings and unpredictable behavior. Yet in practice most interventions are, of design and necessity, much more subtle. They are done with minimal fanfare, sometimes one on one and usually in private. And with adolescents, the more subtle the intervention the more effective the result.

Teachers and coaches are natural experts at intervention, as when they praise a reluctant student for a comment made in class, when they encourage another to take a challenging course or go out for a team, or when they go to a game and cheer on somebody who may be having trouble in class. In other words, and in the broadest sense, working with teenagers is in itself a kind of continual intervention. In this vein, behaviorists have one important lesson to impart to adults who work and live with teenagers. Their research shows that the best way to change a person's behavior is through random, intermittent positive reinforcement. The moral might be: catch your teenagers being good. Every time you highlight their doing something positive, or attempting to, you are intervening and influencing their future actions and attitudes.

Did Karin intervene? Yes, and so subtly that Franny may not even know that it had taken place—often a sign of the most effective kind of intervention. For at least Franny has begun to take responsibility. Karin's intervention places Franny on the right track when she points out to her that the party is, in fact, *not* out of her control. Once Franny subscribes to this notion, all that remains is to work out the details, which will vary from teenager to teenager and from community to community. (Much of the time the most effective intervention simply questions unexamined assumptions: *There is nothing I can do . . . I can't ask for help . . . Nobody else can understand . . .*) There are courses of action to take (perhaps with Karin's help) that will enable Franny to do the right thing and feel responsible for herself. The following are only a few of the possibilities:

Karin talks to Franny's parents in the company of Franny.
Franny can invent a cover story. For example, she can claim that the party is off because another parent heard about it and informed Franny's parents or the school.
After meeting with Karin, Franny can swallow a bitter pill and cancel the party of her own accord, without ever talking to her parents.
Karin can play the villain (with Franny's approval) and go to Franny's parents with the news.
Franny can arrange to come down with a bad case of the flu.

But again, all of these options are secondary until Franny has assumed responsibility for her circumstances. Until this happens, these options will be ruled out one by one. She has to see the bigger picture, and she has to see the possibility of normalcy on the horizon after the weekend.

Usually teenagers know what they should do and want to do what they should do. But they fear that they are not strong enough to do it on their own. An adult can help them conquer such fear by believing in them. Adolescence is a time when teenagers develop decisionmaking muscles, and they only develop them in exacting situations. One way teenagers can acquire the support and earn the confidence that they need to act on their best instincts is through principled, caring relationships with their parents as well as with other adults they trust.

Unnatural Allies: Parents and Teachers

Strangely, parents and teachers are threatened by each other. There are many reasons. Parents can feel their children's shifting loyalties to other adults. They hear that so-and-so is a good listener or is full of great ideas or is an inspiration on the field. But wait, that's the way you want them to think of you. And that's what they have been saying about you. Until high school. As for teachers, well, their lives would be a lot easier if parents would just let them teach and stop trying to micromanage their kids' lives and their syllabus. Or, from the opposite point of view, if only parents would lay down the law and show some authority, then their kids would snap into shape. No wonder their students are talking to them: their parents are too busy or too worried, or they just can't see these kids clearly, which teachers of course can.

In parent–teacher relations, unfortunately, there is enough envy to go around for both camps to undercut each other. Teachers spend many hours a day with your children, and they therefore have much to teach you. But at the same time, parents know their children in ways nobody else can, and teachers can go a long way with their students by listening to their folks for clues and keys.

As for Franny's story, there is a good chance that Franny's parents might never have had a clue as to what was afoot if the party were ultimately canceled. If children roughly eleven years or younger were asked to whom they would turn if they had a problem, most would respond, in order, *parents, teachers, and friends.* If a teenager were asked the same question, the order would be completely reversed—*friends, teachers, and parents.* Ultimately, this means that teachers are confidantes of teenagers and frequently become aware of certain issues and concerns before parents. In fact, often parents don't hear about the near misses until after the event has passed— sometimes years later. This means that as good parents you need to form alliances with your teenager's teachers. This does not mean tracking down scandal or encouraging espionage. Rather, it means supporting and getting to know the adults who play pivotal roles in your kids' lives.

When you hear positive reports from your teenager about a teacher, make sure to let that teacher know. A simple note or a short phone call will work wonders. Why? The overwhelming majority of parent communications question, encroach upon, request an accommodation from, or take exception with a teacher. Certainly, those kinds of contacts may be suitable, even necessary. The fact remains, though, that unexpected, affirming phone calls and notes (to even the most outstanding teachers) are rarer than rainbows. But do not misunderstand: this is not to suggest that you politick on behalf of your child, which in any case probably wouldn't be effective even if it were proper, as of course it isn't. Still, a teacher who learns that your child values her class or values her as a person, something that may have heretofore gone unnoticed by her (she may teach five overflowing classes a day), and that you value her contribution to your child's life, is naturally much more receptive to your responses and suggestions. Furthermore, she can become an invaluable resource for you when you need to get caught up on your teenager's life. That is, even without your explicitly asking, she can let you in on what your son is like at school, which is usually very different from what you might otherwise assume. This information is vital to you. If you acquire some sense of the emergent adult he is at school to balance your sense of the regressed child you all too often observe around home (when he's present to be observed at all), you'll feel more confident letting him exercise his independence.

Freedom and Responsibility

Sometimes, though this is the farthest thing from our minds, we inadvertently set up our children to make poor choices. Even the best of kids with the best of friends from the best of families will, given the right set of circumstances, make unwise choices. Yes, by all means, trust your teenagers, but do so within reasonable limits and according to your own values. The pressures to succeed in their social world are tremendous; they are greater—much, much, much greater—than any of us wince to remember. You may have all the best intentions and your children may subscribe to them, but they are not yet adults. Show that you trust them, of course, but do so in ways they can handle.

Battle lines between parents and teenagers are usually drawn over the twinned conceptions of freedom and responsibility. Every single hot button relates to freedom and responsibility: curfews, dating, grades, telephone, Internet, money, and so forth. In general, for parents freedom flows from responsibility; that is, freedom is earned through demonstrably responsible behavior. Teenagers view the continuum differently. For the teenager, freedom is necessary before responsibility is ever possible. That is, they are not abstract concepts for a teenager. They need their freedom in order to show you their responsibility. They construe freedom to be a right and responsibility to be something learned from the practice of freedom. These divergent viewpoints are dramatized all the time in families. Parents grow anxious when their kids demand freedom, and kids grow angry when parents question their ability to act responsibly.

A representative instance of the conflict involves the teenager's getting her driver's license. Most teenagers expect to get their license as soon as legally possible and are shocked at your reservations, not to mention the state's. You, on the other hand, need to observe conscientious behavior in order to feel better about granting them the privilege of driving a car. For a teenager, parental anxiety here amounts to something like this absurdity: "They're afraid to let me drive until I've driven for a few years." Teenagers are tuned in to the ironies. Society is rife with such monumental disconnects. At fifteen they can give birth, but they can't date the person of their choice. At seventeen they can pay taxes, but they cannot vote. At eighteen they can be drafted to fight in a war, but they cannot buy beer.

Some parents are good at assigning responsibility, others on granting freedom. It's a rare family that metes out both proportionately. Yet teenagers need freedom and responsibility in equal measure, and they grow from having both. They cannot be asked to assume more responsibility than they can handle. Sometimes they are going to fail because they have too much freedom and sometimes because they have no freedom to show responsibility. The one constant is mutual apprehension.

Sometimes they are not up to the responsibilities assigned them; as a result, they let both you and themselves down. For instance, when you and your son agree on a curfew for a Friday night and he comes home forty-five minutes late without a phone call, he has failed to keep his responsibility. As a result the next time you will give him less responsibility (an earlier curfew) and/or you will curtail his short-term freedom (grounded for the next evening). Of course, even when we give them too much freedom our hope is that they learn from the consequences and are able to show more responsibility in the near future. (*Stay home tomorrow night and just think about how you let us down and what you're going to learn from this.* Don't pour salt on the wound: let the consequence speak for itself.)

A teenager's maturity cycles between not enough responsibility and too much freedom. In this sense every negotiation is an experiment in action, and your "scientific method" will, as a result, inform you each and every time if your initial judgment was correct. If your teenagers come home on time or call with reasonable notice, then your judgment was perspicacious. But when they come home late with no notice, your judgment was off. This does not mean your teenager is bad or irresponsible, just that he wasn't responsible enough for the freedom you offered. He may very well be responsible enough in the future, however. But nobody will know this if he is not granted the freedom to try again.

After the Party

Let us imagine that Franny for some reason went ahead with the party. Fifty or so kids showed up, the furniture was rearranged, the trash overflowed with beer cans, and carpets were stained here and there with red wine. Suppose furthermore that nobody was arrested or hurt and that the damage to neighborhood relations was not irreparable. What happens when her parents find out? (And the chances of their finding out are roughly equivalent to the chances of the sun coming up tomorrow.) Her parents should be happy that—and this is no overstatement—Franny is unharmed and that the house is relatively intact. After that, however, things get complicated.

Her parents would have a number of feelings to sort through, including fear, disappointment, rage, relief, and more fear. In addition, they would have to stare unflinchingly into the mirror of parental responsibility. Yes, this is the parent version of the freedom–responsibility continuum. Are parents free to spend the weekend away from home? The short answer is no. But the longer answer is maybe. If you wish to go away, you will need to make considerable arrangements, for instance, having an adult stay at the house, being continually accessible by phone, spelling out your expectations, and facing in advance with them their temptations. That is, you have to take some responsibility for their freedom.

This is why it is fitting for Franny's parents to begin their hard conversation by admitting—and this does not get their daughter off the hook by any means—that they are sorry they left town and left her on her own. That apology will liberate Franny to take all the other responsibility for her decisions, and it will enable her to let go of the resentment directed against herself. There is a lesson for parents here. You never lose face and never compromise authority when you concede you are wrong. In fact, quite the opposite. You solidify your relationship with your children, and they trust you even more.

Some parents in such a situation would take a different course of action. Some would take the car away, along with other privileges. Some would go into family therapy. Some would compel their child to earn the money to compensate for any damage done at the party. Some would take away their teenager's cherished activities: the band, the team, the play. Some would restrict and monitor their child's every move from here on out. Some would ground their teenager for months. Depending on the specific circumstances, any of these responses might well be effective. The key is to be mindful of the course of action that will produce growth and promote responsibility.

It is impossible to prescribe an appropriate action, but it is possible to describe the parental state of mind most conducive to their children's character development. Parents cannot proceed from anger (though they may feel their fair share) or from fear of alienating their children's affections (because they will come off as timid). Whatever you do, you must act with respect for your teenager and with awe as to the fragility of their lives. Your respectfulness will allow them to learn from your disappointment. That is, your daughter will see herself reflected not solely as the failure she fears herself to be, but as the person capable of rising above her failure. This is the essence of adolescence, a time when kids thrive when entrusted with second chances. Another way to put this is that forgiveness is the lifeblood of parenting. Forgiveness is hard, gut-wrenching work. Fortunately, you will be given lots of opportunity to practice.

Party Guidelines and Other Leaps of Faith

If your teenagers are attending parties, you are worried and you should be. And be advised, by the time you finish reading this section, your anxieties will not be allayed. Parties are a parent's worst nightmare: beer kegs, bongs, locked bedroom doors, and police cars. To keep our teenagers out of such troubles, we are tempted to fall back on black-and-white policies:

> *Over My Dead Body:* "You will attend no parties and host no parties as long as you live in this house." Good luck with that one. It certainly is a very clear boundary, although it's more like an attempt to establish a demilitarized zone. True, you may very well succeed in keeping your teenager away from a disaster or two. And by virtue of such an edict, you will minimize a few possibilities of their life spinning out of control—the way Franny's is on the verge of doing. But you will also eliminate the chances for them to take control of their lives and to make important decisions—also the way Franny is on the verge of doing. What's more, you will

escalate resentment and encourage deceitfulness. And you will
convey, too, a mistrust that you will have trouble surmounting.
And that will be a major loss—for both of you.

The Ostrich Position, or, Don't Ask, Don't Tell. "Have a nice time,
wherever you're going." What you don't know doesn't hurt you.
Does anybody believe that? Is this a boundary? More like a black
hole. You might think that your child will feel relieved. You're
right. He will be relieved, but unfortunately for both of you he
will feel relieved of responsibility. And he won't feel loved because
love is courageous and there's no backbone to this stance. And the
worst thing is that if something does happen, if he does get into
trouble, he won't feel able to come to you. Why? Because you
indicated to him in so many words that he's on his own. The last
thing a teenager wants to feel going to a party is that he has no
safety net.

The Coconspirator, or, I Remember Being a Teenager: "All teenagers are
going to drink and have sex and . . . , so they might as well do it
right here in my house, where I can keep an eye on them." Is this a
boundary? If you were a country, this would be the equivalent of
renouncing your territorial prerogatives. But in a way, parenting is
a country and your home is a sovereign state, and that's why this
position leads to anarchy. This raises issues of authority and
governance germane for teenagers. They don't want to be the
queen of the realm, though they may want to be freed of chores.
And they don't want to be your loyal subject either because they
want to know that you love them. And they don't want a
democracy because they don't want to be your equals. *What do
they want?* is the wrong question. *What do they need?* is a better
question. What they need is a kind and benevolent dictator, one
who understands that soon they are going to leave the kingdom to
begin one of their own.

The party is symbolic both for teenagers and their parents, and for the
same reason. Anything can happen at a party. Which is why a teenager
wants to go and why the parent does not want her to go. But at least that is
one proposition they can both agree on—and that's why it's not a bad
opening for a conversation.

When your teenager tells you he is going to a party where alcohol will be served and he says he is not going to drink, he may mean what he says. But he really doesn't know if it's true, and he won't know it's true until he goes there and finds out. If your response is, *That's not a chance I am willing to let you take* and you put your foot down, you will eliminate the temptation *that night*, but you will miss the chance to let your child make his own decision. You will have plenty of opportunities to say, *That's not a chance I am willing to let you take*, plenty of times when that is the appropriate response (for example, when he is thirteen or when he is driving or when he has recently broken up with his girlfriend). Just don't miss those rarer opportunities to take a leap of faith—and by faith we do not mean irrational, unfounded, and burdensome expectations. We mean faith that is grounded in knowledge and intuition: *That party worries me, but I trust you to do what you say. So go and I'll be waiting up for you, and, remember, you can always call.*

As we promised, this discussion has not divested you of your anxieties. Faith, so saints testify, is always frightening, and for them life without faith is meaningless. Similarly, parenting without faith is merely a self-defeating attempt at management. But when we go beyond management as our ultimate objective we are free to love our children. And they are free to love us in return. Whoever said parenting was easy?

10

Divorce

I realized that school plays were invented partly to give parents an easy opportunity to demonstrate their priorities.

—Calvin Trillin, *Family Man*

Were it possible for us to see further than our knowledge reaches . . . perhaps we would endure our sadnesses with greater confidence than our joys.

—Rilke, *Letters to a Young Poet*
(trans. M. D. Herter Norton)

It's Beginning to Look a Lot Like Ex-Mas

"Sam, come in here for a second, would you?" The dean of students had called him in before to discuss problems surfacing in his progress reports, so Sam knew her office. "Got something in the mail from your dad today."

"Was it the old Season's Greetings with his three pugs in Santa suits again?"

"I must not have made the list this year. Wait. Pugs? Never mind. Have I met him?"

"He's not the kind of guy you would tend to forget."

Winter break was only a week away. The dean picked up the letter and read out loud: *Please excuse my son, Samuel, from school Thursday and Friday prior to vacation. He and his younger sister, Katharine, will be flying across country for Christmas. Thank you very much for your cooperation. Please contact me if this presents any difficulties that I can address.*

"Sounds like Pops all right."

"You've missed a fair amount of school this year, Sam. You were out with the flu twice for, what, almost two weeks?"

"Second time, that was a pretty bad one."

"And—let's see—maybe I can phrase this delicately."

"I know I'm not really enjoying what you'd call a good semester."

"Well, those midterms were dicey. Still working on that Incomplete in English?

"Making headway, you bet. But you're right, I should be doing better."

"So leaving early could pose a problem?"

"Who says I want to leave? You should hear Katie—she's broken up about missing her school pageant. You know how hard it was to make those antlers? I helped."

"Why don't you tell me what's going on here? Or should I be talking to your dad or your mom maybe?"

"How much time do you have on your calendar today?"

"I've got a few minutes."

"In that case, everything's fine."

"Come on, Sam."

"It's my dad's turn, every other year for Christmas. It wasn't a big deal at first, but each time it gets harder and harder. When I grow up I'm going to get married, build a house in the woods with my own two hands, and stay there for the next eighty years. I get kind of sick just thinking about airports. Not to mention airline food. I can't even fake it anymore. Since my parents split up, it's so weird, the holidays are just the worst time of year, though summers aren't far behind. And they make it even worse by competing with each other. You know, to give the best presents. The way I figure it, my sister and I are due for new cars pretty soon."

"Sounds complicated."

"Complicated? I love my dad, and I know he loves me and Katie. I just wish he didn't live so far away."

"You think things would be a whole lot different between you if he lived across town?"

"Good question. Maybe, I guess. I'll get back to you. I've got lots of friends who have two bedrooms with two sets of posters, two sound systems, two TVs, two sets of books, two sets of clothes, two sets of stepparents, two sets of rules, and you know what's the worst thing? You can't believe it, but it's two holiday dinners!"

"Should I call your dad and point out that you're missing a test on Friday, not to mention the school assembly?"

"Trust me, save yourself the trouble. Two years from now, when it's his turn again, I'll be in college, and it's going to be different, right? Besides, Katie would be crazy without me on the plane."

"All right. I'll check with your teacher, see if you can take the test early."

"You'd do that?"

"I can try. Let's talk when you get back."

"Oh. That a condition?"

"More like a request."

"OK then. But you won't take it personally if we don't talk, right?"

"You know, Sam, my parents split up when I was in high school."

"I could tell—there was something about you."

A Conversation with the Attendance Secretary

The woman who runs the main office is a legend. She has worked at the school for decades, and she has cultivated relationships with kids to such a degree that a couple of years ago they dedicated the yearbook to her, her photograph appearing with the legend ALWAYS THERE FOR US. Her husband taught English here up until his death at age seventy, and she loved conversations with kids about books, and about everything else. There was also always a big jar of candy on her desk, which she had to refill every single day.

—Happy Channukah, Happy Kwaanza, and a Merry Christmas to you, Mrs. T.

—Thanks, Sam, you've covered all the bases. Doing anything fun for break?

—Fun? That's a concept.

—It's not a concept, it's an eleventh-grade requirement. Better brush up on your handbook.

—Must have missed that. Hey, maybe you can give me a pointer. It's not about me, actually, it's about Katie, my little sis. She's having a tough time.

—What's going on?

—My dad's pulling her out of the fifth-grade winter pageant. She was Donner or Blitzen, I forget. I helped her make the antlers. Man, what a project that was, finding the right twigs, gluing them on the headpiece, and balancing the sticks so the thing wouldn't tip over.

—Why is he doing that?

—Well, let me rephrase that. He's putting her on a plane so she can go spend Christmas with him. Quality time.

—She talk to you about being upset?

—I can tell. She handed off the antlers yesterday to Raynal, her best friend.

—And she's getting on a plane by herself?

—I didn't mention I was going with her?

—Might have missed that.

—No, it's the two of us. It's his year, you know.

—You're worried about—Katie's her name?

—Yeah, she's my partner. Of course, she *can* be a pain, but, hey, that's what little sisters are sometimes—it's all right.

—So you're flying together. Done this before, traveling across country together?

—Oh sure. But she's upset. So here's what I want to know. How can I help her out? Make her feel OK about missing the pageant and all?

—Tough one, Sam. How are *you* feeling about leaving town?

—Me, I'm used to it. Sort of. If I'm not strong, how can I help her, right? And it is his year, and I do miss him a little bit, his being around and all. On the plus side, next year we stick around with my mom. Not that I'm saying I side with her or anything. You have any idea what it's like having a parent who's a lawyer? Anyway, it's none of my business. It's between them, their shit. Maybe I shouldn't have said that.

—What's it like going there?

—Oh, the regular. Maybe I can get into the eggnog brandy punch bowl if I'm lucky like last time. And of course since I've got a late paper due when I get back, I can use his computer. He's got a really cool one. He gets a new one every year. Then I'll just hang out. It's not that long, really, six nights, seven days is all. But I need some help with Katie.

—Sure. Go ahead.

—I feel terrible for her. She's still not over it, the divorce. But it's like years already. Mom is worried about her, I can tell. She said she could call as much as she wants, that might help, right? What can I do?

—One thing I know, it's hard watching people we love go through pain, isn't it? Especially when there's nothing we can do about it. You OK, Sam?

—No problem, I'll be OK. I thought after a while it'd get easier, but it just doesn't. When's it all supposed to get better?

—These things take a long time. Think Katie's worried about you too?

—She's ten.

—It's an important age, ten, a great age. I would guess she knows how much you love her, and I would also guess she knows you two are together in this.

—That's just what she said, the little imp, how'd you know? Anyway, you ever read *Catcher in the Rye*, about Holden Caulfield that maniac and his little sister, Phoebe? Sometimes I think I'm living in a book. And you know what? That's the book I couldn't finish my paper on, which is why I have a dumb Incomplete in English from the quarter. I read it five times and started fifty papers. You know how the book ends? He says don't ever tell anybody anything, because if you do you start missing everybody.

—I've had that feeling.

—The way that book ends, it made me sad. I'm beginning to know why people write sad books.

—Why do you think so?

—Because they don't have any choice.

Notes Home

No Guilt Trip

Let's begin with a couple of provisos. For one thing, the discussion that follows fleshes out the discomfort children may still be feeling after having gone through a divorce, even if the divorce was years ago. Our purpose, understand, is not to place blame or to make parents feel guilty. If you are divorced, and if you are anything like most divorced parents we know, there isn't much of a need for us to provide this service for you. The truth is you probably feel bad enough without any prompting. For another thing, our central focus is on your children. We do this with the full conviction that children are resilient, more than you probably know. We also do this with the assurance that the best way for you to deal with your guilt is to put your children first. Most families are not unfamiliar with trauma of one type or another. Poverty, illness, racism, unemployment, illness, addiction—there are plenty of traumas to go around. You are intensely aware, if you are divorced, of at least one of your family traumas.

Your Divorce and Your Teenager

This story of Sam and Katie and their divorced parents takes place long after judges and lawyers have parted the scene, long after visitation schedules have become fixed, long after all the messiness of money and property negotiations. But divorce is never done, not even after all the papers are filed. Renegotiation is an ongoing fact of life for everybody involved in the divorce, including the child, whether he's fifteen or twenty-five.

On one level Sam seems resigned, even mature, about his changed family circumstances. But on another level it is clear that he is not quite able to shake the lingering effects of the past. Therefore, it is wise to remind ourselves of the originating crisis that divorce visits upon a teenager. That crisis is nothing less than monumental.

Constance Ahrons, author of *The Good Divorce*, creates a helpful model in her discussion of divorce. She distinguishes three stages: stress, crisis, and adaptation. Applied to divorce, stress comes about as the family begins to dissolve. Crisis occurs when the stress reaches a breaking point, when conflict is no longer manageable, when family members can no longer cope with the recognition of their dashed hopes and dreams. Adaptation, writes Ahrons, "requires change—restructuring or re-inventing some portion of life, changing the way stressors are perceived or managed, learning new skills, and finding new resources."[1]

When it comes to Sam and Katie, they are clearly in the adaptation stage. But before reaching this point, here are the sorts of things they—and every child of a divorced family—had to deal with.

In *Reviving Ophelia*, author Mary Pipher explains how divorce is "particularly difficult for teenage girls. . . . When their families break apart, they have too much coming at them too fast. . . . Some [girls] get depressed and hurt themselves, either with suicide attempts or more slowly with alcohol and drugs. Some withdraw and sink deep within themselves to nurse their wounds. Many react by rebelling."[2] In *Real Boys*, author William Pollack remarks that the situation for boys is just as ominous and is trickier in the sense that boys are expected to "tough out" these hard times. Consequently, boys pay a price if they opt to express their feelings, if they reveal that they are vulnerable and needy and ashamed. In Pollack's view the trauma of divorce is every bit as disruptive as the universal shock of adolescent separation from their parents.[3]

The pain teenagers feel in divorce cannot be neatly typed according to gender, however. Some girls hunker down and take refuge in their private world; some boys (like, to some extent, Sam) talk and emote relentlessly. Each individual copes, or doesn't cope, in his or her own individual way. Although it is dangerous to generalize, most teenagers and their families experience certain common denominators.

Loyalties Are Divided Equally Between Parents

The threat of the loyalty oath shadows many teenagers. The very *mathematics* of loyalties is unnerving. What they give to one parent, they sometimes feel they're keeping from the other. This kind of scorekeeping leads them to say things to one parent in defense of the other parent that they might not even believe themselves. The whole problem is insidious and it implicates both parents and children.

For instance, if a dad is typically late for appointments and pickups, a mom might be tempted to offer solace and support, saying, "That's just your father. He's been that way since the day I met him." Her voice may be calm; she may have intended that to be innocuous, even protective of the other parent. Given a separation or divorce, however, don't be shocked to find your teenager rationalizing, even defending, your ex's behavior—and totally missing your intention of helping *them* with their disappointment. He might snap back, "Why don't you give Dad a break? He's doing the best he can, and besides he's gotten much better since the two of you broke up." This comment is not meant to represent the truthful analysis of Dad's behavior; rather, it represents the dynamic of split loyalty—the need to defend the absent parent to the present parent. A teenager who trashes the absent parent creates an untenable situation for himself. His parents may renounce their relationship with each other, but he needs them both to be his parents. This is why it is so difficult and frightening for a teenager of divorced parents to entertain the slightest possibility that one parent is incompetent or worse, such as mean-spirited or abusive. This is why even abused children often defend their abusive parents' actions, often to the point of wanting to stay in their custody.

The real crusher in this split-loyalty dynamism, however, is that the teenager, if not extremely conscious of what he is doing, can go a little crazy. That is, he is saying things that he is not certain of and saying them with a force and vigor that make them sound like absolute truths. In the long run, this leads even the most savvy teenagers to question their own judgment: "Is Dad just spacey when he's an hour late, or is he being selfish and rude?" "Is Mom just making Dad jump through hoops for her own satisfaction—or is she trying to make my life easier?" In drastic cases, they may even question their own identity. "Am I different person when I am with Dad?" "Do I become a better person at Mom's apartment?"

The golden adage of divorced parents is never to disparage the other parent in front of your children, and that's sound. The instant you do so you will feel the backlash of the split loyalty, and much worse, too: you will set into motion the follow-up backlash, which your child will suffer in private, of self-questioning and self-doubt.

Teenagers Need Their Friends

Teenagers from divorced families need their friends just as all teenagers do, only more so. Their friends, besides just being friends, are also their mediators, translators, and sounding boards. Teenagers of divorce go to their friends with the strange feelings and behaviors generated around the divorce in order to make sure they are not crazy. For instance, a teenager who was furious with his dad for being late to pick him up after school but minutes later defended his dad's behavior to his mom, will, after the dust has settled, seek out his friends to reassure himself that he is sane. His friends offer him the understanding that he is looking for, since with his friends his primary preoccupation is not loyalty to his parents but his ongoing health and self-confidence.

Especially during any heightened family drama—holidays, graduation, vacation—teenagers need access to their friends. In essence, they need to debrief with their friends after any and all emotionally laden events. Expect this kind of retreat to friends. In fact, plan on it and, by all means, do not take these sorts of behaviors personally.

Reading Between the Lines

Children from divorced families are expected to articulate everything twice. They are besieged by questions—the same questions from Mom and from Dad. They are continually expected to account for their where-abouts and for their connections to the other parent. Because both parents worry about their ongoing relationship with their child, they are going to press for connection, for information, for support. This is all going to feel like a tremendous hardship for any teenager of divorce, who, because of the hardship, more than other teenagers periodically needs to shut down, go into himself, and be silent. They need parents who can sense when silence is not a threat and not a signal of disengagement. Teenagers of divorced families have to decide consciously how much to share, or not share, with each parent. In this regard, unlike other teenagers, they cannot afford to be spontaneous. They parcel out their emotional energy as if it were precious currency, knowing that sometimes their parents are hoarding it to use against each other.

For example, imagine that a child of a divorced family wins a special prize. Good news, right? The problem is, what to do with the news and, more to the point, whom to tell first—Mom or Dad? This is no trivial matter. This teenager knows that whoever he tells second is going to know he or she wasn't first. It's enough to take away *some* of the pleasure of winning the prize in the first place, and it also takes away *most* of the pleasure of telling parents the good news. And this lost connection and lost pleasure is something that teenagers from nondivorced families never have to contemplate. It's no wonder that teenagers of divorced families often do not share much of their good news with either parent. They rely on their parents' learning through the grapevine. And they rely on their relationships with siblings and friends to take an added measure of joy in their accomplishment.

Therefore, perhaps more than any other group of teenagers, they need adults who can read between the lines of what they are saying, not saying, and struggling to find the words to say. (In this regard, teenagers have the uncanny ability to reach out or make gestures to those adults around them who have the best chance of understanding what they are really asking for. In this story, it is probably more than coincidence that the dean of students knew firsthand the adolescent struggles that come with the territory of divorce.) Teenagers are anything but opaque, though; they just need people around them who know how to read the signs. Not incidentally, most teenagers look to adults who can accurately read the signs and in some unobtrusive way reflect this reading back to them in a comment, a look, or a simple gesture. When they need full-scale conversation, they'll find the adults who are capable of having, and are eager for, such talks.

What Divorce Teaches a Teenager

Teenagers in split families quickly become rueful connoisseurs of the absurd. TV privileges may be limited in one home, and three sets may be blaring all day long in the other. One parent may have a curfew, the other not; one is affluent, the other is counting pennies. In one household, teenagers may have their favorite clothes, and in the other they keep their music. How can they live authentically, torn as they are between two worlds? It is not only a philosophical question, it is also a boringly, ruthlessly pragmatic one.

For one thing, teenagers of divorce believe that they are especially singled out to shape their own destiny. They sense that they must now rely more than ever on themselves, and so they depend on their own resources. No wonder some teenagers carry around enormous backpacks stuffed with their books, CDs, earphones and cell phone, tennis shoes, and favorite sweatshirt. They cannot risk being without some of their essential equipment, their markers of personal identity, just in case. Their burdens can be, in every sense, backbreaking.

All of these crazy complications in their daily life may tempt these teenagers to give up: there is no way they can keep things organized, no way to compartmentalize their lives. They live one life, and that is all they have and are. The problem is that the divorce has assigned them two different lives, one with each parent. Even if one parent is absent, a teenager imagines a life with him or her.

Particularly in times of perceived crisis and powerlessness, teenagers feel thrown onto their own devices—music, sports, school; drugs, alcohol, sex. They invest in new ways to distract themselves, to deflect the pain, to redefine their values. At the same time, because they are thoroughgoingly idealistic and wishful, they may even attempt to reconcile the unresolvable differences between their two homes, two families. They may come to assume that it is their burden to make everything a little bit all right for everybody else involved, even while they endure their own isolation and disappointment. In the story in this chapter, for instance, Sam chose to focus on taking care of Katie instead of himself.

Even the most hardened teenage veterans of the divorce wars have sympathy for their parents. That sympathy, though, is roughly equal to the anger they feel. All teenagers, by definition, gradually see their parents' inadequacies. For a while, their limitations and problems are all that they can see about them. But divorce exacerbates and hastens this process.

A Cruel Fairy Tale:
Holidays Can Be the Worst Time of the Year

The stylized images of supposedly happy homes during the holidays are unavoidable on television, in songs, in ads and in stores, when everybody seemingly subscribes to the mannered fiction that life is perfect and home is unremitting bliss. Teenagers of divorce know firsthand that this is simply not true. With harsh and repetitive irony, the omnipresent holiday decorations highlight all that is wrong.

Even for teenagers in a relatively stable household, the holidays are an unpredictable and intensely vulnerable time—when reality pales in comparison to fairy tales. But those living in split families are more vulnerable to anxiety and frustration. If they feel abandoned by one of their parents, or for whatever reason live primarily with one parent, they are liable to feel shame and culpability, not to mention sorrow over the losses and failures of the other. They may well blame themselves for the fate that has befallen their family and themselves.

If families are reconfigured after divorce, teenagers register every tiny shift in the weather of both families. Such consciousness is enervating. The cost of their picking up every single emotional nuance, no matter how subtle, is very high, emotionally and psychologically. Inevitably, some actively negotiate the tensions that the former spouses, their parents, seem to escalate at this time of year. They are tempted to mediate. How can they afford to stand back? How can they manage not to?

For all of us, and especially teenagers, the holidays are memory mirrors. Because the holidays are special days and events, we tend to remember them and use them as markers in our lives. (For example, we stand a better chance of remembering what happened on Thanksgiving Days than we do of remembering what happened on any fourth Thursday of any particular month.) On every major holiday, teenagers are forced to reminisce about their family history and the way things were growing up in their family. In divorced families this means yearly grieving the lost family (no matter how dysfunctional) and coping with the new family situation(s). Even while parents attempt to move on and redefine their own lives, children continue to be the site of the unresolved family drama.

The first few times that they look into the memory mirror are the most poignant and difficult for teenagers of divorce, and in many ways create no-win situations for kids. Most of these teenagers (especially from recently divorced families, meaning the last four to five years) simply aspire to get *through* the holidays. Merriment and wistful moments of joy are too much to imagine and too painful to hope for. Reduced expectations make it easier for them to deal with their expectedly winnowed down reality.

Self-Destructive Behavior, Divorce, Holidays, and Teenagers

We can see why the teenagers of divorced families often stand at greatest risk during the holiday season, the time when they are confronted with realities that they spend much of their lives trying to ignore or escape. During these times it is not unusual for the "model" teenager to embrace alarming risks, for instance, reckless driving or binge drinking. Why? Quite simply, these behaviors are ways of coping, through avoidance, with the painful realities they would rather not face up to or, most important, that are out of their control.

At the same time, these actions are useful attention getters. Teenagers have no say in their parents' divorce, and yet it radically upends their lives. No wonder they feel powerless and try to influence their families in any way they can manage, including counterproductive and self-subversive ways. Somehow they pack into the weeks before holidays all the trouble they can. This is the time when cars have accidents, when tests are flunked, when credit cards are maxed out, when lies are told, when sweats or CDs are shoplifted, when cigarette smoking is taken up, when expensive textbooks and sports equipment are lost, or when romantic relationships escalate or precipitously taper off, or both. Such teenagers feel that disaster is happening to them.

Teenagers in a divorced family feel betrayed and confused. They don't hate you because you divorced their other parent, but they will say and do things sometimes that make you feel that they do. Don't expect them to help you navigate your pain. They have their own to deal with. You may have cut your ties, but they haven't. They can't. That's why all the logistical roadblocks placed in the way of their free and full connection to both parents can be so infuriating. We all know what we want to do when we see a roadblock. We have to stop, but we would rather plow right through it.

That's why it's a good idea to take as many of them down as you can. That starts with trusting your child's connection with the other parent.

In this story, what is at stake for Sam in his struggles is nothing less than making sense of his fragmented life and his family relationships. On some level, he knows he cannot influence his parents' happiness, but on another, he keeps trying anyway—subverting his own needs occasionally to serve theirs. (For example, he does not insist on staying in school to complete his obligations.) That also partly explains why he ferociously keeps his commitment to his sister, Katie. His connection to her is much more than symbolic. Divorce, much like death, brings siblings closer together. Why? For one thing, siblings in this situation are the only people in the world they can count on to understand what they are going through. For another, they are the people who can take care of *him* because they need him as much as he needs them.

If You Believe That
You Have Ruined Your Child's Life . . .

. . . you probably haven't. Your kids are irrepressible and your home is likely no more "dysfunctional" than the next. (Someone once defined "dysfunctional family" as any family larger than one person.) Yes, you have changed their life, no question about that. But guilt is not going to help anybody now. Unless, that is, it helps you focus on your kids' issues; in that case your guilt can come in handy.

If you are divorced and not angry or upset or worried, if you are divorced and your vacation and weekend arrangements work with clocklike efficiency, if you are divorced and your children regularly express their appreciation for the creative, sensitive custodial adjustments made in their lives—you should write a book as a public service and explain your secret. The rest of us who struggle with the problems, the insecurities, the doubts, and the loss, will value your contribution.

The actualities, especially in the near term, are usually bleaker. After your divorce, you want to put your life together again. You may hope, as the saying too facilely goes, to put it all behind you. The problem is, teenagers cannot put anything *behind* them. Perhaps nobody truly can— maybe the best we can do is put it all *inside* instead. Of course you want to move on. But the problem for your children is this: they move on when they move away. (In extreme cases, this is one reason why kids run away. In

their minds, they are not running away from their family, but they are flee-
ing to a place where they can create a single, whole life.) Does this imply
that your children *need* therapy? Usually, no, but they do need extra doses
of understanding and talk—and a little more slack, too.

In practice, as long as they are dependent on their parents for their basic
needs, they will actively be adapting to the divorce. Not if it happened last
year, not if it was ten years ago. In the meantime, every significant family
moment—every ornament and candle, every celebratory dinner, every
family trip, every gift and card and phone call—is achingly symbolic.
Everything that *is* there is a shocking reminder of what is *not* there anymore. Inevitably, it is tempting to take that short step from disappointment to distrusting the entire world. And that's where you come in: to do
everything you can to keep that from happening.

Even though no two divorces are the same, there are ways we can all help
our children through the crisis.

Be open, but avoid acting on confessional, political, or needy urges,
which are natural under the circumstances. Of course, you have your own
needs and you have your own pain, but your children can't be asked to
help. Let them know in no uncertain terms that you have liberated them of
this burden. Instead, give them every opportunity to talk about what they
are going through. Keep the focus on them, even when you want to talk
about your own struggles or, in particular, your former spouse. Yes, it may
seem palliative to ventilate, to bemoan the irrational judge and the devious
lawyers, and so on. But unless they directly indicate that they need to talk
about the other parent with you, for instance, you shouldn't introduce the
topic. In fact, a guiding principle should be this: your child now gets to
lead the discussion. You cannot shape the terms of their emotional turmoil. If you are talking about the family crisis to serve your own interests,
you won't help your child.

Check with them regularly. How are the arrangements affecting their
daily lives? Is there anything they think can be done to make things a little
easier? Not perfect, of course, because it won't be, but a little easier. It
might be something very simple, something you're missing. Maybe it will
have to do with installing a separate voice mailbox (so that friends and the
other parent can leave messages) or perhaps buying a few extra clothes (so
that getting dressed in the morning does not precipitate dejection).

By the way, checking with them regularly does not mean every weekend
or every single time you see them, either. As we discussed earlier, such hy-
perattentiveness can constitute its own burden.

Family Is Family Is Family

After a divorce, your family is not the same and, what's more, it never will be. But here's the important thing you cannot afford to lose sight of: it is still a family, their family, your family. In other words, let your children have their grief and realize that sadness is usually seasoned with a good measure of rage. That means being ready to bear the brunt and to fight through thickets of impenetrable emotion.

This does not imply, however, that holidays will be grim affairs from now on, only that they will indeed be different. Even though they may want the old traditions, and you or your former spouse may—in your individual styles—want that, too, you must now make something new. That's your best hope. And that is a big hope worth cultivating. Just do not expect your children to help you in this regard. They are too busy helping themselves, which is as it should and must be. You will need all your imagination and faith, and all your love for them, to get yourself—and them— through the tough times that loom ahead. With enough imagination and faith and love—and good fortune—you may one day begin to look forward to holidays in a whole new way. And, believe it or not, so will your teenagers.

Another Conversation Between Sam and Mrs. T.

—Hey, Sam, you're back.

—In the flesh. Have a nice vacation?

—Not bad, thanks. You?

—They didn't spike the eggnog this year if that's what you're asking. But I guess it wasn't all that terrible.

—Did you have a good time with your dad?

—Sure. He even made breakfast every morning, omelets and pancakes and French toast and everything. I forgot he liked to cook. Then every night, a party, or a dinner, a movie, a video . . .

—Did you get a chance to talk? I mean about what you mentioned to me?

—Oh, not really I guess. Where do you begin, and what can he do anyway? It's not his fault.

—I understand. Still, sometimes it's important to say what you feel, as much for yourself as for your dad. In fact, more for yourself than your dad.

—I guess. But I don't even know where I would start. Besides, well, my dad's not the kind of guy that is comfortable talking about that kind of stuff. I can just see him now, getting all fidgety.

—You know him best, so you're probably right. But you know something that works when you have to say something complicated to someone who's important to you, is writing a letter. No, really, honest. Maybe you could write him a letter. You don't necessarily have to send it to him, just write it for yourself, to get it all straight in your head.

—I'm not much of a letter writer. Besides, wouldn't it be weird to write a letter you weren't going to send?

—Possibly. But I do it all the time. Sometimes just writing it down helps you to think through stuff.

—Never thought of that. OK, maybe. Would you look at it, if I wrote one, that is?

—I'd be honored.

—Does e-mail count?

—Sam.

—OK, but something kind of goofy did happen with Katie. Guess who I caught reading *Catcher in the Rye* on the plane? I mean, isn't she kind of young? It's a pretty mature book, and it's not Mister Roger's Neighborhood or anything.

—You're her big brother, maybe you two could talk about it.

—That's true, too. I don't have to write her a letter, too?

—By the way. Did you finish it, the paper?

—It's a beauty. When I finally started writing it, I couldn't stop. The longest paper I ever wrote. Go figure.

11

Weapon on Campus?

....

The woods are lovely, dark, and deep,
But I have promises to keep.

—Robert Frost,
"Stopping By Woods on a Snowy Evening"

It was very sad, he thought. The things men carried inside. The
things men did or felt they had to do.

—Tim O'Brien, "The Things They Carried"

Miles to Go Before I Sleep

– One –

South Side High is one of those post–World War II schools built originally
for around a thousand students. Times have changed. If you are one of the
two thousand or so attending South Side these days, you can forget finding
a parking place if you're late. You can hardly even walk down a corridor
without bumping into somebody. And every semester you take classes
where there are other students you never saw before, and there are teachers
who do not recognize you.

It isn't surprising, then, that Miles didn't know the name of the student
whose locker was three over from his own. Perhaps he could have picked

him out of a crowd, but probably not, at least until yesterday. That was when he accidentally glanced into that locker and saw the steely glint of what might have been a gun. But it all happened so fast, and before he could take a closer look, the locker door clanged shut and the student merged into the crowd, never noticing how Miles was still staring at the plastered-on Raiders bumper sticker. Miles was amazed that some administrator hadn't peeled it off yet.

Twenty minutes later during Geometry class all the figures chalked on the board reminded him of the gun he had seen—if it was in fact a gun and if he had really seen it. No matter how hard he tried to block out the images, they kept haunting him. This wasn't the first time he had seen a gun up close, but it was the first time he had seen a gun at South Side. Guns at other schools, that he could understand, but not at South Side. His school was no urban jungle. It was different. But maybe it wasn't. After the carnage at Columbine, maybe everything was different everywhere. The bell rang and Miles let himself take his eyes off the cylinders sketched on the board. It didn't help as much as he hoped.

"Miles," his buddy Jack said to him once they were out of the class, "what did your mom make us for lunch?"

Miles began working his locker combination but he kept watching that other locker with a sinking feeling, hoping that the other guy wouldn't show and the locker door wouldn't open again to whatever was or wasn't inside. At the same time, he desired a second look, to be sure.

"Hello, you coming to lunch or not?" Eddie, his other best friend, said. "I want to get some hoops in before fifth period and that crochmos test."

As they walked down the corridor, Miles paused before that locker. "Who's the Raiders fan, and I thought they didn't let us put stickers on."

"He's a bass player, some wannabe metal band—what's his name," said Eddie. "How should I know and I'm hungry, let's get out of here already."

"Jason," Jack added, "he's a junior, I think, and the band's supposed to be not bad, and why do you care about a sticker anyway? You the hall monitor?"

"Never heard of him."

Eddie was exasperated. "He probably never heard of you either. Let's go eat." To him, Miles was a good guy, but he sure got worked up about some funny things.

– *Two* –

Spring had arrived early that year, and the three friends were sitting on a patch of dirt overlooking the only stretch of lawn at the whole school, turf the upperclassmen staked out every single day. Staked out? They owned it. As he looked out across the campus, Miles was thinking how few students he knew. True, he was a freshman, but it was funny how easy it was to feel lonely in the midst of the crowd. He was glad for the friends he did have, though, Jack and Eddie, mainly. They were guys he could trust, and they could trust him if they had a problem. When Eddie's parents separated for a while or when Jack's little sister got very sick and missed a whole semester, they were there for each other. Today Miles had a problem, and he didn't know how to talk to them about it.

"What do you guys know about Jason?"

"Jason who?" Jack looked puzzled.

"The band, the Raiders sticker."

Eddie couldn't believe it. "Again, Jason? What is up with you today?"

"I'm not sure, but I'm pretty sure, I saw a gun in his locker." There, he said it out loud. He didn't know for sure that he could. He looked around, as if he were afraid somebody else was listening.

"No way," said Jack. "You sure?"

"Well, I didn't get the serial number if that's what you mean—I don't know. But I know a gun when I see one, so I'm pretty sure."

"What kind of gun?" Eddie wanted to know. As far as he was concerned, not all guns were the same. You needed to make distinctions. He himself owned a rifle, took target practice, and went deer hunting with his grandfather and uncles. "Like a handgun, or like a rifle?"

"A handgun."

"Man," Eddie wondered out loud, "why would he have that in school?"

"Like there's some kind of good reason to have a gun at our school," Jack said.

"What do you guys think I should do?"

"Why do you have to do anything?" said Eddie. "It's none of your business. Jason's not some psycho. And it's not like he threatened you."

"Like that's important," Jack argued. "A gun is a gun, and besides you don't know shit about Jason, just that he's in some band. Ever heard of Littleton, Colorado?"

"Everybody's got Littleton on the brain. Those two guys were losers. Besides, just because Jason's got a gun in his locker—if he does have a gun in his locker—doesn't mean he's going to use it."

"OK, give me one reason," Jack snapped, "to have a gun in your locker."

"Maybe he needs it for self-defense. This is a big school, maybe he's got a beef with somebody. Maybe somebody's harassing him and he has to scare him off. Maybe he's showing off. Maybe he forgot to leave it home. Maybe it's a ceramic sculpture of a gun, how the hell do I know? I didn't see it. And, hey Miles, maybe you didn't see it either."

"More we talk about this, the more I know I saw a gun."

That gave Jack an opening. "What are you going to do, Miles?"

"If he's smart," Eddie jumped in, "he'll do nothing. This has nothing to do with him."

"What if Jason threatened him?"

"That'd be different. But that didn't happen."

"What if Jason was in Geometry with us? Would it be different then?"

"Obviously."

"But Eddie, think about it, he's in somebody's math class—don't you care about them?"

Eddie tossed the remains of his sandwich into his bag. "What are you going to do, call the police? And suppose there isn't a gun. You're opening up a world of trouble for yourself, and for what's his name."

Finally Miles spoke again. "You think I haven't thought about all that already?" If he were 100 percent sure that he had seen a gun that would be one thing. He could almost be sure he would have talked to the vice principal by now. But he was only 90 or 95 or 99 percent sure—and that trace of uncertainty made his life so much more difficult.

"Don't listen to Eddie, Miles. You have to do something. I mean, what if the guy is crazy, what if he does plan on using it? And what if he uses it, how would you feel then?"

"What would you do, Jack?"

"You've got to tell somebody."

Eddie wanted to take a stand, however. "You guys are making a mistake. I'm not telling anybody, but I'm not going to rat you out if you do either. Do what you've got to do."

Jack repeated his advice to Miles. That was when Eddie said if they were going to tell somebody it shouldn't be a teacher or anybody who worked at the school, because they had no choice. They would bust into that locker and be all over Jason before Miles could get out of the office. What's more,

Miles would have a reputation he would never live down at South Side. "You've got three more years and your life is going to be pure hell from here on out if you're not real careful."

"It's *my* reputation."

"Whatever." But Eddie recognized that serious look in Miles's eyes. It was a look Miles gave you when he promised you something or when he was working on a class that was hard for him. "OK," Eddie said, "it's your ass on the line. What do you want from us?"

Miles didn't know what exactly he needed, but it felt good to hear a friend like Eddie ask him anyway. Maybe that's all he needed.

Miles's Conversation with His Minister, Reverend Abigail Cummings

—Good to see you, Miles. It's been a while.

—Been kind of busy, you know, high school and everything.

—You almost missed me. I was on my way to lunch in a minute. Hungry?

—Just finished lunch. At school.

—Speaking of school, why are you here and not there?

—Good question. Remember about eight months ago, I think that was the last time I was at Sunday service, and you were talking in your sermon about working on your orchids, I think.

—Sounds familiar. Winter was hard on them and orchids can be temperamental, like people. You interested in gardening?

—No, not really, but you said something that I can't exactly remember but that I can't really forget. Maybe it was just the way you were talking about them. You know what I mean?

—Not really, but just keep going.

—Well, anyway, the way you were talking that day made me want someday maybe to talk to you.

—And that's why you're here now instead of school, because of my orchids?

—Right. The way you were talking that day makes me think you can help people with a big problem, like the one I've got now.

—All right. Why don't you sit down and tell me what's going on with you today?

—I think I have to do something I don't want to do. Problem is, if I don't do it I'm going to end up regretting it even more than if I do do it.

—You in trouble, Miles?

—No, no, not me. I saw something at school. I think I did, I mean. I just can't forget about it.

—What did you see, Miles?

—A gun.

—A gun.

—Yeah, in this kid Jason's locker. I don't know Jason though. I just caught a glimpse when he was closing the locker, that was before geometry, and then there was lunch, Eddie and Jack, and then I came here. I couldn't think of anywhere else to go.

—OK, Miles, this is a very serious situation. Do you know what you want to do?

—Probably, I just don't know how.

—Well, what is it you want to do?

—I need to tell somebody at school right away. But I don't want to get that kid in trouble if I'm wrong. And I don't want to get a reputation as a narc, whether I'm right or wrong. And I sure don't want to see anybody at school, or any of my friends, get hurt.

—Who else have you talked to?

—Eddie. Jack.

—What did they think?

—Jack's with me and Eddie'll stand by me. I told you, they're my friends.

—OK. You've done a brave thing coming here. It takes a lot of guts. But we've got to act now. How do you want me to help you?

—You got any ideas?

—Do you want me to call the school? I can keep your name out of it.

—How can you tell the vice principal and keep me out of it?

—I'll just tell him I have confidential information and I will never mention your name. Believe me, he'll care more about the information than the source. I'm a minister, but he will probably trust me anyway. We'll call your parents soon as we're off the phone with him and come up with a cover story about you leaving school sick, OK?

—OK. I just want this over with.

Notes Home

Gray Areas

At least one school district in the United States offers a monetary reward to any student who turns in weapons violators. Miles's story dramatizes the complications with such policies. From an adult perspective there is no gray area when it comes to a gun, and it may seem preposterous perhaps that Miles is struggling over what to do. But for a typical teenage boy who is in the ninth grade, fourteen or fifteen years old, this is a complicated assessment. For Miles it involves at least these four questions:

1. Is there really a gun? In other words, is there a benign explanation for his perception of what might be a gun in the locker?
2. Whose gun is it and what is the possessor's intention? It's just as important for Miles to know who Jason is and what he stands for as it is to determine whether or not what he might have seen was a gun.
3. What is the social cost of coming forward with the information? If he's correct about the gun and about the possible perils, there is one kind of cost. If he's wrong about either the existence of the gun or Jason's designs, there is still another kind of cost. Either way, the cost is high.
4. What is the personal cost of *not* coming forward? What if somebody is hurt? How will he live with himself? At the same time, in some school cultures, somebody could sustain tremendous benefit by holding on to this information, keeping it away from adults, and sticking to the boy's code of loyalty.

Although schools and families absolutely need policies and limits, adolescents are capable of seeing ambiguities. For instance, a teenager might see a weapon and rationalize not reporting it, while continuing to endorse zero tolerance about weapons on campus. The same is true with drugs and alcohol: some teenagers experiment while simultaneously supporting Just Say No. In practice, if teenagers do not have a sense that adults can grasp gray areas, they are less prone to cooperate with zero tolerance policies they otherwise endorse. Teenagers are more likely to trust adults who grasp the subtleties that they struggle with while simultaneously holding the high ground. And if we truly want to keep schools safe, we must acknowledge the ambiguity.

Once the phone call is made, both Miles and Reverend Abigail know that the situation is absolutely out of their control. What's more, Miles's life will never be the same. Will he second-guess himself afterward? Possibly. Will his friends Eddie and Jack second-guess him? Perhaps. In the long run he will realize he did the best he could do under the circumstances, and he will begin, upon reflection, to grasp how much he has depended on his trust in relationships with people he respects—both peers and adults. In other words, he is growing up. Beyond that, he is discovering a major truth: doing the right thing isn't nearly as difficult as figuring out what the right thing to do is.

The Post-Littleton World
According to Adults

Most of us feel that the world of schools and teenagers changed because of the killings in Littleton—just as the world of colleges and university students seemed to change drastically after Kent State in 1970. After the Columbine shootings, and after all the similar assaults, are schools actually more perilous? And will parents ever be able to send their kids off to school without worrying about their safety?

Statistically (if we can ever trust the safety of our kids to statistics), schools are becoming safer. As Dr. Jim Mercy of the Center for Disease Control and Prevention said in the aftermath of Littleton, "The reality is that schools are very safe environments for our kids. . . . It would be very hard to predict or identify ahead of time the kinds of kids and the constellation of factors that are likely to lead to this kind of event. . . . They are so rare, and there are so many school kids, and our understanding of what motivates people to be violent is so imprecise, that this would be a very difficult task."[1] Yet the fact is that weapons appear on school campuses in alarming numbers; for instance, in California in 1997–1998, over 7,000 weapons were confiscated, or 1.23 per 1,000 students.[2] Poll after poll indicates that a significant number of teenagers claim to have seen a gun on campus.

To combat the problem, policymakers discuss increasing police presence on campuses, installing more metal detectors and surveillance cameras, criminally profiling teenagers, and even requiring that student backpacks be made of transparent materials. At the same time, however, viewing this challenge as merely making it more difficult for kids to bring guns to school would be an oversimplification of adolescence and of schools. The danger with this line of thinking is that it may unintentionally foster mistrust and suspicion on our campuses, which will undercut our noblest intentions. Certainly, metal detectors may give us all a feeling of increased security. But if our goal is to stop violence on campus, there are many ways to address the underlying problems in those kids for whom violence seems to be an attractive option—or a last resort. Established practices proven to work include peer counseling and mediation, small regularly scheduled advising groups, accessible counselors, conflict-resolution training, reduced class size, faculty and parent seminars, and crisis intervention teams. Over time, these practices create confidence and mindfulness in teenagers that will reduce the appeal of weapons and violence. As James Garbarino, author of *Lost Boys*, writes, the reason kids carry weapons is that "they feel threatened and can't count on adults to protect them."[3] When kids feel taken care of, schools are safer.

The Media's Complicating Influence

Adolescents are driven to extremes by the allure of drama and celebrity. Wherever the line exists, they want to push past it and with as much fanfare as possible. This is consistent with their psychological and emotional development. In essence, the extreme nature of school shootings, along with the sensationalistic attention the media gives to them, contributes to the allure for teenagers.

We are not questioning the First Amendment. But the imaginable behavioral extreme has now been definitively adjusted after these events, and the media, intentionally or not, has dramatized for everyone exactly how far the new extreme has been extended. While television and newspapers and the Internet are not responsible for pulling the trigger, they have—wisely or not, unavoidably or not—provided a forum and a huge audience for the most desperate deeds of some alienated teenagers. (For related reasons, the FBI investigation of the aftermath of Columbine High School pointed out that school surveillance cameras, intended to protect schools, may have actually increased the potential for violence by providing criminals with a means to broadcast their depredations.)

Teenagers are also swayed by their impulses. But now, with the fairly easy accessibility of weapons—and a heightened awareness of how anyone can play so spectacularly to the media—this impulsivity can have menacing, if not literally life-threatening, consequences. If teenagers are alienated enough, they may confuse impulsivity with strength and their recklessness with personal accomplishment. That is, they may be willing to leap onto the big stage by giving in to their darkest impulses, and they believe that the rewards will be worth it. The proof? They will be televised. They will have an undeniable impact on their world, and, what's more, everybody will know who they are. Impulsivity, lethal weapons, and reporters make for an explosive combination.

If you are a parent who owns a firearm, you can make all our schools safer by keeping it locked up. Beyond that, we all need to encourage media literacy in our children. We should take every chance to promote critical thinking about the power of the media and the cult of celebrity. That means taking the time to discuss and analyze the images and information that inundate our media-drenched teenagers—a movie, the evening news, an out-of-control talk show, an editorial, the cover of *Time* or *Newsweek*.

Do Teenagers Tell the Truth? To Whom?

Teenagers frequently do not tell the whole truth, but it does not mean that they are liars. They leave things out. ("Is there gas in the car?" "Yes." "Enough for me to get to work?" "Maybe.") Faced with a crisis, though, they can be usually counted on for their honesty.

Even today, some adults are suspicious of teenagers who make serious allegations and consider their information unreliable unless and until independently substantiated. Experience with teenagers, however, demonstrates otherwise. (Indeed, teenagers' unfortunately realistic expectation that they will be ignored explains why crimes against them go unreported.) Teenagers do prize the truth. Though exceptions exist, hardly ever do they weave such stories out of whole cloth. Teenagers who for whatever reason manufacture reckless accusations usually wreak havoc on their own lives.

Clearly, Miles understands the risks he is running. He has enabled himself to do the right thing within the limits of what he can do and still be who he is. Better than anyone else can, he grasps the complexities of his life in high school, and he appreciates the ramifications of his choice. He has selected a complex, mature course of action, in this case reaching out first to his friends and then to his minister, one that allows him to keep one foot firmly placed among the community of his peers even as he lives up to his obligations to his friends, his community, and, most importantly, himself.

Like any ninth grader, Miles has been struggling to make a place for himself in school, and in one sense it would have been easier for him to convince himself that this gun is none of his concern. So it required an unusually principled, strong, and courageous young man to conceive of, and act upon, his decision. Specifically, he is resisting the code of absolute peer loyalty, which is especially powerful for a younger teenage boy. (See Appendix A, "Where Am I? Being 14–15.") But teenagers often face daunting situations and to their own amazement often do the right thing. No wonder a teenager is stunned when adults spot these moments and highlight them—exactly as his minister did.

Teenagers come to adults with the truth when they are in a crisis of a certain magnitude because no one absolutely unambiguous path suggests itself to them either. What is more, teenagers don't select an adult under stressed circumstances arbitrarily or accidentally. They are continually assessing the adults around them to determine whom can they trust, when, and to what extent. Teenagers are always seeking adults to play the role of confidante, advocate, and institutional support. They don't expect them to be therapists, law enforcement officials, or even necessarily counselors, but simply to be responsive—as well as responsible—adults. In the eyes of teenagers, this role is the most natural dimension of being an adult, an essential extension of mature life experience. For instance, as far as teenagers are concerned, teachers don't just teach science, or any other subject—they teach *kids*. And ministers, fortunately for Miles, do not just lead institutionalized congregations but also minister to individuals. Because Miles has come to Reverend Abigail in this spirit and under these circumstances, he expects to learn from her. He is watching her closely, counting on her wisdom, judgment, and perceptiveness.

In a crisis, there are always middle-ground positions available, and they occur to an adult who tries to keep in mind the objectives of sustaining safety and health in a family or a community. Finding these positions isn't easy, but this kind of thing happens all the time with teenagers who invite us to assist them in their struggles, for example, when they say, "I need some help—my friend's taking steroids, my friend's in a gang, my friend's not eating . . ." Miles does want to be involved, but he may not know *how* or *when* to be involved. He wants the engagement with an adult, a teacher, and he wants to take responsibility, but he doesn't quite know how. The adult needs to hold on to the anxiety, not hand it back and not let herself be overwhelmed by all the clashing variables.

Viewed in the largest sense, there's nothing less than everything at stake in this episode—and both Miles and Abigail know it. The school's safety must be assured, and Miles has given his minister all the information he has in order for her to act judiciously. Furthermore, Miles should ideally come away understanding he did a difficult thing that required integrity and courage. Given the circumstances, he himself may not fully appreciate what he has done. But no matter. He will understand in time, and this understanding is called moral education.

Miles's Friends

What's interesting about Miles's friends is the manner in which they helped him work through his dilemma. Before talking to them, Miles was anxious, unclear about what he saw, and unsure about what he should do. Never during this exchange did Miles unthinkingly accept their suggestions. And never did his friends hold back their honest thoughts. At the same time, however, Eddie and Jack also maintained their support of and belief in Miles as a person and as their friend. In other words, they gave him room to make his own decision.

Teenagers do this all the time with one another. These discussions constitute their trying on a variety of possible responses without committing to any. For example, when Eddie advised Miles to simply let it all go and do nothing, Miles had the opportunity to consider seriously this option. Then, after entertaining this possibility, he was able to reject it once and for all and move forward in his thinking. Miles has chosen his friends wisely. Imagine, for instance, that Eddie had tried to bully Miles with his opinion. If this had happened, Miles would have had a problem virtually as important as the gun—not only deciding what to do about what he saw but also preserving (or learning how to live with losing) his friendship with Eddie.

After he rehearses all the possibilities with his buddies, Miles is liberated to be himself. That is why he can move on. And that's why he can proceed to a conversation with Reverend Abigail knowing what he wants to do, albeit unsure of how to do it.

Males and Females

The conversation between Miles and his friends also generally illustrates some of the profound differences between boys and girls. With school shootings so far perpetuated exclusively by males, adolescent boys have drifted under the microscope. And for the most part they have been found wanting in the area of what has been termed emotional literacy, defined by the authors of *Raising Cain* as "the ability to read and understand our emotions and those of others."[4]

If there is any indirect benefit to those shootings, it may be that we have grown more sensitive to the emotional needs, and the emotional life, of boys. Boys have much to gain by becoming more articulate emotionally, and important books have appeared on this subject (*A Fine Young Man, Real Boys, Raising Cain, Lost Boys*). At the same time, let's be careful. Boys and girls are different and therefore attend to and act upon their emotions differently.

In this story we see three boys working through a difficult situation that is laced with powerful emotions: fear, vulnerability, courage, care, empathy, and generalized anxiety. Although these emotions charge their dialogue, Miles and his friends do not focus on them. Rather, they focus on the action to take, not the current feeling state. No one is asking questions designed to elicit or expand on an emotional response; no one is pausing to reflect self-consciously on the emotions in the air. But that does not mean that they are trying to deny either their feelings or the value of these feelings. Their emotions are abundantly, richly, complexly, sincerely felt, though often expressed indirectly. Emotions are considered in the course of developing an action, but they are not the boys' focus of attention.

Now, what if somebody named Sarah had been in Miles's place and talked with a girlfriend?

Oh my God, I'm so scared, I don't know what to do. My heart's going a mile a minute.

I can't believe somebody'd bring a gun to this school. You OK, Sarah?

I'm a wreck. You would be, too. My hands, they're shaking.

Let's get out of here and go somewhere we can figure out what to do.

I know I've got to tell somebody. I just don't know if I can get myself to do it.

You can do it, I'll go with you.

Stereotypes notwithstanding—that girls lose themselves in their feelings and boys are able to feel only rage and anger—what does this show? Sarah may eventually reach the same conclusion Miles reached, but the way she arrives at her decision is different. She focuses explicitly on her own feelings, for one thing, while at the same time relating to her friend, who is also focusing on Sarah's feelings. They never lose sight of the gravity of the issue, however, and as they continue to talk they will not lose sight of the need to act. Miles consults with his friends and acts independently. Sarah opens up to her friend and they act together. She acts, to invoke a term of Deborah Tannen's, "interdependently." This does not mean that Sarah is weaker or more dependent, and it also does not mean that Miles is stronger or less emotionally articulate or less invested in his friends.

It would be counterproductive to advise a boy to embrace and discuss his feelings about the gun prior to doing something, and it would be equally ineffective to disparage a girl for talking about and focusing on her feelings prior to doing something. Boys and girls, then, may reach the same moral conclusion, and arrive at the same choice, but they do so traveling along different paths. And parents must not lose sight of these differences as they encourage their teenagers, both boys and girls, to feel and to act appropriately.

Miles's Parents

Where are Miles's parents in all this? Is it a good sign or a bad sign that he never consulted them? If Miles's parents routinely rescue Miles from tough decisions, it makes sense that he never consulted them. He wanted to resolve this situation on his own, since from his point of view it is his problem alone and he is going to live with the ramifications of his decision. In other words, he may be afraid that his parents will push him aside and rush into the principal's office and start the ball rolling with no regard for him.

On the other hand, Miles may not have consulted with his parents because they routinely support his solving his own problems. As a result, he is more than able to assess the predicament (on his own and with his friends), come up with an action plan (talk to Reverend Abigail), and do what he feels is the right thing (have Reverend Abigail call the school). Most likely he will report to his parents all that happened as soon as he sees them. Although they might feel tempted to be hurt because they were left out of the decision, they can also feel proud to have raised such a mature decisionmaker. This is the sort of parenting that can make us feel marginal in the short run, but in the long run—where we should always be concentrating—will better serve teenagers.

Jason

And what about Jason, the boy who might have a handgun in his locker? His is going to be a long and complicated story, however it turns out.

Enormous social issues come into play in any attempt to understand why a teenager would carry a gun into school and how a teenager comes to resort to violence. Garbarino notes that his research on the "lost boys," who kill and inflict violence on others, shows that they are not easy to generalize about. Yet factors such as poverty, abuse, abandonment, a desire for justice, and a withering sense of disconnection are typical, if not universal.

Assuming that Jason does have a gun, though, something monumental, and mysterious, is going on. But is he intrinsically evil, intent on inflicting harm, possibly even death, upon his classmates and teachers? Nobody can say for sure, including perhaps Jason. But at the same time we can presume that, even while he constitutes a grave threat to others and to himself, he is also a teenager in need and at risk—and need and risk are flip sides of the same coin.

When confronted with the possession of a weapon, Jason may unleash a string of nearly credible explanations. But none of them, upon reflection, will ring true to anybody—including himself. On some level Jason is in trouble and he knows it. Doing something outrageous may be the best way he has of asking for help; it is guaranteed to get everyone's attention. He is in serious need. Is this harmless need? Far from it. Unless Jason is caught and unless someone is patient and understanding enough to help him make sense of his actions—and to hold him responsible too—there is a significant likelihood that someone will be hurt by his gun now or later. Simply catching him is not enough. He must be led to understand why he has chosen such a desperate course of action. By doing so, adults fashion lifelines that no teenagers can live without. For an adolescent, especially an adolescent boy, doing something—obliquely—about his anxious pain (which is what psychologists mean by the term *acting out*) feels much better than doing nothing. But working on an understanding of his feelings through a relationship with an attentive adult results in both the hope and the feeling of doing something for oneself that obviates the urges to act out violently these anxieties.

In any case, Jason is dangerous, but he may not necessarily be a demon or a sociopath, and he may not be beyond reclamation. Based on Miles's perceptions, he cannot conclude anything about Jason except that he might have a gun. Teenagers live in the moment, and in the moment, Miles is dealing with the probable existence of a weapon. The weapon arrives on campus along with Jason and his load of problems, but that is not something for Miles to deal with. That's where adults come in quickly and decisively, first, in order to defuse the danger, second, to address Jason's under-lying crisis, and, third, to parcel out consequences.

The Risks of Being a Teenager, and the Risks of Being the Parent of a Teenager

It is hard to imagine that there exists one school in the country, whatever the high-mindedness and virtue of the mission, whatever the sterling qual-ity and commitment of faculty and administration, whatever the address, that isn't free of risk for teenagers—drug dealing, sexual harassment, phys-ical violence, alcohol abuse, and so on. No family or school can afford to be blasé because these possible perils come with the territory of adoles-cence. If we are not careful, though, our expressions of legitimate parental concern might come across as sounding paranoid to our children (and teenagers believe they are expert diagnosticians of this clinical condition). Therefore, we cannot chance infantilizing our teenagers. When they were children we held their hands crossing every street; though we know it's dif-ferent now, we also need to communicate that we *know* it's different. In re-sponse to the general helplessness we feel, and because we do mean well, we may adopt measures to restrict our kids' vulnerability, attempting to limit every variable of exposure they can conceive.

The problem is, however, that there is no curfew in existence that can eliminate risk entirely, and there is no teenager absolutely and finally im-mune to the allure of excitement. Including your teenagers. Yes, you can monitor their hours, their friends, the time they spend on the Internet, the car. But you cannot control teenagers twenty-four hours a day in every an-ticipatable context. If you try, everyone stands a chance of going slightly insane. If you try, you are virtually compelling your children to cover up. The world can be a threatening place for a teenager—in a car, at the movies, at a game, wherever. Your fears are not baseless, but you can't al-low these fears to translate into a fundamental mistrust of your teenager's judgment—or even the *appearance* of mistrust, for that matter. If this hap-pens, you will be left feeling even more exposed and helpless.

Health and Safety, Revisited

One way to reduce that feeling of insecurity, however, is for parents to be direct and realistic with themselves and their teenagers. For instance, if you hear about a weapon being confiscated or a tragedy occurring in a school, be direct in your conversation with your teenagers. Do they think something like that could happen at your school? What would you do if you saw a gun at school? What person would you go to? Why that person? Just as important, what person would you not go to, and why? What if the one who has the gun is one of your friends? What can we do as your parents to help make your life safer?

In the early stages of conversation, the goal is to get them talking. Practically, this might mean watching their eyes roll as they politely decline the invitation to talk. But you need to plant the seeds of engagement. The next time you try, you will hear more. This is when to listen, ask follow-up questions, and listen some more. This is the time to learn from your kids. Later on is the time to share your views, and your anxieties, too.

As early and as often as possible, then, speak together frankly about the real-life issues that growing up invariably poses. More than likely, you won't be discussing anything that they already don't know about the world, but you will be opening yourself up for them to understand and trust. If you are committed and available, you might talk together in a way that, with honesty and openness, will help all of you be prepared for the exigencies that might occur. This additional strength will better equip them to deal with what comes their way, and if they have exercised their judgment-making muscles they will stand a better chance of doing the right thing.

You can't make all the judgments, in other words. For starters, acknowledge your own anxiety—just don't be paralyzed by it. You might be surprised to hear an answering response from your teenager. Create together mutually appropriate boundaries—what *you* need to keep your sanity and to promote your values and what *they* need to feel trusted and protected. The trick here is to walk that fine line between recognizing the realities of the world and creating a fantasy world of controlled possibilities. You want your teenagers to embrace the world in all of its fullness and joy, but you want them to be vigilant at the same time. Believe it or not, you can get that message across because they also want to hear that—even if sometimes they may roll their eyes.

12

Being Gay, Coming Out

I go on writing so that I will always have something to read.
　　　　　　　　　　—Jeanette Winterson, *The Passion*

Mothers of America
let your kids go to the movies!
　　　　　　　　　　—Frank O'Hara, "Ave Maria"

Wherever You Are, There You Go

Everybody loves Sheila. If you could say that anyone in particular sets the social rules around school, she does. For instance, whatever she wears on Monday somehow becomes the height of fashion by Thursday noon. Some teachers find her shallow but some find her interesting, and a lot more substantial than she appears. Usually adults can't help but like her, though, and they think she is amusing in that just this side of sarcastic way. Others wish the girl would give the old act a rest. As for her friends, her legion of friends, they say she's already a party animal legend, and it's only her junior year.

Although Sheila made it a point of personal pride to get along with everybody, she knew she wasn't really that close to anybody. Stacey Witte was a teacher she liked, even if she was a teacher. They used to chat, very friendly, before and after class, stopping on campus, that sort of thing.

Sometimes Sheila went out of her way to cross paths with her. Actually, though, they had never had what either would have termed a serious conversation, a good conversation. It was always that playful banter they were both good at.

Then last week it all changed.

It was last period, and Sheila had been singularly quiet and distracted, remote as an island. Stacey Witte could guess something was up, but there was no reason to make a big deal and call attention to it. When class was over, though, and Sheila was slouching away, Stacey asked her how she was doing. She intended to sound casual but must have sounded like somebody who was trying to sound casual.

Sheila whirled around and flashed that chiseled, absolutely counterfeit smile. "Oh, everything is fine." Then her tone darkened as she added, "As you would say, just peachy."

It so happens that "just peachy" had never once been uttered by Stacey. In the moment, though, it didn't seem opportune to point this out.

Still, Sheila's gaze seemed to lock them both in place, and they stood still—both feeling a little silly in that stock pose—while the other students departed. Finally, they were alone.

"You sure? The reason I ask is, it doesn't look like it."

At this point, Sheila clambered into a desk as if it were a life raft. In no time, the tears were flowing. Stacey shut the door, found a box of tissue, took a seat next to her, and waited. "Take your time," she said.

Finally Sheila looked up. "Well, I guess everything isn't fine after all! You might even say, life pretty much sucks right about now."

"Want to talk about it?"

"Not particularly."

An opening or a closing? Impossible to tell so far. "Let's start with what's troubling you right now."

Sheila leveled her eyes and said, "You asked for it. Top three list of things that are troubling Sheila these days. One, the girl drinks, like way too much. Two, last Friday she had an abortion. And three, hey, guess what, the girl's gay. How's that for not being OK?"

It was Stacey's turn to be speechless for a while.

"I don't even know why I bothered you. There's nothing you can do for me. There's nothing anybody can do for me."

The whole world seemed to have shifted between them. Stacey was frightened for her, concerned about her, and sympathetic, not to mention a little lost.

And self-conscious too. It was impossible to speak from personal experience about an abortion or about drinking, though Sheila could be guided along to help if that was what she wanted. On the other issue, though, Sheila had hit home.

"How do you think those three things are connected, Sheila?"

She seemed caught off guard. She may have been counting on, or possibly half hoping for, an everything-will-be-fine, you'll-get-through-this sort of response. She sagged even deeper into the desk and stayed there while rethreading the remnants of her voice.

First, she let out an ocean-size *OK, you asked for it* sigh, and then she laid it out: "Basically I first realized I was gay when I was fourteen. Welcome to high school, Sheila! Ever since, I have been terrified. If you knew my family you'd know this is one topic they're not going to bring up for polite conversation. When I was growing up, I heard all I needed from them to know they wouldn't understand. The thought that I might be gay—that I was gay—just made me freak. I chose not to deal. In fact, I came up with a brilliant solution! If Sheila stayed high all the time she wouldn't have to think about it. I know, don't start. I know I'm right out of the textbook, which is probably the hardest part for me to take in. Then once I numbed myself drinking I was able to act heterosexual, like maybe I would suddenly somehow snap into place. Hey, if I could *act* that way maybe I could *be* that way. The easiest way to act heterosexual is do it with lots of guys, the more the merrier, which of course was bound to lead me you know exactly where. A couple of beers or a joint, you know, and the idea of birth control seems pretty quaint, I mean, if the concept registers at all. That's right: I'm textbook. And don't even think of the Lecture. I know it by heart. Given it to myself. One week late, two weeks, three weeks, then I got the news I didn't want to hear. Abortion seemed the easiest way. Some kind of easy."

She glared at the box of tissue offered her.

"Never mind." But she took one and dabbed her eyes.

The seconds ticked by. "Who else have you talked to?"

"Kathy Best Friend drove me to the clinic. I wish I could have gone alone. My parents were entertaining all weekend and barely noticed that I never left my room, never even got out of bed till school. When Monday came around, I loaded up my trusty backpack and painted on a smile for first period, because, hey, I was good as new. Right. The other stuff? My folks—and a couple of the Good Kids I keep in reserve for company on a rainy day—they've talked to me about the partying. They even persuaded me to get involved in a substance-abuse group at the youth center. But you're the first—I mean, I've never told anybody I'm gay." Then, although it didn't seem physically possible, her eyes opened wider still, and she looked directly at Stacey. "Of course, I knew if anybody would understand me, it was going to be you, right?"

Conversation with the
Support Group Leader

Sheila has driven about an hour away from home, into the next county. Support groups exist at the local community center, but two or three times she has attended gatherings of gay teenagers several towns over. So far she has never run into anybody from her school, which was, of course, the plan. Tonight no group meeting is scheduled, but she has made an appointment with the group's facilitator. She arrives fifteen minutes early.

—So.

—So, Sheila?

—So I did it.

—Really.

—I told somebody. Never mind who. That's important but not important right now. Just telling somebody, that was important.

—What did it feel like?

—Great. Better than great. I felt honest, like I was myself for the first time. It was better than getting high. You know how like when you're hiking and when you're thirsty and you drink cold water and you think you maybe never tasted water ever before. Like that.

—Good for you.

—Was it like that when you came out?

—I remember like it was yesterday. It was exciting and terrifying at the same time. But I was lucky. And so far you're lucky. It's not that way for everybody.

—So far? What's that mean?

—Means you took the first step, but it's a long journey. Not everybody's going to be as understanding as your person.

—You know how some people fool other people all the time? They're not who they say there are, but they get so good at just being somebody else it becomes like another person inside?

—Keep going.

—It's like they're not even lying anymore, they're just being somebody else, which is what people want them to be anyway. And you know what? I don't have to be that way anymore. Of course, there were advantages. You could experiment around, with your life. Try on new identities, play at being something else, you know, just for practice.

—Sounds exhausting.

—But I'm all done with that now. There's no holding me back.

—Slow down. That's exactly what I mean by *so far*.

—I don't want to slow down. This feels too good.

—Believe me, when I came out I wanted to shout it from the rooftops, but the person I came out to helped me see that would have been a mistake. And that's what I'm trying to do with you.

—How can it be a mistake being your true self?

—Great question. A very sad question, too. Even though you're ready, your world may not be prepared for your arrival.

—Well, if they don't respect me for what I am, why should I respect them?

—This is not a matter of compromising yourself. This is a matter of taking care of yourself.

—I'm not going back to wearing the mask anymore. I'm not going back to what I used to be.

—I know that. You know that. And that's why we need to keep talking. Take some time to enjoy your freedom, don't rush to repeat the experience. You have time, Sheila. You have your whole life to be you.

—What about you? Everybody knows about you. You don't make a secret about being gay.

—I'm not in high school anymore. I'm thirty years old. And even now, I have lots of rough days. People aren't always ready to hear the truth, and I never let myself forget this.

—For real?

—For real.

Notes Home

Gay Teenagers

Adolescents who are gay are at great risk. In comparison to other teenagers, they have a much higher chance of adopting addictive behaviors like drug and alcohol abuse. They are also more often inclined to contemplate or commit suicide. It is important for everyone—all parents and teachers, families and schools—to understand why their plight is so serious and complex. And it is important whether or not our children or their friends may be gay, or, for that matter, whether or not we ourselves may be. For whether or not your teenager is gay, and whether or not you are asking yourself if your teenager is gay, you can be sure that your child interacts with gay kids everyday, at school, at work, in games, in plays, at parties. In other words, the issues of gay teenagers affect everyone.

Few topics can polarize people more quickly than homosexuality; few can comparably mobilize, antagonize, and titillate. Yet while everyone around seems intent on taking a stand one way or another, a gay teenager simply wants to be herself in a world in which being herself may constitute a threat to somebody else. Gay adolescence is, in a manner of speaking, the most extreme manifestation of adolescence. While all teenagers struggle to come to terms with their identity and with their perceived exceptionality, gay teenagers often struggle in shame, radical uncertainty, and anonymity. That is, they consciously conceal their sexuality and pretend to be someone or something they are not while they simultaneously search out their true identity.

Why do they do this? For one thing, they are afraid, and there are several legitimate reasons for their fear. They fear that once peers discover their homosexuality they will become the target of unrelenting and vicious ridicule, sometimes even physical abuse. This dread, however, pales in comparison to the apprehension that close friends and family will be irrational or distraught and, in either case, reject them. For many teenagers, acceptance from loved ones predicated on a false image is, bitter though it may be, preferable to rejection. As the psychiatrist Harry Stack Sullivan suggested in his developmental theories, once a person arrives at puberty, the most significant organizer of behavior is the avoidance of loneliness.

Almost all gay teenagers endure an excruciating period of denying their feelings for the same sex. In the same instance they do all they can to nurture those same feelings for the opposite sex. During this time of working against themselves, they are most prone to self-destructive behaviors—promiscuity, substance abuse, extreme risk taking. Such behaviors distract them from facing their discomfort and at the same time effectively, and usefully, mislead others.

This is an expensive price to pay for some breathing room, and it's no wonder gay teens are so imperiled. Rea Carey, executive director of the National Youth Advocacy Coalition, declared it remarkable that gay youngsters survive at all. "That, in and of itself, is a miracle." She cited one study showing that students might hear antigay remarks seventeen times a day. Other research indicates that gay youths are up to three times more likely to become pregnant, or to get someone pregnant, than their straight peers. "If you know it's not cool to be a lesbian," said Carey, "what's the best way to prove you're not a lesbian—get pregnant."[1]

The Sense of Difference

For most teenagers, being gay, and therefore "different," is the exact opposite of what they want more than anything, which is simply to fit in. A teenager's deepest anxiety is that she does not truly belong. For a gay teenager, however, not belonging is the substance of self-description. Of course, some gay men and women never accept their sexuality and never "belong." As a result they lead lives of repressed emotion and form relationships that torment them, or they avoid relationships altogether. Some gays even cultivate homophobia. They begrudgingly acknowledge their own sexuality but do not care to be affiliated with other gays. It's little mystery, therefore, that adolescents have a tough time navigating this rocky terrain.

As Sheila herself said in her acute self-consciousness, she is a "textbook" case. What she means by that, partly, is that she has been striving to disprove, or maybe deny, feelings she has for other girls. Deep down she knows she is gay; in fact, she says she has known the truth about herself since she was fourteen. But rather than affirm these feelings she pushed them aside and worked even harder to fit in according to the prevailing high school social conventions, most notably through her out-of-control partying and her promiscuous behavior with boys. (Gay boys, of course, have parallel issues and are tempted by the related fateful choices.)

Although most teenagers can sort through some of their identity crises in public, gay teenagers usually have no such opportunity. No other conceivable rite of passage has the same promise of turning their world upside down. For instance, a teenager raised in a religious family, perhaps attending a religious school, might grow restive about her faith, perhaps even flirt with atheism. Even in the most circumscribed environments, though, she can probably find many ways to discuss or argue with others, in so doing she makes a very private matter appropriately public. Doing so is essential to her personal growth and to her coming to terms with her faith concerns. Normally, staring down conventions and embracing iconoclastic ideas and lifestyles is seen as a badge of honor among adolescents but, strangely, not when it comes to homosexuality, which seems perennially taboo for most teenagers in most communities. A gay teenager struggling with his sexual identity likely senses that no venue is suitable or safe. It is one thing for a spiritually restive teenager to refuse to bow her head in prayer during services. It is quite another for a teenager to announce the next meeting of the Gay Youth Association at a school assembly.

Coming Out

To come out or not: This is a monumental issue. The innocent-sounding term "come out" both suggests and deflects the hidden burden of sexuality. It discloses the precarious nature of the risk run before friends and family. But even more, coming out connotes at the same time a hope for liberation: a desire to live a more genuine life, to step from the darkness and the shadows into the light. In this sense, coming out is an act of hope and trust courageously performed before an often uncomprehending, hostile world. In other words, coming out is a complex act with deep implications.

Once a teenager comes out, he gains a glimpse into the heart of his family, his circle of friends, and his school community. He sees himself reflected in their understanding of "gayness" or "homosexuality." He becomes, at exactly the moment when he is asserting his individuality, a representative of a group. (Of course, the other side of this issue is that by coming out he gravitates toward another community, which is always important in the project of avoiding loneliness.) He may even be called on, ignominiously, to provide the "gay point of view." In no time, he is wondering whom can he now trust. Which peers and adults will really listen and support him in his struggle? Which of them will patronize him? And can he tell the difference between support and condescension?

After carefully assessing their world, some teenagers will decide not to come out—or at least not now. In their judgment, the immediate environment may not be conducive or safe. How do they make this determination? How can they fail to miss the cues? Gay teenagers have their ears and eyes wide open to every homosexual joke, every grimace, and every raised eyebrow in response to a mention of gayness, every instance of "fag" or of "gay" as a term of scorn and disapprobation uttered within a square mile. How could it be otherwise? First, to be blunt, they often have to be concerned for their physical safety. Gay bashing, unfortunately, is twisted sport in some circles. Second, feeling alone and isolated by their sexuality (not something, given the biology of sexual orientation, they had any choice in either), they constantly scan their horizons. Who will be sympathetic to their coming out? Who will have to be avoided from now on? Who will need lots of time for talk, for answering questions? Such anxiety and such vigilance is wearying and often degrading, too.

Once a teenager does decide to come out, he will tend to want to come out to everyone right away, for no other reason than to relieve his residual ambivalence and dissolve any lingering ambiguity in the minds of others. At some juncture along the route of their reasoning, they determine that any expectable slur is preferable to living inauthentically. Obviously, this is risky and exhilarating at the same time. Risky because the old world is being abandoned; exhilarating because a new one is swimming into view. Now they need for all their friends, family, and acquaintances to know about their sexuality. Sadly, given the prevailing cultural landscape, that is often a big mistake, a mistake that the facilitator points up to Sheila—to her disappointment.

When teenagers decide to come out, it is usually advisable for them to err on the side of caution and patience. Just because they are learning to accept, and even to celebrate, their sexuality does not mean that those they care about (and those whose care is mutual) are suddenly capable of making the shift in their view of someone they used to know. Now out of the closet, they magically reincarnate as the gay pal, the gay child, the gay sibling, the gay student, the gay employee, or the gay teammate. Such a transformation is a trial for everyone involved. Genuine acceptance takes time, patience, and, usually, lots of conversation. Pragmatically, it's much too exhausting to come out to more than one or two persons at first.

To come out responsibly takes time and forces one to go much more slowly. Tough choices insist on being made. Who needs to know, and when, and where, and how, and why? Coming out means spending lots of time with these people answering, and anticipating, questions and concerns.

Although initially Sheila's life seems out of control, we see, through her conversation with the facilitator, that she has started to take charge of her coming out. Her conversation with Stacey was not as spontaneous as Stacey thought it was. An exchange of this magnitude is almost never totally spontaneous, which is something to keep in mind when working or living with teenagers.

Boundaries Between Teenagers and Adults

Teenagers look for kindred spirits among their peers and among adults, too, even though they also like to consider themselves separate, the exception to every rule, the originator of themselves. Sometimes they look to adults in their world for something precious that they can't find with friends or family: a confirmation of their sense of themselves.

Although adults may feel invited to do otherwise, they need—for the good of everyone—to maintain clear boundaries. In particular, adults should only share personal details when such revelations can help a teenager. For instance, a teenager who wants to talk about his problem drinking and makes personal inquiries usually will not be helped by hearing all the details of anybody's history on the subject. When adults start telling their own stories they remove the focus from the teenager and inhibit her from dealing with her own life. When kids come to adults, it is the perfect time for us to be quiet and listen. As the updated adage suggests, whenever possible, and certainly at first, don't just do something, stand there. At the same time, a well-placed and concisely revealed bit of personal history at the right moment can open the doors for the teenager who is looking for understanding and support.

Such support and understanding can make a tremendous difference to someone who is acting self-destructively, like Sheila. For one thing, Sheila has begun to realize that she now belongs to a more often than not beleaguered high school minority. She may very well begin to feel like a wretched outcast. Those intense feelings of loss, disenfranchisement, and confusion are exacerbated if she does not believe that those around her can or will accept the reality of her newly embraced sexuality. (Sheila, who always prized the admiration of her peers, had told nobody except the facilitator—not even her friends—about her sexuality. Perhaps she valued her popularity so highly and would do anything for it because it enabled her to do without a close friend, which would bring about other complications and intimacies she was not yet ready to face.)

With Sheila, it could be appropriate—depending on the teacher—to speak, within limits, from personal experience. (Within limits means saying less than 50 percent of what you are considering saying.) After all, Sheila has struck a particularly resonant chord. Stacey could speak from personal experience, could make the implicit explicit, as long as Sheila's experience was kept paramount and as long as Stacey felt the confidence and comfort to speak. To go to the substance of this issue, though, Stacey need not come out in order to support Sheila or sanction Sheila's coming out, just as the teacher need not deny the existence or orientation of her own sexuality. The boundaries may be somewhat porous under the circumstances, but they are still boundaries.

Intimacy

Intimacy is predicated on mutuality and equality and interdependence. Teenagers can be intimate with their peers on these terms, and adults can be intimate with their peers on the same terms. But for a teenager in relation to an adult, intimacy means something different. It means trusting that adult with personal revelation and counting on her respect and support, that is, not expecting to hear comparable revelations. Interdependence is the last thing teenagers need with adults. Pushing away a teenager in need will not help, but neither will drawing her into your personal life. Teenagers benefit most when adults stay adults: separate but nearby. Adults who understand this dynamic make a difference in the lives of teenagers who seek them out.

Stacey is exactly this sort of adult for Sheila. She was insightful enough to recognize the different perspectives of "closeness" between teenager and adult. Stacey was ready when Sheila opened up because they had an existing relationship, even if the news itself turned out to be surprising. (With adolescents, however, it is not at all unusual for the floodgates to simply burst wide open, and what is released is sometimes astonishing to take in. Remember, too, that a teenager seldom discloses the full story all at once.)

Of course, for adults who work with teenagers it is not unusual to have experience with the perennially needy one, who seems to be in the office or in the classroom ready to talk during every free moment. While these teenagers' issues should not be taken lightly, what we have in this narrative is not a needy student but, much more seriously, a student in acute need.

Health and Safety: No Compromises

Sheila's health and safety are crucial, and so is her relationship with Stacey. When the *immediate* health or safety of a teenager is in jeopardy, however, everything else, even maintaining relationships, shifts to the background.

If, for instance, Sheila had come to Stacey and revealed that her drinking was overwhelming her and she was, say, concerned about her party plans that night, Stacey would have an obligation to intervene in some way, at school or with the family. Or if she had observed Sheila drinking or drunk at school, she would have notified school officials immediately. This is the equivalent of intervening by seizing the car keys of somebody who has been drinking.

Nonetheless, some parents may be shocked to realize that Sheila's teacher did not automatically make a call home after their talk. But that does not necessarily seem appropriate now. Why not? Stacey has assessed, in consultation with Sheila, that she is dealing with her drinking (she has discussed with her parents the problem drinking, and they encouraged her participation in a substance abuse group). Sheila also has given Stacey signs that she is addressing the deeper issues of her sexuality. Because Sheila's circumstances are so complicated and interwoven, her relationship with her teacher assumes great importance. How Stacey responds to Sheila's revelations is crucial to Sheila. Here's why.

Sheila's worst fantasy is that her revelations will overpower everybody or that her selected adult confidante will back away, pretend not to have heard what she just said, or quickly shuttle her off to an "expert." She might well feel pathologized. Essentially, the humiliation that she feared at the hands of the biased and ignorant would be realized by somebody she respected. If she could not hope for Stacey's sympathetic understanding, what will it be like for her in the rest of the world?

Therefore, no matter what is happening inside you as the confidante, no matter what alarms are going off, it is primarily important to focus on Sheila's experience. Adults in such charged conversations need to indicate that they have, as Harry Stack Sullivan often explained, "withstood the blow" of intense, personal disclosure. This maturity, this composure, this strength on the part of the adult implicitly says, without being dismissive or judgmental or patronizing, that this crisis, too, can be confronted.

Sheila is not seeking advice or facile reassurance. She requires, instead, what we would colloquially term a reality check. She wants to hear that what she suspects is true: she is dealing with some tremendous problems and some hard-to-break behaviors. But with hard work, trust in the right people, and faith in herself, she can successfully deal with them—even if that will not be easy.

Beyond that, what Sheila is requesting, simply, is the wholehearted acceptance of an adult she respects. She needs this almost immediately and without a flinch of hesitation. Sheila may be (perhaps unconsciously) thinking that Stacey not only *can* but *will* speak to her crisis from personal experience; she may be assuming (seemingly, in this case, correctly) that she and her teacher share a common bond. Like most teenagers, Sheila assumes that teachers expend imaginative energy speculating about their students' lives. She feels like an open book and she assumes that her teacher feels exactly the same way.

Risks and Opportunities

There are only two mistakes Stacey could make; first, to demonstrate to Sheila that she has erred by coming to the wrong person and, second, to play the therapist role. Sheila is open to direction, however. She will need the time and expertise that a teacher (or any other significant adult in her life) simply cannot furnish. Therefore it is important for Stacey to understand how to make an appropriate referral. How can an adult signal to a teenager that she would benefit from additional help, without conveying a trace of rejection or abandonment?

Providing this transition to a professional and helping Sheila subscribe to the notion is a delicate process indeed. But it is essential. Unquestionably, Sheila is going to need help coming to grips with her new identity. She is going to need help addressing her abortion and everything she might associate with it—the grief, the conflictedness, the sadness, and the regrets. She is going to need help taking a look at her alcohol abuse, its roots and its dangers. And she is going to need help looking at her family's dynamics, which are, in her understanding, hindering her development.

Yet Stacey must be careful. Sheila has just opened up and may fear she is being shipped off if Stacey quickly refers her to a professional. This is where Sheila needs to be provided a rationale that does not diminish her experience and that, at the same time, acknowledges Stacey's boundaries. Not every teenager in crisis who comes to an adult needs a psychological referral, but, considering the nature of the crisis, Sheila and her teacher should talk through the possible benefits of her working with a counselor. The rationale that a successful transition hinges on is this: the third party allows Stacey and Sheila to sustain their invaluable connection. Otherwise, without this third party, their relationship is headed for confusion, as Sheila's overarching needs and the Stacey's limitations will not mesh.

It is important to get across to Sheila that she is not being shunted off; she is to be cared for in different ways by *both* another professional and the caring adult she wisely trusted. Having such a discussion may well provide Sheila with a key to regaining control of her life. Unless Sheila gets additional assistance, Stacey will eventually be overwhelmed, personally and professionally, by the burden of Sheila's disclosure. By Stacey's keeping her focus on caring for Sheila and helping her find the help she needs, Sheila will have the chance to grow tremendously.

Schools Need to Be Safe Places for All Students

When teenagers feel alienated and exceptional, they are most vulnerable. A school should have a coherent program of support for gay students because how it treats them ultimately reveals how everyone in the community is valued and treated. Schools risk fostering exactly the wrong attitudes when they set gays apart from other teenagers, or ignore them, because in so doing they intensify their alienation. A policy supportive of gay teenagers, then, should be the essence of any school's mission: the fostering of the individual.

Given that a significant segment of the population is gay (most researchers calculate roughly 10 percent), schools should ideally dedicate considerable resources to gay youth. At a minimum, this means that sexuality (heterosexuality and homosexuality) should be treated responsibly at school, including in and through the classroom. (It should also be talked about at home, of course.)

In addition, schools should be safe enough places for gay employees to feel that they do not have to necessarily hide their sexuality. Like all teachers, they should be free to use their discretion in terms of self-revelation that is appropriate to the teenager they are working with. In practice, the lifeline for isolated gay teenagers is frequently an adult who is comfortable being both adult and gay. Implicitly, a school, a faculty, teaches teenagers how to survive this crisis of self. Creating such an atmosphere of openness does not make for inappropriate relations, necessarily, at least no more than a heterosexual teacher's interaction with a student of the opposite sex. After all, as we see in this story, Sheila was fortunate: she found an adult who understood what she was going through. Remember, as much as gay teenagers cannot fail to register every single degrading reference to homosexuality, they also never miss an instance of empathy and care.

Be Conscious of What You Communicate (And You're Communicating Everything)

It is usually in those casual, unguarded moments that teenagers discover where their parents and siblings stand on any hot topic: at dinner with the family, in the car on a family trip, during an overheard phone conversation between you and one of your friends, at a family reunion. Teenagers will make sure that your words and actions are congruent with the high-minded beliefs you express, and they will point out precisely when and where one value does not align with another. Of course, if your values do not strike them as sufficiently high-minded and idealistic, you may expect to hear all about it. Though this may sound fatiguing, not to worry: teenagers will continually remind you of any inconsistency on your part. Again, in this fashion, teenagers continually hold mirrors in front of us and repeatedly demonstrate their need for us to be the best people we possibly can be.

Discovering Your Child Is Gay

If you yourself are not gay and you learn that your son or daughter (or a teenage friend of yours or a friend of your child) is—take a deep breath and try to stay calm. You have quite a bit of catching up to do. Even if you are the most liberally inclined person you know, even if you actively support and vote for gay rights, even if you have a gay sibling, you still have lots of catching up to do.

Now that you have heard the news, you will likely review everything you've known about your child and wonder if you ever knew anything at all. You may feel wounded, even betrayed, for a while. After all, from the birth of your child you couldn't help but have fantasies about your future lives. For most this means heterosexual marriage and grandchildren. Now you will have to modify these visions. But these long-held dreams are not easily forgotten. You'll have to grieve over the loss, which in no way implies disapproval or rejection of your child.

The truth is, though, that attending to your own feelings and reflections should be secondary to taking care of your child. Make sure they have the support they need. Are they talking to people they can trust? (Don't be surprised if they have told one or two people already, including a few adults.) In other words, make sure they are doing all right.

It is wise to get as much knowledgeable assistance as you can. Fortunately there is plenty available. Talk to your community counseling centers for the names and local addresses of support organizations. One prominent support source is P-Flag, Parents and Friends of Lesbians and Gays, P.O. Box 20308, Denver, CO 80220. Above all, be honest with yourself. Of course you love your child and you want to accept your child's sexuality. But realize that it is going to take time, patience, and imagination. To expect anything else would be naive and unnecessarily hard on yourself.

Author William Pollack writes that it is "homophobia—not homosexuality—[that] makes the lives of gay people so tough."[2] He also makes a related point, one that may serve as a tonic in your own coming to terms with your child: your gay teenager is just as likely as a heterosexual teenager to grow up a happy, healthy, productive, successful adult. So do not undervalue your own significance. You have not been excluded from their lives. You have been invited instead to help them shape their future.

13

Making Decisions

One moment you're the honey,
the next you're the ant.

—DEAN YOUNG, "POST-OVIDIAN"

If my mind could gain a firm footing, I would not make essays, I
would make decisions.

—MONTAIGNE, "OF REPENTANCE"
(TRANS. DONALD FRAME)

I Quit, I Think

Dale was a senior and he had this fantasy: at the sports award banquet in
May, Coach would stand up and make a speech about how one particular
player had hung in there through adversity and then would make the following announcement: *This year's winner of the Most Improved Player
Award . . . Dale, come on up here and get your trophy.* Not that Dale was the
kind of teenager who lives in a fantasy world. The truth was, he had
worked at his game—on the freshman squad, through two years of junior
varsity, every summer at baseball camp, daily workouts throughout the
fall, and winter league ball, too. This year he was finally going to get his
chance to play regularly as a varsity starter. He knew deep down that he
wasn't the best player on the team; no, not even close—though there was a

time not too long ago when he was the star of his Little League and Babe
Ruth teams. He had baseball recollections that were wonderful memories
of those days, playing, winning, and being with his dad before and after
the game. Those same memories were beginning to haunt him now because he had just realized that he had probably lost his starting position on
the team.

"Someday I hope I run across the guy who said high school's the best
four years of your life and ask him what was he smoking. If these are the
best four years, I don't want to know the other kind." Dale was talking to
his good buddy Kip. Last game he hadn't played. A tenth grader, Manny,
started in his place and got a couple of line-drive base hits and made a very
nice play in the field to end a rally and pretty much sew up a victory. *A
tenth grader.* The humiliation of it all. In the local paper, which Dale had
tucked under his arm, Coach was quoted to the effect that Manny was a
natural, that he had skills and instincts you couldn't teach a baseball
player.

Dale knew that he had a good eye at the plate and could always be
counted on to get his fair share of walks. He was a good base runner, too.
He was proud that his head was always in the game and that he was always
alert to every opportunity to take advantage of the opponent's lapses. The
mental part of the game, that's where he was strongest. He knew how to
position himself in the field, and he knew when to hold the ball, when to
make a risky play and when not to, and when to take the extra base. As
somebody said, 90 percent of the time the game is 100 percent mental.
When he and his dad watched a major league game, they talked fine points
of strategy, and sometimes they could call the pitch selection ahead of
time. His dad used to make him imagine every conceivable circumstance
and anticipate the right play: "OK, one out, you're in center field, men on
first and second, ground ball up the middle—where's the throw?" Dale always felt a little bit sorry for people who never saw all the subtle aspects of
the game, which were so beautiful, so difficult. Some people actually
thought that baseball was merely about blowing the ball past a batter for a
strikeout or blasting one over the fence.

Dale had never got two base hits in a high school game, not that he
could ever remember—and he would have remembered, because every
single play he was involved in was imprinted on his brain. Dale and his dad
would go over the whole game, every single pitch in every at-bat. That was
almost as much fun as playing the game, the remembering. He was going

to miss the remembering. In fact, he could vividly remember his youth league days, when he played shortstop and led the team in hitting. He made the all-star team, and they won the league championship. High school, of course, was a whole different story. The competition was tough. Everybody had been an all-star, and he wasn't going to play shortstop at this level. He was a team player, though. That's what he always thought about himself, and here he was moping the day after his team won. That didn't make him feel good, not at all. But there were issues, weren't there? "Like start with fairness, that's an issue."

His friend couldn't stop himself. "Life's supposed to be fair?"

Dale ignored that. "Man, I can't believe it," he went on. "For three years I sit around waiting for my chance, and I think finally this year I can count on playing regularly. Now I get the old shaft. The old see-you-later, thank-you-for-your-support."

Kip tried to sympathize, though he was not absolutely sure he got the point. Sports just weren't his thing. He never once tried out for a team and hardly ever went to a game. "Did you piss off the coach or something?"

"I must have. But heck if I know when."

"He a good coach?"

"I used to think so. He used to encourage me, he used to give me tips. But lately he's all about Manny. Manny, the tenth grader. OK, I agree: Manny's got talent. He can probably hit a little better than me, but I'm better in the field, which everybody knows. Just go ask any of the guys. Plus, he's got years left here at school, and this is it for me. This sucks. I'm gonna quit, I'm not gonna sit around waiting for him to beat me out." Dale hated that he was whining like this—it just wasn't him at all. The whole thing was out of his control. "It's not *fair*," he said again. Saying the word over again made him feel even more bitter. Was fairness too much to ask for? At the same time, he could hear the chatter in the back of his head: *What's fair for the team, Dale?* And then still another voice: *Work hard*, his dad is saying, *good things'll happen if you work hard.*

"What'll your dad say?" Kip said, as if he had been reading Dale's mind. He and Dale had been friends since the early grades. Dale's dad tolerated and, almost despite himself, even liked Kip, the kind of kid who loved computers, played weird music, and wore funny clothes and that earring. There used to be an old cartoon series called *Chip and Dale*, and sometimes Dale's dad used to make that old joke about the two of them, *Kip and Dale*. He used to be funny, his dad, a long time ago, for a dad, that is.

"Kip, you quit the newspaper last year. What was that like?"

Kip shivered and squinched up his shoulders.

"Why'd you do it? Remind me. Was it because of the editor, Miss I Got a Deadline?"

"Tina wasn't the problem. It was the adviser, Mr. Zamora. He didn't respect my work. Every time I gave him an article to look over, he would rip it to shreds or tell me it was not appropriate subject matter. Man, I would have never joined the paper in the first place if I couldn't write about inappropriate material."

"Sounds like Coach."

"Your coach did let you start the first part of the year, though, right?"

"Let me start? I earned the start. What are you trying to say?"

"Nothing, just trying to understand."

"You going to defend him too? I should have known better. I don't know how I'm going to tell my dad."

Suddenly Dale realized that Kip didn't get what he was saying, or what he was going through. Was it possible that Dale was on the verge of doing something crazy? Or was everybody letting him down these days? He remembered the bus ride back from that game when he scored the winning run, he remembered hanging out with Woze, with Hector, with—

"Hey, you know, man, maybe you had the right idea," said Dale. Somehow the image that popped into his mind at just that moment—clearing out his locker by himself while the team was taking infield—was exhilarating. He wasn't going to let everybody see that tear drop from his eye.

Dale's Conversation with His Former Little League Coach

Dale's old team, the Yankees, wearing the same uniform he had worn, was practicing at the same field where he once played. A couple of assistant coaches were running drills, and his former coach took a seat on the bench in the tiny dugout to talk with his favorite former player.

—What are you doing here, All-Star? You get the day off from practice?

—Kind of. Hey, Coach, you need any help this season? Because I'm available.

—I'd love to have you but our practices run same time as yours, and what about your games?

—That's not a problem.

—What's wrong? You get kicked off the team?

—Quit.

—What happened?

—Nobody's as good a coach as you. You should be a high school coach. You made us want to play every game. You encouraged us.

—You have a problem with your coach?

—I'm over it, I've got to move on. I just want to go to college and get the hell out of high school. They can mail me my diploma. I'm tired of being jerked around. I'm a senior and I worked hard, for what?

—OK, but why'd you quit now?

—Oh, I get it. I'm supposed to be more worried about my loyal teammates, my pals. Excuse me. They love Manny, who took my job. He's batting lead-off now, and they haven't figured out how to pitch to him yet. But change speeds on him, and he's useless.

—So, you lost your starting position.

—My ass is riding the bench now, at least it was before I quit.

—Dale, what do you want from me?

—What do I want from you?

—Yeah. What do you want? Do you want me to help you feel better about quitting the team? Do you want me to try to talk you out of your decision? Do you want me to help you understand why you quit?

—I don't know, I just feel awful. No matter what I do, it's wrong. And nobody seems to understand. It's weird, I never felt so all alone in my life.

—Oh, you mean it's like when you're going around second—and the ball's out there in right field—and you're looking for a sign for what to do from the third-base coach, and his back's turned, that kind of thing?

—Knew you'd understand.

—Thanks. I guess. So what'd your coach say when you told him?

—I didn't tell him. It's not between him and me. It's like it's between me.

—So you quit and you want to help us out. You sure you don't want some time off?

—I miss the game already, and it's only the first day. I've never not been on a baseball team.

—OK.

—OK what?

—OK I can use you. But first you have to talk to your coach.

—There's nothing I have to say to him anymore.

—Then that's where you start. You figure out the rest as you go.

—I don't owe him an explanation.

—This isn't for him—this is for you.

—I'm not going to change his mind and I'm not going to change my mind.

—I'm not expecting that. But you have to finish what you started. The way you do that is by telling him where you stand. That'll be the real moment of decision for you.

Notes Home

Connections and Disconnections

Teenagers passionately yearn for independence, even as they simultaneously long for community and identification with others. Clubs, teams, publications, service opportunities, dramatic and musical performances, and student government all serve to join kids with others and enable them to make a contribution to their world. Sometimes these are called extracurricular activities (and sometimes, perhaps more fittingly, cocurricular), and considerable resources are usually expended to their end. It is a very rare teenager who at some point or another does not aspire to forge such a connection or two through these activities, and if this never happened it would be a reason for scrutiny. As any parent knows, for many kids these activities become all-consuming.

At different phases of teenagers' lives, group identities acquire different meanings, but at every interval they are noteworthy. (This is especially true for second-semester seniors, like Dale. See Appendix D, "Where Am I Going and Where Have I Been? Being 17–18.") For instance, schools and communities justify interscholastic and intramural athletic programs on the grounds that such participation pays off in valuable dividends earned from team work, cooperation, commitment, and desire. Of course, those values—often hopefully labeled "character building"—are also available through class projects, painting a mural, tutoring, or many, many other activities, including playing bass in a garage band. As teenagers' dreams evolve, so do their modes of expression. Even when they lose interest in activities they used to devote themselves to, or maybe seem to outgrow them, we know that they are creating important psychological and emotional markers in their lives. One day he stops playing chess or the piano, or she refuses to go to another dance class or pay attention to the dog she used to fawn over. Or he forgoes running for class officer reelection. Some teenagers grow bored, some become distracted, and others discover more compelling alternatives for their energy and time. This is natural. In other words, for some teenagers moving on is no big deal and is appropriate, while for others moving on may provoke internal crises, since nothing less than their self-definitions are at play and at risk, too, in these decisions.

When Dreams Collide with Reality, Teenagers Grieve

For some teenagers, moving on from one activity to another means they have recognized the limits of their abilities, whether on stage, behind an easel, or, in Dale's case, on the field. High school gives every teenager experience with limits and failure: being cut from the team, not getting a part in the play, being rejected by a college, not getting the A they worked so hard for, losing the class election, or missing out on a job for which they thought they were perfect. These are never pretty moments, and they are the ones every adult wishes to forget and hopes do not come up at their twentieth reunion. Painful as these moments are, they are also turning points.

As adults, we realize much later that being rejected by Green University opened up the opportunity for us to attend Blue College, which turned out to be perfect in ways we never could have expected. And when we didn't make the volleyball team, we took up tennis, a sport we still play today. We now know that the inevitable was never anything remotely like inevitable, and that our personal history is largely a sequence of accidents, choices, mistakes, lucky breaks, triumphs, and failures. Sometimes what we thought was a triumph becomes anything but, and sometimes what we cringe to recall as our greatest failure opened up doors we could never have imagined. What makes teenagers teenagers is precisely that they do not have this perspective. They cannot take the long view. For them, the long view is the game next week or the movie on Saturday night. And that's why the pain of disappointment is so overwhelming: they think they just lost their last chance.

Dale is slowly facing up to his loss. Whereas baseball used to mean team, pride, identity, and driving purpose, Dale's lost status as a starter has overlaid upsetting new meanings onto playing baseball—loneliness, shame, and bewilderment. Nobody is ever quite prepared for abrupt shifts of such magnitude, but at least Dale is struggling and engaging himself in the quest for understanding. Sure, he has lots of potential blame to assign (Manny, Coach, his father), but underneath it all he himself catches a glimmer that Manny is a better ballplayer and that the coach has no alternative but to do what he thinks is best for the team. Therefore, Dale decides for himself to move on. This may very well be a courageous move, one with ultimately momentous and possibly positive repercussions.

Now, after quitting the team, Dale is at the most vulnerable point in his grief. He has walked away from an old identity but has yet to replace it with a new one. Unfortunately, when kids are lost to themselves like this (for example, after a rejection, a death in the family, a fire), many choose risk-taking behaviors, such as driving recklessly, cutting school, smoking, and drinking. Although none of these behaviors resolves the questions produced by forsaking his former identity, they may create exciting diversions and appealing false identities. For example, Dale could even indulge himself in theatricalized, grandiose illusions: *I'll hurt myself and show them what happens when they betray a good guy like me . . . I'll take up with exactly the kind of guys I never would have before, but why not, who cares, nobody really respects me anyway* . . . What can a parent do to help a teenager spiraling out like this?

In order for teenagers to understand and grow after loss and grief, they need both to come to terms with their emotions and to initiate a plan of action. Until and unless that happens, they can wallow in their private world of isolation, doom, and powerlessness, which is the last thing anybody wants. Some find it easier to articulate their feelings and to investigate the sources of their sorrow and pain. Others rush into new activities and relationships. (Girls are usually more comfortable with the former, boys with the latter, though exceptions—like Dale—abound.) This is the time when they look not only to their peers but to adults for empathy and wisdom. We help them make sense of their feelings and encourage constructive courses of action. We do not attempt to take away their responsibility for dealing with their suffering by infantilizing them *(you'll get over it sooner than you think)* or by trivializing the experience *(try something new)*. Instead, we build on their strengths, which, until they go through their crises, they may never have known that they possessed.

Encouraging Natural Interests and Letting Your Kids Fail

Predicaments like Dale's furnish veiled opportunities. Once he accepts that he is an average baseball player who has outstanding work habits he is free to express that passion in a new relationship with baseball. In the short term he can serve as a Little League coach, for instance. In the long term, he might be drawn to a career as a sports reporter, coach, play-by-play announcer, or athletic trainer.

Will Dale regret his decision to quit the team? Who can say? And when? Will he regret the decision next week, next year, in twenty years? Who knows? Maybe never. Or maybe he will regret it forever. Furthermore, do his parents have an obligation to express doubts, even disagreements, with their son when he is on the verge of doing something they feel is not in his best interests?

Absolutely, but it isn't going to be a lot of fun for either of you. As Mark Twain said, "Good judgment comes from experience, and experience comes from bad judgment."

So go ahead and try to give your teenagers the fruits of your wisdom and tell them what to do when they have a tough decision to make; you'll soon make your face-first acquaintance with the brick wall of legendary fame. Sure, they may ask you what you think they should do, but they'll resent it—and you—if you actually tell them. This is because, on some deep level, they know that it is their life and that they need to make the difficult decisions, especially when there is no clearly right thing to do. Beyond that, there is nothing you can do if they are determined to fall, or if they are making what you believe to be a mistake. The most you can do is cushion the landing.

As for Dale, he will likely respond to supportive friends and adults who ask him the hard questions and give him the room to make his own decision—right or wrong by their standards. Either way, Dale will learn a great deal about life and himself if he makes his own decision. Obviously, the more he wrestles with the problem the more he will learn. And this is why, if you have confidence and hope for your child, you will be ready to let him fail. His making mistakes, his letting himself down, paves the way—if anything does—to adult success. Needless to say, parents will always struggle here, fearing that in not doing enough they will let their children down. But at some point, doing too much is a sure formula for misery for one and all. You cannot save them from themselves and you cannot stop them from growing up.

If a teenager is going to be a success, she will have to do it in her own way and on her own terms, not the way you would do it or for your satisfaction. You are not your teenager. If you let go of your own judgment and avoid seeing your child simply as an extension of yourself, you can view her in brilliant relief. This is why you learn the most about her and she learns the most about herself in these lonely moments of failure and success. This is when she will astonish you and mortify you. Both success and failure set us apart from others, and the cost of both is the same: loneliness. No wonder so many people fear striving for excellence. And no wonder she will soon open up a space for you to come back into her life.

Teenagers Do Not Want to Disappoint Their Parents

Contrary to popular belief, teenagers do care what their parents think, even though they hardly ever show this side of themselves. Unfortunately, teenagers can also misread their parents because they project their own misgivings onto them. For instance, it is entirely conceivable that Dale's dad may not care whether Dale plays baseball at all. He may really only care that his son is happy doing what he loves doing. He may have been supporting Dale's baseball life because that is what he felt Dale wanted and needed. (Secretly, because he may have seen this day coming, he may be relieved that Dale has realized his athletic limitations, even though he may also feel guilty that he feels relieved.) But if Dale does not know this, then it does not matter, since in Dale's eyes his dad will be deeply disappointed in him as a son and a man if he quits baseball.

Suppose, however, that Dale's father was living vicariously through his son. He himself may have played college ball, or he may never have played at all and envied an athlete's fame. Dale would have sensed his father's disapproval, and he may have been unable to quit the team for fear of disappointing him, even though that was what he felt he should do. Here his father would be of no assistance to him in his internal struggles, since those would pale in comparison with his struggles over his father's blinded conception of him. In short, Dale would stay on the team for all the wrong reasons, and his resentment of his father would grow instead of his character.

All this points to why we ought to support teenagers in their multiple identities. When they outgrow or leave an identity behind, they know that their parents, although they may be confused or even troubled, will never abandon them. They know this because their parents supported them in their various identities, from skateboarder to poet to yo-yo aficionado to loyal friend to social organizer to movie lover to intellectual to jock. In a way, then, as with all the big moments in a teenager's life, parents and their children have been practicing how to act and how to be for as long as they have known each other. Only now parents are relearning who their teenager is becoming, even while simultaneously their teenagers are coming to see their parents in a whole new light.

Is Quitting Ever the Right Thing to Do?

Sometimes quitting is exactly the right response to a difficult situation. Hanging in there just for the sake of hanging in there does have its merits, but it makes no sense when damages outweigh gains. Stubbornness is not a virtue. This means that under certain circumstances quitting may not be only right but also courageous. Sure, there may be more than a few grains of truth in the maxim *Winners never quit and quitters never win*, but there isn't one "winner" anywhere who at one time or another hasn't resigned from something—a class that was beyond his capacities, a job that didn't pay enough, or a relationship that wasn't working.

It is easy to imagine circumstances under which some senior baseball player would make a regrettable mistake by quitting. For instance, suppose the team was mediocre and by midseason was securely out of the race for the playoffs; suppose he was relegated to the bench because of a disciplinary infraction, because he was insubordinate to the coach, or because he had picked a fight with a teammate. Suppose Dale was habitually lackadaisical in practice, and suppose he thought he was owed extra consideration just because he had hung around for a long time. *Sour grapes*, we would say, and probably should say to him. *Keep your commitments, that's all you have. You're letting yourself and the team down, both. Grow up, the world doesn't revolve around you.* Or suppose, more generally, Dale had a lifelong pattern of quitting everything. Clearly, however, those conditions do not seem applicable here, and Dale's real predicament is sadder and deeper than that.

The trick for both the teenager and the parent is to recognize when the act of leaving is an appropriate, if reluctant, response to an accurate assessment and when it is a sign of timidity or weakness. Certainly we want to encourage moral stamina and strength of character in our children—but this doesn't happen the same way for every teenager and is seldom a black-and-white call. To become adept at making these kinds of decisions, most of us have to experience some bad decisions from both sides of the equation—quitting in preemptive, fearful anticipation of failure and *not* quitting due to a timid desire to maintain an image of not being a quitter. Although the following observation may scandalize some, Dale has earned, by virtue of his history of commitment and hard work, the right to quit the team if that's what he needs to do, though the way he comes to his decision is the key.

Two Kinds of Decisionmakers

When brainstorming possible solutions to a problem, some of us flee to a decisive resolution as soon as we hit upon the first viable notion. Our brainstorming stops, we make and act on our decision, and we move on. Others of us brainstorm possible solutions, land on the first viable alternative, put it aside, and brainstorm dozens of more feasible options. Each style has its shortcomings. If we use the first style, we may act too precipitously, before we have had enough time to consider alternative ideas that may be much more elegant and effective than the first idea we came up with. With the second style, the danger consists in never acting. We get so caught up brainstorming the best possible solution that we become paralyzed. The Meyers-Briggs Personality Inventory calls the first style "judger" and the second "perceiver."

We all have a temperamental predisposition one way or the other. For parents, this means understanding your preferred style and your teenagers' style, since this will enable you to better understand how you can help them grow. For instance, if you are a perceiver and she is a judger, you will be continually frustrated by her impetuosity. When you say *Slow down a second*, she will ask *What for?* Conversely, if you are a judger and he is a perceiver, you will be bored to tears by his navel gazing. And when you suggest *Get up and do something*, he will consider at length *Like what?* If you're both perceivers, there will be lots of long midnight conversations and little action. Conversely, if you're both judgers, nobody will be inclined to stop long enough to imagine alternatives. Consequently, you may benefit from experimenting with decisionmaking in a mode that you are not instantly comfortable with. Why? Because perceivers and judgers have to rub shoulders in the real world, which is where your teenager is headed any minute. More than that, perceivers and judgers have much to teach each other in and through their decisions. You don't want to change your teenager's temperament; you merely want her to imagine and appreciate the alternative perspective.

Some Advice on Giving Advice

This above all: to thine own self be true,
* And it must follow, as the night the day,*
* Thou canst not then be false to any man.*

Speaking of decisionmaking, Hamlet is famously (if erroneously) regarded as one of literature's greatest "perceivers." Of course, *Hamlet* strikes some first-time high school readers as a string of quotations and hackneyed phrases they've heard all their lives:

"To be or not to be ... "
"Something is rotten in the state of Denmark ... "
"The play's the thing ... "
"Sweets to the sweet ... "
"Words, words, words ... "

Or as one adolescent critic once intemperately inquired, "How'd Shakespeare get away with using all those clichés?"

The words quoted from *Hamlet* as an epigraph to this section are spoken by Polonius, a father giving instruction to his son Laertes as he embarks on his journey to school. Although Laertes pretends to be attending to this sage discourse on life, honor, and the eternal verities, it's a rare director who won't play to the comic possibilities of the way his sister Ophelia is doing all she can to lighten the mood and distract him. That is not all, however. Although the audience is listening to a speech that is beautiful, and possibly even wise and profound, on another level it is attending to the speechifying of Polonius, a hypocritical character who is full of himself, short on integrity, and tireless of expression. To put it charitably, Polonius is not the best father in the world—though he does have advice that would be useful and important for any teenager to hear. As we see in the play, Laertes can barely hear what his father is saying. Polonius is somebody to keep in mind when you're about to launch into tribal wisdom or poetry. He's also the long-winded character who ironically opines that "brevity is the soul of wit," an injunction forgotten to the pain of too many innocent bystanders—and teenagers.

The shape of advice, the love and care with which it is delivered, then, is as important (or conceivably more important) than the substance. It's certainly what will be felt and heard. The best advice is like the rock thrown in the lake. The rock plummets beneath the surface but the ripples leave a wonderful, though transitory, impression.

If you feel the need, though, and the opportunity presents itself and you are called upon to give something like advice, try to frame it as indirectly as possible. Say what you have to say so obliquely that your teenager can make the idea his own. In the moment your child can reject the idea as wrong, insane, or off-base—but it is something he can mull over later.

This is another good reason to consider putting your thoughts in writing. You don't need to be a writer to get across your ideas and feelings this way; too much artifice may even constitute a distraction. But if you put your thoughts on paper, you might be more careful and precise than you are capable of being in the moment of utterance. Beyond that, the very act of writing sends a precious message to your child that you want to communicate, that you value his or her attention, that you don't want to risk misunderstanding, and that this is something you want him to contemplate at his leisure. Oftentimes, a letter like that will make all the difference in a complicated situation. When talking to each other, people sometimes can be misread, sometimes can overreact or overdramatize, sometimes can be swept up in the moment. But a letter can always be kept, can be reopened, can be reconsidered—and these are benefits a teenager will treasure.

Sending a Message, Teaching a Lesson, and Other High-Wire Acts

The idea of sending a message to your child is a tricky one. Yes, you want to convey in no uncertain terms your grasp of the gravity of a given situation, but beware of acting symbolically. Measure your responses appropriately. Don't be seduced by the now-or-never idea of getting across some abstract principle. Besides, it's very rarely now or never when you're in the teenage time zone. Understatement and indirection usually work better. Don't pull out and refer to the manifestoes. Don't make helpful references to the past unless they will help; and nobody is likely to feel that they do. Ratchet down your emotions in a crisis. It's rarely do-or-die. Remember it's your child's life. Whatever you do must be done with the idea of helping him or her grow through this experience. If you take up all the available emotional terrain, where can they stand?

Parents, like their children, can be blinded by ideals (loyalty, commitment, etc.). There's nothing wrong with ideals and plenty that is right, but don't let ideals get in the way of seeing your teenagers in and through their experience. What's the best you can do with this as a parent? Listen and seek to understand. The two biggest errors are trying to make it OK (it's no big deal, you'll get over it) and rushing to the rescue (calling the principal, the coach).

This brings up a related matter that can be counted on to be unpleasant: dealing with a coach, teacher, or authority figure who seems incompetent or unfair. At the risk of asking a rude question, Have you ever heard of parents whose children are receiving excellent grades or awards complaining? Still, parents have a tough time restraining their anger when their teenagers' hard work is not acknowledged, much less prized, by an adult in a position of authority. Could Dale's coach have been subtler in his approach to a sensitive and deserving young man? It certainly seems on the surface to be so. And yet dealing with a coach, a moderator, or an assistant manager at work is always a tricky proposition, and the world is full of less-than-heroic adults.

As a parent, you have some complicated alternatives to work out, though, if you perceive that your children are not being given their due. You cannot take much solace in the maxim that life isn't fair, and you can't expect to sell it to your teenager, either. On the one hand you naturally wish to protect your child from feeling the pain and suffering of unjust treatment; on the other, you want to—or should want to—demonstrate how to confront adversity independently and with dignity. This involves asking yourself some hard questions.

What do you expect will result from pressuring the coach to play your daughter, who is, to your way of thinking, much more talented than her replacement? If she does consequently get more playing time, what do you think the state of her relationship with the coach or her teammates will look like? If you think it will be helpful to give the English teacher a piece of your mind about the grade on that paper, do you believe that your teenager's quality of life in that classroom will be enhanced? No one would expect you to stand back from malfeasance, to be sure, but those instances are comparatively rare.

Ask yourself, instead, how you can model taking responsibility for a difficult situation. Take the long view: your teenager, who is incapable of doing that, will be amazed. Instead of attacking the adult in question, which does admittedly have its momentary appeal, contemplate ways you can show your child how to discuss and address his or her problems. This is also one of those definitive teenager moments when, whether you know it or not, they are putting the mirror up to your face. They want to know what you stand for, how much you trust them, and if you are willing to let them take the consequences for their actions.

Dale's Father's Big Catch

—Dale, got a call from your coach.

—Coach called here?

—He was wondering where you were today.

—Why?

—I guess because you weren't at practice. Something wrong at school?

—I don't know. Is it wrong to quit a team?

—Are you thinking about quitting?

—No. I already quit. I'm going to talk to him tomorrow, but I wanted to talk to you first.

—You always loved baseball. What's going on?

—I do love baseball, and that's exactly what happened. I can't believe it, but I lost my spot. I'm really sorry, Dad.

—You sure?

—Of course, I'm sure. Manny . . .

—No, are you sure you want to quit?

—That's what I'm trying to explain to you. Manny . . .

—What's this have to do with another guy on the team?

—It has everything to do with him. I'm not going to get the innings anymore.

—That's why you're quitting?

—If I'm not playing, why should I stay on the team?

—Plenty of reasons I can think of.

—Like?

—Commitment. Self-respect. Your love for the game.

—Love for the game? That's *why* I'm quitting.

—This is a big decision, are you sure? Shouldn't you at least sleep on this?

—Dad, I know you always wanted me to be a great baseball player, but face it, that's never going to happen.

—When did I ever tell you that?

—It's obvious, Dad. I knew it from the first glove you ever gave me. It was a Pete Rose special. We still have that glove in the garage.

—Dale, hold on now and listen to me very carefully. I don't care one way or the other if you're playing for the Los Angeles Dodgers or if you're second string junior varsity as long as it means something to you. I come to your games to watch you, whether you're on the field or on the bench. I supported you because of that bright look I saw on your face. When I looked at you, I saw Dale playing baseball, not a baseball player named Dale. If you never pick up a baseball again in your life, I'll still be proud of you. I was always thrilled that you had something that you loved so much.

—Would you be thrilled if I walked away from it?

—Depends on what you're walking away from and what you're walking to. Don't you get it? I'm thrilled that you are who you are.

—That makes one of us.

—It'll feel like that whether you quit or not.

—So I don't get to feel better for a while?

—Not today anyway.

14

The Breakup

My bounty is as boundless as the sea,
My love as deep; the more I give to thee
The more I have, for both are infinite.

—SHAKESPEARE, *ROMEO AND JULIET*

Yes, I can write about a lot of things
Besides the summer that I turned sixteen.
But that's my ground swell. I must start
Where things began to happen and I knew it.

—MARK JARMAN, "GROUND SWELL"

Endless Love

– One –

Jaimey's mother knocked again on her door. When was the last time her daughter had been home on a weekend night? That wasn't the only odd thing happening these days. She guessed it had something to do with Jaimey's being a second-semester senior and the breakup days earlier with her first serious boyfriend, Corey. She still wasn't sure why they split. Reading between the lines suggested that it was Jaimey's initiative.

Whatever the reason, it had been quiet in her room for hours now, since dinner, and here it was past eleven. She knocked once more. Still no answer. She didn't want to panic, but she opened the door anyway, her heart racing.

Jaimey was in her sweats, lying curled on top of her bed, listening to music with her headphones on and her eyes closed.

"Sorry," her mom gasped. She felt self-conscious, too, since she never entered her daughter's room without permission. "I've been knocking."

"What!" Jaimey shouted.

Her mother pointed to the earphones and Jaimey pulled them off.

"Sorry," Jaimey said, "I was spacing out."

"Sorry I barged in on you."

"Come sit," said Jaimey, and she patted the bedspread by way of invitation. Her mother complied.

"What are you listening to?" Her mother didn't recognize the CD. Then again, she didn't expect to.

Jaimey looked confused. "I have no idea. Something Pita gave me, said it helped her when she broke up with Neils. You'd think somebody named Pita would never break up with somebody named Neils, wouldn't you? Anyway, so far I haven't figured out how anything could help."

"You want to talk?"

"I just need to be miserable for a while. Tomorrow, maybe."

Her mom placed her hand over her daughter's and kept it there.

"Mom, you ever make a decision, without ever realizing you made a decision till after you start doing things like you already made a decision?"

"Not sure, though probably. Sometimes things fall into place without our being exactly conscious of how or when."

"You can color me surprised. I had no idea I was going to break up with Corey. I did break up with him, didn't I? Things had gotten a little stale: we were just doing the same old things with each other, not like when we began seeing each other. But is that a reason to break up? If you ask me, I don't even know if I wanted to. I just did. I love him, much as I ever did. What's that supposed to mean?"

"Have you two talked?"

"Does it count that he called up and screamed into my ear for fifteen minutes till I hung up? And then he called back and apologized?"

"I don't know. It's tough. It'll take time; you guys were together for a long time."

"Tell me about it. I feel like I chopped my own arm off, and it's like still there, throbbing, the old phantom limb. What was it like when you got divorced?"

Jaimey's mom clasped her hands together and sighed. She had been married once before, right out of college, but she and Jaimey's dad had been together for almost twenty years now. Part of her sympathized with her daughter's ordeal with Corey. Part of her fantasized that Jaimey and Corey would stay together after graduation, even though she was a realist and knew the odds were long. Another part of her was almost relieved to know they had broken up before college. Jaimey could meet new people, enjoy a new life away from home and all that she had known. How come being sensible was always at war with being in love?

"It was pretty bad at the time. I was surprised at how difficult it was, though at the same time getting the divorce was the best thing for me—for both of us actually. I'm happier now than I could have ever imagined back then."

"You got over it, right?"

"But it still hurts to think about, like when you just asked me."

"Right. How come I feel like that'll never happen to me, that I'll never get over it? And at the same time I'm more sure than ever that we shouldn't still be going out."

"Because that's what you're supposed to feel now. On the one hand, breaking up was the right thing to do. And on the other, it causes more sadness and pain than you ever bargained for."

"No lectures, Mom. I feel lousy enough."

"Sorry. I didn't mean to, honey."

"Want to go out tomorrow, Mom? Lunch, or something?"

"Sure. That would be nice."

"OK, maybe if I'm in the mood I'll join you."

"Very funny. Good to see you smiling like the old Jaimey."

"Hey, you know what I miss? His sisters. They were almost like my sisters. And I miss the way the sun feels when I'm with him, and I miss the way the air tastes, and the way my skin sings. I love how time slows down with him and . . . Do you think I'm weird?"

– Two –

Corey and his best two buddies, Bruce and Marcus, were driving around on a Friday night. They used to do this all the time, hanging out, driving around. But it had been a while. Things changed when Corey hooked up with Jaimey. It meant he was usually out with her.

Maybe because he was a little out of sync with them, Corey was talking nonstop about anything. It took the other two over ten minutes to get him off the subject of the prom, which deeply bored them. They were going to go all right, but Corey was obsessed with it. He had been going through the list of eligible girls and was crossing off one name after the other. One had an attitude, one was too perky, one was on the rebound from a loser boyfriend, and so on. When that topic was used up, he talked about every college he could think of and tried to imagine what it would be like to go there. That was getting tedious, too.

Bruce said, "You've been spending too much time in the counselor's office with the *Peterson's Guide.*"

"Excuse me for living," said Corey. But he knew Bruce had some kind of point.

Usually, Bruce never said much. He was behind the wheel because it was his car and he was proud of it. Proud of a dented, green-hornet, slashed-dashboard of a gas guzzler, but with monster speakers that he installed himself. The radio and the clock were the only features illuminated, dimly, on the dashboard.

They had nowhere to go, and it was a night when there should have been somewhere to go. So far they had ruled out going bowling, getting a six pack, watching the game on TV, renting a video, playing pool, shooting hoops at the Y, taking a few swings at the batting cages, and stopping by that sophomore's party where everybody else was going to be. Technically, though, *they* hadn't ruled out these options—*Corey* had. In fact, he had ruled them out as quickly as they had been introduced.

"Man, Corey," said Marcus from the backseat, "you're a dud. It's eleven already, and when the sun comes up we're going to have to return to our crypts and we'll have no stories for the other vampires."

"What's up with a party of tenth graders?" sneered Corey. Something had changed with how he felt around his old friends. He couldn't imagine going to parties with tenth graders.

"You afraid she'll be there?" Marcus risked asking.

"*She?*"

"Come on, Corey. *Jaimey*, all right?"

"What makes you think I'd be afraid? I'm over her." He did wonder, though, after Marcus made that wise-ass remark, if Jaimey would go to a party now. He knew he couldn't, that he wasn't in a partying mood, but, you know, it would be just like her to show him up, and it would prove she never really loved him that much in the first place.

"I've got to get some gas," Bruce said.

"You can't see the gauge," said Corey. "How can you tell?"

"I know my car and my car knows me."

For some reason, that was the saddest thing Corey had ever heard in his whole life. It made him think about Jaimey, how they knew each other and never would again. Unless he could make it right again. "Take me home, would you, please? I'm coming down with the flu, or something."

Marcus answered his ringing cell phone. "Nothing . . . Driving around . . . Corey and Bruce . . . Really? . . . She said what? . . . OK, I'll see you maybe." He flipped closed the phone and made one last try: "You sure you don't want to go to that party? Phil says it's happening."

"Home, James." Corey insisted. He couldn't believe these guys had turned into guys who wanted to go to some sophomore's party. The cell phone intrigued him, though. At one point, he and Jaimey were going to buy them together.

"All right," said Bruce, and he reached over to change the station.

Corey stopped him: "Could you leave that on for a second." It was a song he never liked, but Jaimey had given him the CD for his birthday. He'd been wrong about so much lately. Maybe he was wrong about that, too.

"You want to go to the game tomorrow night?" asked Marcus.

"Sure. Not really. I don't know. I'll call you maybe." Corey was having an all-of-the-above kind of night. He missed Jaimey and hated missing her at the same time.

Jaimey's Conversation with Cheryl, Her Camp Director

For the past three summers Jaimey has been a counselor at the local summer camp for little kids—the same camp she attended when she was young. Cheryl, who was in her thirties, started as director during Jaimey's first year as a counselor, and Jaimey has just stopped by to check in with her about plans for this summer.

—You're still planning on being with us this summer, aren't you, Jaimey?

—Definitely. As of right now it looks like the highlight of my dreary summer.

—That's not what I expected from a college-bound senior. Is everything okay?

—Sort of. Corey and I broke up.

—Ouch.

—Yeah, it's a real drag.

—I can tell. How to say this nicely? You've looked better, girl.

—Hey, maybe I'll just leave.

—Don't you dare. Have a seat.

—I can't believe how I screwed up everything. But I think I did the right thing, breaking up with Corey. He's a sweetheart and all, but a girl's got to do what a girl's got to do. It's not him, it's me. I think we just grew right past each other.

—Did you tell him any, or some, of that?

—Every time I started to, it came out wrong. I want to tell him I still love him, but I don't want him to love me back. Makes me a bitch, doesn't it? And that's the worst part: I feel so totally mean to this guy I used to love so much.

—It would be worse if you felt just fine and effortlessly moved on with your life. At least this means you really cared for him.

—You know, he is the only guy I ever had sex with—no, make that the first guy I ever made love to. Amazing, it was just amazing. I can't imagine that with anyone else. Problem is, I can't imagine that with him anymore either.

—Been there. You'll get through it; you're more than strong enough.

—Yeah, but I'm worried about him. He talks crazy sometimes. Then he doesn't talk at all. And of course there's nothing I can do, because I'm the reason he's so upset.

—Give it some time. He's got to go through his thing too, and it'll be different for each of you, and you're going to go through it apart from each other.

Corey's Conversation with His Neighbor, Mrs. Domingo

Corey and his mom have lived in the same place for the past eight years—since his parents divorced and his dad moved out of state—and during that time he has developed rapport with Mrs. Domingo, his neighbor four houses down. She is in her seventies and has five grandchildren. She counts on Corey for intermittent yard work in exchange for what she likes to call some walk-

ing-around money. Corey just finished raking the yard and is sitting down at the kitchen table for his ritualized glass of homemade lemonade.

—Ain't worth it, being in love. That's Corey's Theory for the Day.

—You're too young to talk that way, but I can't say it's a foreign idea.

—Sometimes I just want to close the door and hibernate, stay inside for a month. Put my dinner on a tray outside and tell everybody who calls I'm unavailable. I could use with a good case of mono.

—Something wrong with you and that young lady of yours? What's her name?

—Jaimey.

—Real nice girl. Can't imagine what she sees in a rascal like you.

—Seems not much these days. We're officially in that "let's-just-be-friends" stage of the relationship. Everybody knows what that means. Has that ever happened, that you can be just friends?

—That sure explains your gloomy Theory of the Day.

—I'm pretty miserable company. It's just all so confusing. I don't think I am dealing. I feel like such the jerk. I didn't know what I had. I took her for granted. I've got to stop seeing her. Got any more lemonade?

—Wait, I thought you said you broke up.

—Well, technically, we're broken up. But last week, in fact, the day after we broke up, we got together, to talk, and the next thing, there we were, just like old times. Except it isn't like old times. I can't be with her but I don't want to be anywhere else.

—I think I read something in *People*, some survey about how after divorce most couples keep getting together for a while.

—A month ago that would have sounded insane, but this ain't a month ago.

—You two were together for a long time.

—Yeah, I feel like somebody inside me died. I'm not sure if the somebody's her or me. It's crazy, or maybe it's me that's crazy. I'm depressed as hell but I can't sit still either.

—Corey, are you taking care of yourself? Eating enough, sleeping OK?

—No way. All food tastes pretty much the same—lousy. And whenever I close my eyes my brain starts going a mile a minute.

—I know it's hard to believe, but you'll come through this, Corey.

—Yeah, yeah, I know. That's what everyone tells me, including my newfound best friend, Dr. Engstroter that my mom makes me see.

—Does she help?

—More than I expected. But I've only seen her a few times.

—I'm glad you found someone you can talk to.

—We'll see.

Notes Home

Parents Whose Fools Fall in Love

When you discover that your teenager has fallen in love, you are not the first parent to feel terror and elation in equal measure. Unlike the case of your adult friend who has fallen in love, when you are glad and hopeful, this is your child you are seeing heading out the door arm in arm with a stranger. For one thing, when it comes to your teenager, you see your *child* in love—and your teenager in some sense is always, say, about five years old in your imagination. And what five-year-old is ready for an adult relationship? The problem is the five-year-old is now seventeen or eighteen. Of course, you think about the worst cases—you're the parent and that is your job because you know your teenager is not thinking this way. That is why you have nightmares. Pregnancy. Putting off college. Closing off other experiences and—big parent word coming up—*options*. But if there is one moment in your parental life when you know for certain that you cannot control your child, this is it. Welcome to the very large, totally nonexclusive club. *Your* parents have been card-carrying members since as long as you can't remember.

You might think of your teenager's being in love as merely a stage. You might believe that it is a rite of passage into adulthood. You can reference your own personal history. None of this, however, gets to the heart of what is going on, which is this: being in love is a mystery.

Romeo and Juliet will always resonate for a teenager, partly because it is a drama about families' denying love and about love battling with mortality. In other words, it's about the most ordinary experience possible: teenagers' giving over to love, and how the demands of the once-familiar world (and that means to a large extent family, school, and so on) have been pushed aside. Love changes us for better or worse—and that's the concern for parents, the better-or-worse part, and this is the concern we address in the pages that follow. As much as love may fulfill our teenagers, their breakups can also break them. That's the story of Jaimey and Corey. Love, which joined them as one, has left them in pieces to strive separately to put themselves together again.

Teenagers in Love

Just about every teenager harbors the fantasy of falling deeply in love with someone and feeling that love reciprocated. Despite their fantasizing over this prospect for approximately forever (that is, since puberty), they are stunned and amazed when it actually comes to pass. Consider what happens to them.

Being in love provides a new best friend. More than that, it revises their whole conception of friendship. They now have a best friend with whom they can—or might or may or will or hope to—explore their sexuality. This does not necessarily imply intercourse, though it might be useful for you to know that the current average age for first having intercourse is around fifteen or sixteen. This means half of fifteen- and sixteen-year-olds have had sex and half have not. But teenagers do not consummate their relationships to conform to statistical expectations, of course. There's no way to generalize about teenagers who are in relationship, and that is why you cannot assume anything about your teenagers' sexual life—except that they have one, even if it exists only in their imagination. (Look in the Appendixes for how teenagers' notions of sexuality change over the course of their development.)

Being in love mollifies the most intractable adolescent insecurities. For instance, now they always have a date for Saturday night, which on face value is good. (At the same time their whole lives have changed. They are barely conscious of how they have restructured their social lives to accommodate this new relationship. Few teenagers, such as Corey, ever consider the absence of their other close friends—remember Bruce and Marcus?—until it's too late.) More than anything else, now they believe that they are accepted for who they are. They are loved by someone who matters to them. And this is someone whose love is freely given and is not unconditional, like a parent's. No wonder that teenagers can temporarily lose sight of their family and take for granted their parents when they are in love. In short, they have the good in them acknowledged on a daily basis, their humor, caring, tenderness, intelligence, wisdom—their specialness. Teenagers in love see themselves reflected in someone else's eyes, but in an idealized way. They feel powerful, coherent, and desirable because they are desired. They feel that they have found the key to themselves and that there is little to worry about anymore. (Which is exactly what worries their parents to sleep every night.)

Most teenagers in love possess a sense of clarity that gives everything sharp perspective. Teenagers are experts in compartmentalizing. They're different in class from how they are at practice or at home or with the college counselor. Being in love resists this tendency. Love colors everything and everyone, and invests even the most mundane activities with transcendent significance. Every sunset, every true-love song on the radio, every flower, pet, and bird—everything can be the occasion of rapture. Fortunately, as they get dreamy and misty-eyed in love, most of them also do better in all their other activities: sports, academics, community service, acting. Why? Because they feel like adults: they are playing for keeps. With the security of the relationship and the love and responsibility they feel to another human being (and the extra energy not expended on anxiously trying to impress potential love mates) teenagers gain a clearer focus on and a stronger commitment to their well-being. This is why it is not unusual for the average student, after getting into a relationship, to decide to apply herself academically in a way that nobody would have predicted.

For a few teenagers in love, however, the picture darkens soon. Some abdicate personal initiative; that is why their parents worry when they observe that they seem unhealthily invested in each other, that their individuality has become effaced, and that their once-independent teenager is no longer recognizable. Instead of finding themselves in each other, these teenagers lose themselves to each other. For parents, the strategy becomes the exasperating one of waiting and hoping. Yes, you need to find a way to express your apprehension, but don't expect to be heard, at least right away. If you share your concerns in a manner that is critical of the boyfriend or girlfriend (he's a little old for you; she's not worthy of you, etc.), your failure is guaranteed. If you do so with a commitment to your own teenager's welfare (your schoolwork seems to be drifting; your little sister misses you around the house, etc.), your success is possible, though probably not immediately. Either way, once you have made your point, move to the side and return to waiting and hoping. (For another discussion of the topic of parental anxieties about teenagers' relationships, see Chapter 7, "Eating Disorders.")

The darkest side of the teenage love affair, though, is the breakup. More than likely, the breakup is going to invite considerable misunderstanding for everyone. You might well be relieved that the relationship is now defunct, or seems to be. It is not a safe bet that your teenager will feel the same way, even if he or she says as much. You knew all along that the euphoria of falling in love was impossible to sustain, an insight you would do well not to remind anyone of. You know that your teenager probably does not have the experience to know that love has different seasons, that pain will eventually subside, and that love will come again. And this information is useless to impart. You might even recall that no sort of *information* when it comes to love is of much use. That's where experience, perhaps sadly, comes into play, and that's why it is so difficult to watch our teenagers go through the trials of gaining such experience. That's why we knock on our daughter's room late at night. That's when we pour some lemonade. Now finally they need our love more than ever, love that shows up in the little things—in unsolicited acts of kindness and in our sheer presence alongside them in their pain.

"Let's Just Be Friends"

These are four words that can break any teenager's heart. Any teenager? Who wants to hear this at any age? It takes courage to break up—certainly more than it takes to let a relationship die slowly. And because it takes courage and demonstrates strength, and because it hurts somebody, almost everyone wants to soften the blow by offering friendship. No matter how often and how earnestly both teenagers have professed undying loyalty to one another ("if we ever break up, I promise to stay friends"), they seldom are able to keep this pledge.

Naturally, hearing *Let's just be friends* is enraging and confusing. As Corey remarks, everybody knows what it means. But at the same time, it's also open to interpretation at this risky stage. One person might construe that statement to constitute a kind of negotiating position. He thinks, OK let's be friends—that's a step away from a relationship. Another thinks, OK, let's be friends—that means I still have a foothold and I still can work my way back in.

Another thing that makes teenagers' breakups so disturbing is that with teenagers, as opposed to adults, their worlds almost always converge and overlap. When they were in love they remapped the whole world; it became theirs. Only now it is not theirs any longer. High school becomes claustrophobic. There is no escaping the memories, the signposts and tracks of each other. Daily, hourly, they see the traces of a once-cherished person—and both Jaimey and Corey sense this loss, virtually equally. Each must now develop new routines that expressly do not involve the other. Adults might redraw the outlines of their daily life (move, join different clubs, and so on). But for a teenager in high school, this is much more difficult, especially if the couple has melded routines and activities, which most teenage couples who have been together more than a semester have done. This means that things like carpooling, fixing their schedules to have the same classes, eating lunch with each other, and belonging to the same clubs turn into a galling reminder of loss and disappointment. But even if they came from different schools or parts of town, teenagers are narcissistic enough to believe that everybody knows everybody else, and that everybody at the mall or the movies knows them. Swimming inside this perceived fishbowl, they yearn for a privacy and anonymity that will allow them to move on in their lives, yet they don't feel they get the chance.

Let's just be friends? Teenagers who promise friendship are not necessarily being disingenuous in doing so. It's simply a naive attempt to avoid grieving. By trying to move into a redefined relationship, they are hoping somehow to palliate the suffering. They mourn not only the loss of the other but also a deep part of themselves. They loved each other, yes, but they also loved who they were together—and who they were as individuals when together. They were kinder, less judgmental, more optimistic, and more empathetic. And nothing, not even a proffer of friendship, will feel anything other than hollow. Of course, if they ever manage to leap out of that fishbowl, if they let themselves grieve in private, who knows, they might one day become not *just* friends, but friends.

Reality Shifts

After a breakup, teenagers rethink their relationship and doubt themselves. Corey, for instance, wonders if the relationship was ever really good. Did she ever love me? Did I ever love her? Who was she anyway? Did I ever know her? And did she ever know me? I was sure I was in love, so can I ever trust my feelings? For teenagers, who are constantly questioning their understanding of reality, this is an unnerving self-dialogue. After all, they think if they were wrong about that girl or that guy or that relationship, could they be right about anything else? No wonder most teenagers, just like Corey and Jaimey, feel set adrift from life after the loss of an important relationship. Everything, not just the relationship, cries out for reconsideration and reevaluation. This is hard work, but it is necessary. All teenagers perform this work differently. Some will fill out journal pages. Some will rekindle bonds with their old friends. Some will shoot solitary baskets till past dark. Some will talk incessantly on the phone. Some will hibernate.

Given to philosophizing anyway, teenagers are never more drawn to deep discourse than they are at this point. For parents, this might be the first time you enter into enormous, far-reaching dialogue with them about religion, about the purpose of life, and about the meaning of love itself. Keep your ears and eyes open, for these may unexpectedly be some of your best moments. Your dinnertimes may stretch into many hours. Sometimes you're not going to watch the video you rented. Be ready for the tears, the rants, the rages, and the laughs, too. This can be a strangely exhilarating opportunity for you and your teenager to redefine *your* relationship, too.

All of this is conceivable and normal. And yet this juncture can be dangerous. Teenagers' lives can quickly turn precarious. They can jettison everything that mattered to them in an attempt to redefine themselves. They can immerse themselves in cynicism (sleeping around, partying nonstop). They can become timid and fearful (they do not return friends' phone calls, they watch television all the time, they compulsively surf the Net). They can turn fatalistic (what difference does it make anymore?). Every question is capable of being answered with the same single-word response: *whatever*.

Of course, they can also go in another direction. They can go deeper into themselves, and they can reaffirm the values they once held or affirm new ones. Personal crises of this order can forge a depth of character unimaginable before. Teenagers can embrace their newfound identity and face life with renewed interest and vigor.

The Unmasking

At the end of their struggle to understand what they have lost and who they now are, teenagers will arrive at hard-earned self-awareness. They'll come to terms with themselves and their experience and eventually treat themselves and the other with more generosity. They will again trust their emotions and their grasp on the world. While still feeling sad over the breakup, they will accurately remember the good times. Is that a consolation? For some, certainly.

For other teenagers, however, these struggles may well open up old wounds. In Corey's case, it seems that he is going through more than the usual pain following a breakup. On his own testimony, he is not eating; he is not sleeping; he is listless; he is morbid; he is self-loathing. He also seems to be reliving family traumas. The breakup seems to awaken in him memories of abandonment and disappointment. Fortunately, his mother is sensing his apocalyptic attitudes and is guiding him to professional help. There is more at stake here for Corey than simply coming to terms with losing Jaimey. She symbolizes a deeper disconnection within himself—and an elemental loss of meaningfulness. What's more, he may never have been aware of these deeper internal fissures until Jaimey left him and in effect consigned him to himself. And perhaps this unconscious material is not ready to be dredged up until he sits across the room from Dr. Engstroter, whose expertise lies in inviting him to face himself and make the connections. The split within himself, therefore, may very well give Corey a chance to integrate his past experience with his present life.

There is hardly ever a simple breakup for a teenager. He is drawn into relationship for reasons he can only partially appreciate and then is yanked out of the dream for reasons he may be understandably afraid to face. For some teenagers, the ending of a romance is the harbinger of adult life. And this breakup can open doors to other people and happier choices.

The Most Important Sex Talk Is Also the Relationship Talk

The parent's job is, in a word, preparation. Not prevention.

Talk to your teenagers about sex.

Resist giving in to the embarrassment you will naturally feel broaching the subject.

Talk to your teenagers again about sex.

Listen to them when they talk to you. And listen harder when they're not talking.

Some may need a review of the biology. Many more don't. And others won't, out of mortification or shyness, reveal their ignorance. In other words, tell all of them all of what you know, and steer them to the resources for the answers you don't have, teachers, pediatricians, books—resources that you yourself need to tap.

Do you need to tell them everything in one conversation? No. Of course, it would be easier if you could, and that's the fondest hope of many parents who hope to check off *Had sex talk. All bases covered.* Do they need to know the facts of your sex life? Absolutely not. Do they need to know that sexuality is an essential part of your life? Yes, but spare the details. (After all, one expression of your sexuality is embodied in the person you are now talking with.) In general, they need information that is developmentally appropriate; for instance, the topic of sexually transmitted disease will be over the heads of most thirteen-year-olds, while for a seventeen-year-old it may be way past due.

Biology dictates when you begin the conversations. Ideally, you should do so before they hit puberty. The median age for girls is twelve and a half, and falling; for boys it is fourteen. But some kids hit puberty as early as nine or ten while others are not there until sixteen or seventeen. In other words, don't set your calendars by the average ages; watch carefully and listen closely. Your kids will tell you in their own way when they are there. You are the authoritative expert on your child's development, as long as you pay attention and know what to look for.

Yet something as important as your teenager's sexuality requires much more than a one-dimensional "sex talk." It's always easier for the teenager when the parent initiates these conversations. Many teenagers have been known to admit their relief: "I'm glad you asked. I wanted to talk to you about this, but I didn't know how to bring it up." Parents and teenagers mutually need an open line of communication on the general topics of sex, love, morality, and relationship. Do not leave something so important up to your teenager. If you do not reach out, sexuality becomes shrouded in secrecy, and feelings of guilt, shame, and fear attach to what can be the most joyful source of affirmation. In fact, if he hears you bringing up the topic consistently and openly, he is more likely to come to you with his questions and concerns. Your teenager learns that you are a safe resource for questions about sex (or drugs or alcohol, etc.) when you take the initiative. Even when they are staring at the tops of their shoes while you talk, know that they are hearing every word you say and that your reaching out to them on this uncomfortable subject is creating a bridge of understanding, a bridge that they can cross freely.

In order to ground your conversation in reality, you need to grasp the enormous physiological changes your teenagers are going through. Michael Gurian's *A Fine Young Man* details at length these processes for boys. *Changing Bodies, Changing Selves,* by Ruth Bell, and the *What's Happening to My Body* books for boys and girls, by Lynda Maderas, are excellent resources, too. Some parents may feel that being direct and realistic about sex amounts to "giving permission," says June Reinisch and Ruth Beasley in *The Kinsey Institute New Report on Sex.* "This is not true. Providing sexual information has been shown to *delay* the age of first intercourse and *prevent* unwanted pregnancy" (their italics).[1]

In other words, knowledge is the foundation of your discussion of morality and relationship. Instead of simply applying moral discriminations to sex, put sex more generally into the moral sphere of your family. For some, this includes religious beliefs and doctrine. For others, this includes a humanistic, philosophical position. In any case, your clarity is what your teenager needs to make her own decisions, which is not the same as agreeing with you or living up to your ideals. This is not to imply, either, that kids are amoral on the subject of sex. Contrary to popular mythology, very few are, in fact, amoral, and most are very high-minded and idealistic about sex and about love—and they are ready to discuss the connection between the two.

The teenager's first love affair is a kind of rite of passage. Such rites are less frequent than they perhaps once were. During high school, you have, for instance, graduation, the prom, and the driver's license. But love, as opposed to the car, is quite different. With driving, your teenager prepares, takes classes, practices driving with an instructor and you, and so on. There's no course to prepare for falling in love—not even the sex education program at school or church. And there's no formal preparation for falling out of love either. And yet we know our children are undergoing initiations and crises that are, by definition, out of our realm of influence, or so it seems.

The truth is that we have been exerting an influence all along. We have been modeling our understanding of love and relationship in our relationships with our children. This is why our sex talks must take place in the greater context of relationship and include specific discussions about respect, honesty, and vulnerability. It's one thing to speak frankly about the biology of sexuality—and it's essential, even if the school is covering the same ground. But it's still another to make the connection explicit between, for instance, the values you have embodied in your relationship with your children (respectfulness, sensitivity, integrity) and the attitudes you wish them to hold in their relationships with others.

Childhood's End

When teenagers fall in love—when they begin that first serious relationship—what happens to their parents? Chances are your child is at least sixteen, and more likely seventeen or eighteen, and therefore well into the project of separating from parents and family. Your reactions are mixed. At least she's not dating around so much. Good thing that he seems serious about a relationship. But you wonder if they're ready for what they seem to be asking for. You wonder if he's good enough for her or if she's good enough for him. You fight back your skepticism and what you believe is merely pragmatism: no way this will last out the year or survive the next. Are they selling themselves short? Are they missing out on lots of experiences as a result of all the time they are spending with each other? Have they checked out of the family? You remember when they used to be home and you enjoyed untrammeled access to them and to their emotional lives. Now the landscape is changed. Your child is one half of a couple.

Still, at the beginning you are supportive: "I like her." "Why don't you invite him over for dinner?" "Maybe one day we can meet the family." Nobody is prepared for all the complications that will ensue when it becomes clear that they are no longer merely dating—much more seems at stake: they let you know they have professed a deeper commitment to each other. Before you know it, you feel like you have added another member to the family. But that's not quite it, because on some level you feel that you have lost a member of the family, namely, your teenager. Now he or she is finding meaning and emotional connection outside the family. Before, you could tap into their triumphs and failures in school, in athletics, at work. Before, you knew who their friends were (or believed that you did). In other words, you had strong connections to their lives. Now, however, someone has arrived on the scene who inspires (it seems to you) the deep feelings that you always associated with you and your family.

You have friends and you have intimate relationships; you know the difference. And now so does your teenager. There is no turning back. They have discovered a new level of intimacy away from you that is beyond your ability to provide. Now they are in a relationship over which you have no control. In weaker moods, you can become both envious and jealous. You have been replaced (that's why you can be jealous), and you are in awe over the appearance of love (that's why you can be envious). It will bring out the best and worst in you. You will be sad: you have lost your child. And the day that relationship ends and your teenager comes back, he or she will come back radically changed, somehow no longer your child—or so it can feel. Love breaks the hearts of everybody involved, and in the love between adolescents, you, the parents, are involved. Only involved at a remove. This truth becomes accentuated for most during the breakup because you will see close-up the furious and sweet depths of your children, and you will be able to do precious little to obviate their immense suffering. Falling in love and breaking up as a teenager can ultimately be healthy for your child. But it also means that she has taken another step away from you. That's good, isn't it? It just isn't easy for anybody. For these reasons, parents grow up, along with their teenagers, during the seasons of love and loss.

15

Distress, Depression, and Danger

If youth is the season of hope, it is often so only in the sense that our elders are hopeful about us; for no age is so apt as youth to think its emotions, partings, and resolves are the last of their kind. Each crisis seems final, simply because it is new.

—GEORGE ELIOT, *MIDDLEMARCH*

A good analysis will take you to places you don't know are there. You didn't know your tears were there, but they were.

—LARRY MCMURTRY, *DUANE'S DEPRESSED*

This Is Not a Test

– One –

Unit tests took place every four or five weeks in Mr. Hirsch's class. When he was starting out teaching, he used to refer to them as *quizzes*, thinking that might minimize students' test anxiety. And once he even called them, in a lighthearted moment, "quizzies." But that was when somebody piped up from the back of the room, "If this is one of his quizzies, I'd hate to see his testes." Teachers learn fast if they're going to survive in the profession.

In any case, today's was the seventh exam of the year. If you had heard all the weeping and gnashing of teeth, though, you would have thought it was number seventy. Tests are not exactly the highlight of the teacher's day either, to be honest. But at the same time Mr. Hirsch would also like to add—for the record, in case anybody's keeping one—that a test could be a teaching tool. He felt that, if you do a good job, you can design a test that not only reveals the student's knowledge but also teaches something to those who take it. Well, anyway, officer, that's Mr. Hirsch's story, and he was sticking to it.

Luke usually did all right in this class, Bs—never Cs, never As. But Mr. Hirsch was almost embarrassed to make the following admission: he barely knew Luke, who was one of his 152 students this term. Luke did keep mostly to himself, hardly opened up in discussion, and rarely walked into the room in the company of anybody else.

Maybe Mr. Hirsch did get hung up in his classroom, at his desk, in committee meetings, or at games, but he happened to know a lot more about some other students. In fact, he would never have thought much about Luke today if it hadn't been for the incident.

After handing out the test and answering the inevitable procedural questions (whose answers inevitably appeared as numbered instructions in boldface at the top of the test), he sat down at his desk. There he could review notes for next period and, of course, keep an eye out on the whole class. It's not that he is a mistrustful sort. It was just that there's no need to furnish anyone incentives to give in to temptation.

In this school, it's acceptable for students to leave the room after finishing a test, as long as they don't disturb the other test takers and the other classes in session. Compared to other schools, this one was little bit casual in these sorts of matters. A fair number of faculty thought the institution was a little too casual and could benefit from more traditional rules.

On this day, it wasn't very long—maybe twenty-five or so minutes into the period—before Luke was gathering up his things, slinging on his backpack, and advancing to the teacher's desk. When he arrived, his eyes shifting slowly from side to side, he allowed the test pages to flutter down before the teacher.

"Done already?" Mr. Hirsch asked. Not a great question, he would have to concede, but he had been surprised by Luke's finishing so fast and hadn't had time to warm up.

"Oh, I am done all right, I am really done." His voice was so cool the climate in the room seemed to change. "I've had enough," he asserted.

"It's not worth the hassle. I'm going to shut down this circus once and for all."

Mr. Hirsch asked him to repeat what he just said.

"Never mind, I am outta here, I need some oxygen." He wasn't asking for permission to leave the room.

When Mr. Hirsch picked up the test and scanned it, it was clear that Luke had completed about half, and none of it with great care. "Forget to study, Luke?" he whispered. There was no need for students to hear, though everybody seemed wrapped up in their own work anyway.

"No, I didn't forget." His voice carried as he loomed over the desk. "It just doesn't make any difference is all. Why bother? I'm just a choke. Don't waste your time grading the test. It doesn't matter anymore. Adios."

Mr. Hirsch's head snapped back. It took a minute to register that Luke had abandoned the room.

Then Mr. Hirsch recalled the single time when the two of them had talked, and their subject was taking tests. On that occasion he had just handed back a corrected test, and Luke seemed very disappointed with the results. He thought he had been ready that day and he had been counting, he said, on a higher grade. He went on, describing his tendency to become too tense and to blank on what he had studied. Mr. Hirsch made a few suggestions for preparing systematically and doing simple things such as reading the whole test first and then rereading one by one the questions as he proceeded. He had said, "Hey, I want you to do well on a test. I could easily write a test that I myself would fail. What would be the point?"

Anyway, after Luke had left the room today, Mr. Hirsch took a walk around the classroom to get his bearings. Then he settled back in his desk chair. What Luke had turned in was right there, on top of the grade book. On the back of page two was a stick-figure drawing of somebody strung up on a hangman's noose and a caption: "Now it's off to hang myself I go. Thanks for nothing."

The next thing Mr. Hirsch felt was his heart racing as he gripped onto the desk as if it were the safety bar on a roller coaster. What in the world was Luke telling him? Should he do something? There were thirty-two minutes left to ride out before the bell rang and released them.

– Two –

Mr. Hirsch pulled Luke out of his next period.

"What's up?"

"Took the words right out of my mouth. The note, on your test, remember?"

"That? No big deal."

"In my mind, it is."

"I can't afford to miss any more class, so why don't you and everybody else stay out of my life?"

"That's not so easy anymore, after the note you left me."

"I didn't leave *you* anything. And who invited you into my life?"

"You did. Look, I don't know what's going on . . . "

"There's a news flash."

Mr. Hirsch didn't have time to deal with the sarcasm. "But I can't ignore what you did on that test."

"Just requires a little practice. Some of my so-called friends ignore me all the time."

"Can you just give the attitude a rest, Luke, and talk with me for a few minutes? I'm not trying to make your life harder, honest."

Luke was poised to reply—obviously it was going to be another wisecrack—but for some reason he paused and stared at his teacher. Finally, he announced, "All right. Talk."

Mr. Hirsch guided him over to the picnic tables where students ate their lunch. They were empty at this time of day because everybody was in class, so it was a private enough place for them. "Thanks for sitting down with me."

Luke studied his wristwatch.

Mr. Hirsch tried to organize his thoughts. He wanted to be careful. He stared at the carvings on the table, all the black-marker hearts encasing initials and pierced with arrows, all the character smears and phone numbers and more than a few crude words. He hardly ever sat at these student tables and looking at the inscriptions made him feel a little sad, to tell the truth. It was hard being a teenager, and here was plenty of evidence that very few kids were getting out of high school unscathed. "I'm pretty troubled about what you wrote."

"I've been frustrated, is all."

"When you said you were off to hang yourself, it sounded to me like a lot more than frustration."

"I shouldn't have written that, you're right. Had something to eat, I'm feeling better."

"I'm glad to hear that, but you can understand why I'm worried."

"Just keep it between us, would you? You're not going to get sued if that's what you're worried about, because I'm really not going to kill myself. That'd be pretty cheesy."

"Are you talking with anybody? Friends, parents, counselor?"

"Like a shrink? Nah. I can deal with my problems. I just get angry sometimes. Of course, I wouldn't get so angry if people weren't such a pain in the ass."

"But you did put me in the middle, you know, writing that."

"You'll get over it."

"I thought you were going to cut the wiseass."

"All right. I mean, just keep it between us. I'm not going to do anything."

"I wish I could believe that."

"Now would be a perfect time for somebody to trust old Luke, you know that?"

Luke's Surprise Conversation

When Luke leaves school at the end of the day, the last person he expects to find idling in her car at the curb when he turns the corner is his . . .

—Mom? What are you doing here?

—I'm giving you a ride home. You're welcome.

—Well, if I can't have my own car . . .

—And if you're too cool to ride your bike to school anymore . . .

—OK OK OK. Aren't you supposed to be at work?

—Finished early today.

—OK, but I'm supposed to find Joey, maybe Pam, too.

—You can look for them later. Just get in the car, would you?

They drive silently for a while and Luke begins to realize, gradually, that they aren't driving home, but he doesn't say anything just yet. Finally, though, she begins to speak with him.

—Anything going on at school?

—Not really.

—How about History class?

—Same old stuff. Wars, caravans, speeches, dates, more wars. Boring.

—How'd you do on your test?

—I can't believe he calls my mother. What a jerk.

—I got a call, but he didn't really seem like a jerk.

—Trust me. I couldn't get to square one on his test today, and I bet nobody else did either.

—He didn't mention how you did on the test. He was worried about you.

—Hirsch was born worried.

—That note you scrawled scared him, and you know what? It scared me, too.

—Oh, that. I was just pretty pissed off.

—At?

—Him, who else? The idiot who wrote that impossible test.

—Luke, I'm just going to blurt this out. Are you planning on hurting yourself?

—Come on, Mom. I've got to meet Pam, drop me off at her house.

—I thought you two were broken up.

—She might be, but I'm not yet.

—But Luke, you haven't answered my question.

—What question?

—Are you planning on hurting yourself?

—Try to get a grip, Mom. It's my life.

—I'm not letting you out of this car till you answer me. Are you planning on hurting yourself?

—Doesn't everybody?

—I'm not everybody's mother. I'm talking to you.

—Hey, wait. You never liked Pam so don't start talking about her now.

—You're scaring me. I'm not following the way you're thinking these days. I never said I didn't like her.

—Didn't need to. Besides, I'm never going to get good enough grades for the kind of college you want me to go to, so who cares?

—Where did you get that idea? We think you're doing great. We have a lot to talk about, Luke.

—I just wish I could be left alone.

—Not till I'm positive you're OK.

—What are you going to do, follow me around all day?

—If that's what it takes.

Notes Home

Trust Your Intuition

The first thing and the last thing you need to hear on the topic of depression and suicide is simply this: trust your intuition—and be prepared to act on very short notice. If you are going to make a mistake, in the long run it's preferable to accept the blame for overreacting.

If you are like every other parent, the day may come (if it has not already) when you will endure at least one extended moment of acute anxiety about your child's ultimate well-being. It won't feel like normal worry either. Worry is the term for what you endure when you wonder if he's working hard enough in school, if the coach will ever let her get off the bench, if he will really go to the prom, if she can pass the driving test, if he gets the part in the school play. This other feeling is qualitatively different; you can tell because there is a fearful chill running down your spine.

There will be something in your child that strikes you as being odd, as off, as vexatiously strange. It will seem—and we are aware that this is an extremely charged word—faintly dangerous. It will seem as if they have almost, and in some bizarre and subtle way, checked out of their former life. You must determine whether they are growing up by growing a little bit away from you or whether they are going through a crisis that they cannot, or will not, articulate for you.

Depression is different from normal teenage sadness. It is one thing when sadness is tied to a specific crisis, such as a divorce or a failing grade. Depression, by contrast, is vague, is slow moving, and it is only usually in retrospect that you recognize it for what it is. In the beginning, your teenager's grades may drift or even plummet. He may abruptly break up with someone he has been seeing for a long time or claim it is no big deal, or even, as Luke did, question the accuracy of the perception of a breakup. He doesn't seem to care enough even to fight with you on a curfew or a chore. He seems remote and affectless. He doesn't express grief at the right times (it seems to you anyway), and he doesn't laugh at the right times either. He doesn't ask to use the car. He gets angry about something that would ordinarily seem trivial. Overall, he appears to have locked the doors to himself and you have no idea where the keys are.

You search within for understanding and find yourself asking, in disbelief, Is my child depressed? In every magazine you pick up these days you notice articles on the subject of mood elevators and serotonin reuptake inhibitors and ponder whether or not you should schedule an appointment for your teenager with your family physician. Then again, maybe your child is just sad. Life is full of disappointments, right? Or is that precisely 100 percent wrong?

Now What?

Whenever your child speaks of self-harm, however, you have no alternative but to take those words at face value. The stakes are far too high to do otherwise.

For openers, glean all the information you can from all the sources that are available: friends, relatives, teachers, coaches. Above all, ask your teenager unambiguous questions and do not settle for ambiguous responses: Are you depressed? Have you been contemplating suicide? Sometimes parents or other adults who work with kids are afraid of asking such grave questions, as if raising the topic will somehow plant poisonous seeds that will instantly burgeon into a plan of self-destructive action. Of course, there's no guarantee that that won't happen. But we doubt it. What we can guarantee is that by asking the questions in such a clear way you are sending a direct message that you sense suffering, that you care, and that you want to understand and help.

Even today, mental illness and emotional turmoil carry a social taint, and appealing to psychological help may in some circles constitute a badge of shame. It is also sometimes considered stigmatizing to direct somebody to therapy. Help is available in many forms, ranging from counseling to medication, any of which often proves effective under the right circumstances. But first let's take a closer look at Luke's situation.

Is Luke Suicidal?

Luke is being as direct about his emotional state as many adolescents are capable of being. And if he has a strategy, it works—he does get everybody's earnest attention. He makes a seemingly wild gesture and makes frightening remarks to a teacher that certainly merit being taken very seriously. To tell from his talks with Mr. Hirsch, and later with his mother, many issues are pressing upon him, including his academic limitations (or his perceived limitations—he seems to be doing all right, after all), his flagging college aspirations (which also might be imaginary), his failed relationship with Pam, and his uncertain connections with peers (he implies that he has no friends). These are precisely the kinds of problems that instill distress in most teenagers, depression in a few, and thoughts of suicide in a very few. Most teenagers have passing thoughts of suicide. But once they give voice to these thoughts, they have entered another stage. Does it mean, in Luke's mind, that suicide is imminent or inevitable?

Generally, people who are considering suicide but are not yet resolved reach out to those around them. Some do this through a diary entry left open on the dining table, some through graffiti on a notebook cover, and some through a drawing or note directed at a teacher. Others reach out more ominously through a suicidal gesture, say, an overdose of pills adequate to cause illness but not enough to cause death, or slashing their wrists in a way that causes bleeding but does not sever an artery.

Luke's gesture certainly seems to be the proverbial cry for help. At the same time, it does not necessarily mean that Luke is suicidal. Experts differentiate levels of threat, from conceptualization to gesture to real attempts at suicide. Most teachers and most parents are not experts and should not try to be. But certainly intervention is called for here.

First, Mr. Hirsch intervenes when he calls Luke out of class to confront him with the note. He sees into and past Luke's sarcasm and anger to the underlying suffering. Then his mother intervenes, appearing at the school after having heard from Mr. Hirsch. All of these moves are crucial and will be felt that way by Luke. Of course, he is likely to consider them, at least at first, excessive, and he isn't going to be pleased with what feels like anybody interfering with his life. Frankly, that's not important right now.

What Luke mainly needs to know is that others are tuned in to him. They are hearing what he is not saying. What Mr. Hirsch and Luke's mother need to remember, however, is that their work has only begun. His isolation, if it goes unremarked by others, can have terrible consequences. Teenagers often take extreme stands, and it's hard to distinguish symbolic gesture from genuine threat. That's why we make interventions, to make these distinctions. We never take chances, including the chance that this will all blow over in time. It will not.

"Don't Tell Anybody"

The teacher, Mr. Hirsch, has inadvertently sailed into turbulent seas. This happens all the time to altruistic, caring teachers and their students who sense that they have found someone who will listen to them. Certainly, not all of these moments are as direct as this. But let's take a look at what is happening in this extreme situation and try to untangle some of the strands of meaning. Although Luke's example may be extreme, there are virtually no high schools that escape being the backdrop for such potentially serious and life-threatening occurrences.

The legal and moral obligations of a teacher in this drama are worth underscoring. A teacher who has information, or even a reasonable suspicion, as to a child's endangerment (self-inflicted or otherwise) has an absolute responsibility to report what he knows to the administration of the school (at a minimum) and, depending upon school practices and county or state requirement, to the local equivalent of the child protective services agency. A teacher's talk with the parents or even with the family doctor or therapist is not in and of itself adequate. The child's interests demand a dispassionate investigation of the circumstances that may possibly continue to threaten the child. In the broadest sense, the teacher may safely assume that no matter how much he knows, he does not know everything that may be relevant. For instance, what is the connection between the parents and the child's gesture? Are there home conditions that require looking into? (Many schools, fortunately, periodically walk through such problems and exigencies with faculty and staff, spelling out expectations and discussing as realistically as possible obligations, dilemmas, self-questionings, pitfalls, and assumptions.)

The problem here is that Luke is making an appeal to the teacher in a way that is liable to be misread and misinterpreted. He is insisting on loyalty and confidentiality, when he really desires exposure and assistance. What he says amounts to, "Keep this hot material between us," but what he means in effect is, "Help me go to others for help." But Mr. Hirsch has an obligation *not* to maintain confidentiality. Luke is tired of keeping this secret to himself, but the only way he can dispossess himself of its force and allure is to articulate it to somebody else. This somebody else is the perfect audience for his ambivalence, too, because Mr. Hirsch (Luke senses) is vulnerable to the appeal. The teacher in question here has to work through his own relationship with the student clearly and forthrightly so that he presents himself as being not quite at the center of the drama. He must see himself as aiding Luke in his responsibility to be the agent of his own fate. At the same time, he takes no chances when it comes to health and safety. He calls Luke's mother and he probably reaches out to colleagues and administrators at the school, and that's very wise.

Adolescence and Changing Perceptions of Depression and Distress

What makes depression in teenagers difficult to diagnose is that they are mercurial in their moods. Daily life for a teenager is full of challenge and stress. "The early adolescent is always 'on' before 'the imaginary audience,'" writes psychologist Miller Newton. "This involves microscopic examination of self. Most early teenagers, given the fact of physical awkwardness, as a result of disproportionate growth, find themselves wanting. This negative self-evaluation results in down feelings."[1] Clinicians, understandably, make a distinction between the normal distress of teenagers and depression. In practice this means that in moments of acute distress (being cut from the play, being rejected by a college, not being allowed to use the car for an important Saturday night) a fair number of teenagers will display some symptoms of depression.

So what is depression? Gerald D. Oster and Sarah H. Montgomery, authors of *Helping Your Depressed Teenager,* define it this way: "The experience of clinical depression . . . goes beyond normal mood swings. It encompasses an increase in the intensity and length of the everyday expression of emotions and occurs in combination with other physical and psychological symptoms," such as overtiredness, intense feelings of inadequacy and worthlessness, a loss of interest in life itself, restlessness, appetite changes, diminished concentration and decisionmaking, and obsessive thinking about death. And these behaviors and attitudes haunt a victim for weeks at least.[2] Like all definitions of psychological and emotional states, the terms are elusive if not relative, and therefore diagnosis is somewhat subjective and depends on the assessor's insight.

Not everyone who commits suicide is depressed, though people who are depressed are more vulnerable to harming themselves. Partly because suicide is so complicated and because depression is still viewed by many as a character flaw, suicide is a dirty secret in this country. Yet the fact is that

31,000 people committed suicide in 1997; by contrast, fewer than 19,000 were homicide victims. And since 1980 the suicide rate among children aged 10–14 has doubled (Office of the Surgeon General and National Center of Health Statistics).[3] It comes as no shock to learn, then, that the use of antidepressant medicine by teenagers has soared; for instance, over 600,000 children and adolescents have been prescribed Prozac, Paxil, or Zoloft. Some clinical psychologists worry that many teenagers are being medicated for *being* teenagers. Others counter that because rates of depression and suicide for teenagers are rising and approaching rates for adults, they deserve psychopharmalogical treatment when necessary. "We don't want to leave these kids as therapeutic orphans," said one expert from the National Institute of Mental Health.[4] Almost universally, however, clinicians are going to insist on psychotherapy prior to, or in concert with, medication. Like many adults, many teenagers, when they are denied access to therapy or medication, will self-medicate with drugs or alcohol: many substance abusers mask their depression. When teenagers use drugs and alcohol, they may indeed be experimenting; but some are sending a signal that they are depressed and need treatment.

Beyond this, research has begun to erode popular myths about the connection between gender, depression, and suicide. Boys and girls are equally at risk, and boys and girls may conceivably harm themselves even when not depressed. "Adolescence is a time when development and culture put enormous stress on girls," writes Mary Pipher in *Reviving Ophelia*. "So many things are happening at once that it's hard to label and sort experiences into neat little boxes. And there are many casualties. For example, a girl who is suffering from a mild case of adolescent misery may try to kill herself, not because her life as a totality is so painful, but because she is impulsive, reactive and unable to put small setbacks in perspective."[5] At the same time, boys are also subjected to comparably devastating cultural pressures that may contribute to self-harm (see, for instance, *Real Boys*, *Raising Cain*, and *Lost Boys*). Although girls are more likely to articulate their depression and to threaten suicide, boys are statistically much more likely, because of their action orientation as well as their access to and familiarity with firearms, to carry out a suicide attempt.

Some myths about adolescence can confuse and hinder us. One such myth fittingly under siege these days holds that adolescence is, by definition, a time of unceasing trauma and unrelieved tumult. These notions of teenage "storm and stress," proceeding from the contributions of psychologists G. Stanley Hall, Anna Freud, and to some degree Erik Erikson, have taken hold in the popular imagination. But there are other views of teenage development. For instance, Lynn Ponton, author of *The Romance of Risk*, takes exception to the "storm and stress" theory, positing that teenagers are simply engaged in the formative developmental stage of risk taking: "It is during adolescence that young people experiment with many aspects of life, taking on new challenges, testing out how things fit together, and using this process to define and shape both their identities and their knowledge of the world. . . . Their struggle is not all adolescent rebellion, then, but a more complicated and fascinating process."[6]

If swallowed whole, the rebellious youth myth can produce toxic effects by blinding us to the realities of unique, individual teenagers—our own children. That is, if we are counting on kids' predictably acting out and doing crazy things, we may easily miss the more disturbing manifestations of their personal suffering. If Luke's mother, for instance, had explained away his note as being something merely bizarre, as "typical" teenager's histrionics, she could have missed the opportunity to intervene and make a positive difference at a crucial time.

What Is Counseling?

Luke could benefit from, at a minimum, short-term psychological counseling. Such counseling is different from talking with members of the family or other caring adults, or even peers.

There are as many approaches to counseling as there are available conceptions of human being—and for the same reasons, too. Whatever the mode of therapy—cognitive, psychodynamic, behavioralistic, individual, family, systems, and so on—the bottom line is that the counselor must be honest, empathetic, intelligent, and courageous. Most important, the counselor must be effective with your teenager. That is, he or she must quickly develop rapport and trust. Most kids will approach the first session with reluctance bordering on indifference if not defiance, but when counseling is working well these resistances diminish. They will value the safety and support of this confidential relationship. For in this setting teenagers are free to explore secrets, feelings, wishes, sufferings, desires, hopes, and fears. Of course, they do something like this elsewhere in their lives, with friends and family, but it is very different in counseling. While they may deal with parental conflicts in one place of their lives, their sexual frustrations in another, and their existential dilemmas in yet another, in counseling all of these issues are conceivably on the table all the time and in toto. They do not have to protect their father from unpleasant revelations, for instance, or their best friend from disappointment. They are free, in other words, to confront the entirety of their lives with somebody who is able to witness sometimes messy insights precisely by virtue of *not* being a friend or a parent.

Counseling does not work best to solve specific problems. Instead, counseling focuses on what in this person helped bring about particular problems. For instance, doing poorly in school is not approached in counseling with study guides or test-taking advice. Rather, the approach is to discern what the teenager fears by working hard (encumbering expectations, social reprisal, facing limitations), and, as odd as it may sound, what the payoff is for doing poorly in school (increased attention of parents, the avoidance of more pressing problems, deferring personal responsibility). At the same time, the counselor works with the teenager to help him recognize, develop, affirm, and enhance his psychological and emotional resources. Because this quest is neither linear nor straightforward, this investigation takes time, not necessarily years but usually more than a few hours.

The beauty of counseling with teenagers is that, because their worlds are changing so rapidly and dramatically, once they trust the counselor, they are able to confront, without prejudice or constraint, many of the ideas and attitudes you have been fostering since they were children. We are not suggesting that counseling is the ultimate context for growing up, but it is one place where astonishing leaps toward self-discovery routinely take place. In the presence of a counselor, teenagers have the opportunity, independent of you, to affirm—and integrate—these values and beliefs for themselves and on their own behalf. When this happens, problem solving is once again appropriate and effective. Why? Because they cannot understand their problems until they better understand themselves in all their incarnations, as students, as friends, as sons and daughters, as sisters and brothers, as citizens, as males and females, as human beings.

Will counseling eliminate distress in your teenager's life? That is hard to say, but it will provide a sense of meaning and purpose to his struggles. And meaningfulness and purposefulness go a long way in anybody's life, especially a teenager's.

If Luke goes into counseling, does his mother no longer need to speak with him about the hard issues in his life? Absolutely not. Does Mr. Hirsch now forget what transpired and treat him like every other student? No. What is different during counseling, and after, is that Luke will likely be able to have more substantive conversations about his suffering. In addition, he will have a more comprehensive picture of his life and a richer, more complex vocabulary to articulate his concerns and needs. His rage, his notes, and his distancing strategies will probably be replaced by self-scrutiny, self-respect, and honest talk. That is, counseling works in conjunction with conversations with his mother and teacher. You as a parent never hand off your responsibility to a counselor or anybody else.

Into and Out of the Woods

Even if Luke opens up to his mother, engages in dialogue with a counselor, and begins to see himself more clearly, his mother will probably indulge herself from time to time in a fantasy that she can somehow magically take away all his distress so that he can be the happy little boy she remembers him to be. What parent wouldn't wish such a sweet conclusion?

At the same time, the reality is that a certain amount of distress is inevitable in a teenager's life. That's how Luke's mother grew up, and that's how we all grow up. Nonetheless, she herself is going to come close, sometimes, to giving in to her own feelings of helplessness and guilt.

Parents of teenagers who are troubled need to acknowledge their feelings of helplessness and their anxieties, but they cannot afford to be immobilized by them. There is much they can do to help their children. Pointed conversation. Clear direction. Time and support. Reaching out to others for information and help. And yes, counseling, perhaps even family sessions.

Perhaps most important, parents need to take care of themselves. They need outlets and support for their own distress inspired by their teenagers' plight. When your teenager is distressed, you must be able to tap the full depth and breadth of your intelligence, imagination, and intuition. If you do not take care of yourself, you are likely to confuse the voice of fear with the voice of intuition. Now more than ever, your teenagers need to sense your clear-eyed, solid presence in their lives. That can make all the difference for you and for them. In other words, there's quite a bit for you to do. What you are modeling here is that you yourself are able to withstand your own distress (something your teenager is always registering), and that is one message that can save his life.

16

Romance and the Classroom

Tonight I can write the saddest lines.

—Pablo Neruda,
Twenty Love Poems (trans. W. S. Merwin)

After high school in America, everything's posthumous.

Joyce Carol Oates, Broke Heart Blues

What Stars Are For

Every year the Environmental History class goes on a week-long field trip. They climb sheer walls, analyze amazing rock formations, swim in crystal-clear water holes, revel in the spectacle of dazzling flora and wildlife. It is the perfect experiential culmination to a semester of book- and computer-based learning in the classroom. But it's much more than that. The students, all seniors, regard the late-spring journey as a kind of rite of passage, and the whole school culture celebrates the tradition. It is one of the most sought-after electives, and the instructor is one of the most popular, respected members of the faculty. After returning, the class usually presents in assembly a slide show of breathtaking sights, and the student body listens to testimonials from the participants. One of the powerful (unofficial) subtexts of the experience is that during the field trip these seniors begin to grow conscious that their four years together are about to eclipse. As they bond, their emotions are bittersweet and intense, disorienting but paradoxically familiar, too.

It was the last night before going home. After cooking dinner over the campfire, the class and the teacher, along with two other faculty chaperones, sang songs and told jokes and spread rumors until late. Gradually, one by one, the students and faculty chaperones drifted to their tents, sleeping bags, and well-earned rest. One student, Verna, and her teacher, Justin, stayed and tended to the fire. There were pieces of kindling and a few logs between them and the fire.

The stars out here, far away from the city lights, were transcendently glorious, and the teacher identified the constellations.

"See, there's the Little Dipper. And Perseus. And Capella. And the North Star."

"God, you're right! I never saw the constellations so clearly before, at least outside of books."

He named a few other constellations. "It's amazing what's right in front of our eyes, when we get away from our old frame of reference and take a good look, isn't it?"

"Not to mention the cloud cover, the smog, and the bright lights the big city . . . "

There was a long moment of silence that was almost uncomfortable. Verna seemed to be searching for words. There seemed to be something on her mind. Verna had had a tough senior year. She was tanking on her classes. Her board scores were good, but her grades were only so-so, including her grades in this class. She thought she was trying, she believed she was working, but somehow it never paid off for her. Sometimes, when she was honest with herself, she would admit that she was often just distracted in class, that other more urgent things consumed her attention.

Justin felt a desire to fill in the silence. "Anyway, that's why I like this class so much. Maybe that's why I like teaching, period." Science was not solely an academic subject for him, he went on, not merely a set of facts to be absorbed. It was a way of thinking about the natural world. "Reality, the partial explainability of reality, that's the miracle. The existence of stars is as amazing as anything we can make up, anything we dream."

"You're the best," she testified. "You know, when I hear you talk like that, I understand my life in a whole new way."

Then conversation drifted to school, and after that to her college plans. The other chaperones were in their tents, and Justin felt a tug to join them.

"I haven't made up my mind yet where I should go to college, actually. What do you think?"

Verna told him where she had been accepted, and to him they all sounded splendid. He said that his wife had gone to one of the colleges she mentioned and that he had attended another. "I'd trust your own intuition, but I don't think you can go far wrong with any of them."

"The problem is, I'm not sure I trust my intuition about anything these days. I'm just not sure about much. People seem so different when they are getting ready to take off to college or wherever."

"It's hard to leave your friends. It's easy to lose sight of the big picture. It's a sad time, a hard time, leaving school, but it's exhilarating, too. Your real friends will stay your friends, trust me. I still have my good friends from high school."

"I'm going to miss school, I hate to admit. It even sounds so cheesy to me because I never much liked school. A few classes, one or two teachers—like you, Justin—that's what I'll remember."

That last comment flared up suddenly like a distant meteoric disturbance and Justin watched it tail away.

"You'd be weird if you didn't feel a little sad leaving school." To him, that seemed like the right thing to say under the circumstances, whatever these circumstances were.

"The closer I get to leaving the more I miss the school, my friends, the teachers. Even though I want to get out of this place, I'm going to miss a few people a lot, like you."

"We can stay in touch." Immediately he flinched, and he wondered if he had been careless and sent an unintended signal.

"Really? You mean you wouldn't mind if I wrote you sometimes?"

There seemed to be no turning back now, though he didn't want her to misunderstand. "Of course not. Why, I'd be disappointed if I didn't hear from you. I stay in touch with my students all the time. E-mail's great for that."

"Do you want to be friends with me—after high school?"

Wait a second, was that what they were, *friends*? When he used the term and when she used the term, did they mean the same thing? Why was he feeling so uncomfortable? He hoped she understood he was first and foremost her teacher. He also hoped this would be the last time they would talk in this way about their relationship ever again.

Verna reached for a log at the moment he leaned forward to do the same, and her hand brushed his arm. She didn't pull back, and she gazed into the fire and said nothing. To Verna, it felt like destiny. To Justin, it was a sign it was getting too late.

"I think we should turn in," he stammered.

"You're right, Justin." She made no move to go.

"Morning is right around the corner." Did he just need to say something—anything?

"I feel like watching our fire for a while," she whispered, her voice drifting like smoke. She threw on another log and watched the sparks fly. "Sweet dreams."

In eighteen hours, he thought, they would be driving back, back to home, back to school. These were the places they knew from before, or these were the places they thought they used to know. Mostly, these were the places he needed to keep in their place.

Verna's Conversation with the Senior Class Dean

—Remember me?

—Let me think. Verna, right? Didn't you used to be a senior here?

—Yeah, right. Twelve more days, and I am outta here.

—Congratulations. Happy about that?

—Let's see, *happy*. Excited, scared, confused, but *happy*? I don't think so.

—Well, in that case, you sound pretty healthy to me.

—I *knew* you'd say that!

—It's still true. Now, want to fill me in on some of the details?

—Oh, you mean like life at home, relationships with my excellent peer group, college plans, disappointments in love, that sort of stuff?

—I've got a few minutes, if you do.

—I really don't know what I'm doing here. You and I haven't talked, since, when was it? Like, couple of months ago? When I skipped class with Madison that time she was bummed out?

—That long, really? Sit down. How are things going?

—God, it shows, doesn't it? I knew it was obvious. It hurts a little, but I'm not sure I can say what or how and why it's that way or any other way. I don't think I know anything for sure anymore. Only just don't tell me I sound perfectly healthy either. Thing is, not so long ago I used to know everything for sure. I go back and forth. Sometimes I understand my family.

Sometimes I'm like, who are these people in the kitchen in their funny slippers? OK, I know I hurt my parents when all I want to do is go out with my friends, but I don't know what to do about it. Sometimes I know what I want in my life, sometimes it seems so pointless. Sometimes I just feel all these feelings. And the only thing I want is to speed up everything to make it go by faster, so I don't have to think about anything too closely, and so if I do that, maybe it'll be better. Know what I'm saying?

—Not yet.

—Good, finally we're on the same page.

—Very funny. So. I heard the field trip was great. How was it for you?

—It was good. It's always fun to get away for a while, especially with that class. It's all seniors, and besides, Justin is my favorite teacher.

—Does sound great.

—Yeah, it was really cool. Best part was that Justin and the other teachers treated us more like adults, which when you get right down to it, is true. I mean, in less than a month we graduate so it's not like we'll be students for the rest of our lives.

—Are we still talking about Environmental History?

—Everything I say is confidential, right?

—As long as there's nothing involving abuse or intent to harm, it's confidential.

—I know all that. Everything else, though, confidential?

—Right.

—I really don't want to lose touch with Justin. He's such a wonderful man.

—He is a first-rate teacher and a terrific person, I agree with you. But what do you mean, you don't want to lose touch with him and why the sudden concern about confidentiality?

—I think I really might be in love with him is what I mean.

—You think you're in love with Justin?

—Yeah, I think I might be.

—OK, slow down now. What makes you think that you're in love with him?

—It's just that I feel so good when I'm with him. Everything makes so much sense all of a sudden.

—Let me see. Are you the same person who said she didn't know anything for sure anymore?

—Amazing, ain't it?

—A little too amazing, if you ask me.

—I'm telling you I'm in love, and you're going to be a downer now?

—With all that's going on for you now, it'd be easy to be confused.

—Maybe. But I don't think so.

—OK. Let me ask this another way. Is it Justin you're in love with, or is it the way you feel about yourself when you're thinking about Justin?

—I don't need any trick questions. They're the same thing anyway, aren't they?

—Or are you clear about your whole life because you feel you are in love?

—Shit, why are you doing this to me now? I wish for once that somebody could understand me.

Notes Home

Freedom or Flight?

At the end of high school, when teenagers are simultaneously moving forward into the future and reaching back into the past for meaning and reassurance, they are prone to rethink and occasionally misinterpret all types of relationships. Their focus at such times is more self-centered than other-centered, which leaves plenty of room for illusion, not to mention errors in judgment and perception.

Adolescence is a time of romance, but teenage romance takes many forms, not all of them necessarily, or totally, erotic or sexual. No wonder life in the senior year can feel almost unbearably sad, unbelievably sweet, sometimes during the same class period or shopping spree.

Teenagers on the verge of graduation fluctuate between the antithetical, if not paradoxical, feelings that they are being both dismissed and liberated. Giving in to one emotion, they feel betrayal and disappointment; giving in to the other, elation, expectation, and excitement. Partly as a result of their ambivalence over this inevitable event, many seemingly ordinary interactions with second-semester seniors as graduation looms are double- and triple-edged. They can't wait to get away from the place (and the people) they have outgrown. But before they do, they need to know where they stand with friends, family, teachers, and themselves. They want to know that they have in some important way marked the people with whom they have shared the last four years—and they would like to know exactly how.

When it comes to their relationships with adults, especially favored ones, teenagers have an acute need for definition and, if possible, assurances about the future. Are these adults sending them packing along with everybody else, or are they prepared to accompany them, figuratively speaking, into the next stage of life? Specifically, can they come back and visit? Can they write? Can they call? Are they more than student and teacher? Are they friends? Are they more than friends? In other words, right up until the last moment, and even beyond, they look for adults to set and defend the limits.

The issues that are in play in this narrative are plentiful and charged, so let us concentrate on two urgent ones: romance and leaving school. Overnight field trip—a moment of freedom and experimentation. The end of the senior year—everything is saturated with mysterious meaning and deep implication. The relationship between an adult and a teenager—it seems to be shifting.

Teachers and Students

Of course, the romance that is possible between a teacher of either sex and a student of either sex is a theme we all recognize and acknowledge, often unwillingly if not begrudgingly, always self-consciously. The schoolboy or schoolgirl infatuation with a teacher is, when recalled in its seemingly least muddled form, the inspiration of blushes and jokes and provides some adults with those sweetest, most idealized memories of school, of growing up. As we can hardly fail to notice in these tabloid and made-for-TV-movie days, however, often such innocent nostalgia is transmuted into the dark material of litigation, criminal prosecution, pedophilia, and psychopathology. It's deeply revealing somehow that both the figure of Lolita and the image of the predatory adult have assumed such transcendent prominence in our popular culture. It's also no accident that children and teenagers have never stood (according to every statistical barometer) in greater jeopardy of being harmed by an adult authority figure. (Such data, though, may merely reflect our modern interest and capacity for labeling and recording more accurately what has been their perennial victimization.) In short, the theme of illicit romance between teacher and student arrests our imagination because it titillates and frightens us in equal measure.

Relationships, Entanglements, Confusions, Misreadings, and Other Signs of Growing Up

In this story we observe a real, substantive connection between Verna and Justin, each bringing to the relationship powerful and complicated needs, desires, hopes, and experiences. Are all of their emotions and fantasies clean, rational, and manageable? Hardly. Anyone who has ever walked by a group of teenagers knows well that they are swimming in an ocean of hormones and passions. So it would be naive to gloss over the existence or misgauge the power of emotional entanglements between teachers and students, the affection they have for each other, the attraction. But the question that matters between Justin and Verna, as the emotional tides rise, is, Who is responsible here? That is, who is finally answerable for the expression of their feelings? Though there's plenty of room for interesting debate on the topic of student–teacher relations, there's no room for disagreement in a community that supports (and therefore protects) adolescents in their experiential searches. The adult is the one accountable, and the teenager (even the most mature ones) must be safeguarded.

In every school students somehow identify a few stars in the faculty. There is no accounting for how this rough sorting works in each school culture, but we all know that it does. However, one consistent pattern emerges everywhere: not every popular teacher is an excellent one, but every excellent teacher has a loyal following of students and colleagues. To an outsider it may appear that teenagers are helplessly manipulated, drawn to the flamboyant, superficially attractive teachers, but this is not so. Over the course of time, if the teacher is flash and no substance teenagers will see through the glare. When students identify an excellent teacher, or a good teacher, their judgment is (perhaps contrary to popular belief) normally unerring. Students love the teacher who respects them enough to challenge them academically, who brings to class a passion for and a commitment to not only the subject but teenagers as well. And this happens no matter how square or hip, no matter how eccentric or conventional, no matter what sort of fashions they wear or cars they drive or sports they excel in, no matter how young or old the teachers may be.

Justin, then, is probably a charismatic teacher, and may even be excellent. Of course students are drawn to him. How boring schools would be (not to mention life itself) if we did not respond to such a visceral appeal. In this narrative, however, the teacher is beginning to feel insecure about his long-standing boundaries with this student. At first, he thought he was talking about constellations during an exhilarating school-sponsored field trip. What he begins to grasp, almost one second too late, is that he is having an intimate conversation with a student who is in—to invoke an old-fashioned term—the throes of a crush. And the chance exists that Justin is on some level drawn to Verna as well. Or, at the very least, he may be flattered by her attention and interest. And that's every bit as dangerous—for both of them. These feelings are strong, perhaps on the part of both of them, but in and of themselves they are ultimately irrelevant: what matters is what each of these individuals, especially the adult, does with these feelings.

Teenagers Count on Adults' Being Adults Because Teenagers are Not

When adults allow their relationships with teenagers to be eroticized, or sexualized, they have crossed a moral line that can never be uncrossed, and disaster awaits everyone involved. True, principled adults who are also charismatic may unintentionally inspire ideas of romance in their students. Most of a teenager's romantic conceptions glide effortlessly into sexualizable ones, after all. But adults have to carry and manage honestly all the ambiguities, including their own; that is, it is altogether possible that Verna could misread the signal of Justin's interest in her friendship. Justin may indeed mean to promote a friendship, but Verna may construe that to be a stepping-stone, an implicit invitation, to what is presumably a more serious (that is, a sexual) relationship. Can this teenager reveal herself in such a vulnerable way and not be scarred? Yes. Can the teacher respond by both affirming his boundaries and not dismissing her or her feelings? Yes.

Romance and Sex: There's a Difference

For at the same time—and this is tricky—a certain kind of romance does have a legitimate place in education. Though this is a difficult proposition to elucidate, education *is* itself a romance—the romance of learning, of growing, of becoming. Romance does not mean or imply sex. Teenagers are expanding emotionally and are thrilling to the world within and the world without, all of which can make high school such an exhilarating, beautiful, intense experience. Of course, they may identify (out of inexperience) that blossoming within themselves with the person who appears to be the agent of inspiration, and as a result they romanticize their teacher. Ethical, well-balanced adults understand this transferring process and do not cultivate the teenager's illusions; instead, they redirect that romance into a passion enkindling the student's own learning and self-discovery. This is always a conscious decision and it is, finally, that which distinguishes excellent, principled teachers.

Some adults adopt measures in their dealings with teenagers that make it less likely for teenagers to misconstrue their intentions—no private conferences, no hugging, no references to a personal life, and so on. This may be, for the individual teacher, the appropriate demeanor, and obviously there's nothing intrinsically wrong with it. But as a matter of fact such closed doors may tantalize a teenager even more or may overdetermine the teacher's connection to the student. There are huggers who do not have a flirtatious bone in their bodies, and there are remote figures in the classroom who have the manipulative, uncanny power to insinuate themselves into the dreams of their students.

Teenagers and adults themselves ultimately grasp any inappropriateness when they question themselves. If there exists a question in their own minds as to whether or not what they are doing may be flirtatious—it almost certainly is.

Teenagers Trust the Adult to Set Boundaries

Justin eventually insists on maintaining a boundary. Could Verna misinterpret his final signal and press a romantic interest in him? Of course, and some teenagers certainly would. But actually, that prospect seems unlikely in her case, because, tellingly, her question *Do you want to be friends with me—after high school?* is also her subtle insistence upon the maintenance of boundaries with which she herself is comfortable. Will she test these boundaries again? Very likely, and deep down, she hopes Justin maintains them, since this would allow her to address the inner turmoil occasioned by her imminent graduation.

Seniors are simultaneously reaching forward into the future and backward into the past. Most eagerly anticipate the end of high school and fantasize their second semester as one of nonstop fun and celebration with all their friends, a time of sanctioned irresponsibility. However, they are disappointed when the carnival never shows. Instead, second semester is often a somber phase in their lives, shadowed with dark, conflicting recollections and reflections. First, they are leaving behind an established identity in high school for the unknown world of college or work. In school they are secure enough with who they are, which is different from feeling they have resolved all their identity questions. People know what to expect from them and they know how to respond. This is both safe and frustrating. Safe in that it is easy to blend in; frustrating in that it is difficult to change in this setting. Second, friendships are changing as some people pull away while others draw closer, all this happening against the unknown social backdrop of their next stage of life. Everybody is furiously assessing and desperately solidifying relationships. They are also creating memories about which they can reminisce in the future.

In particular, second-semester seniors are looking for recognition and approval from the adults who have shaped their adolescence. For them, second semester is as much about these relationships as it is the class work. The preferred way to test these relationships is to push the boundaries, to make adults define the parameters—again and again. This is what senior pranks are all about: bonding with one another through an eye-grabbing act that brings everyone closer together for having broken the rules. (This prank becomes class lore and is one of the first items of discussion at every gathering of classmates in future years.) This is also when we see amazing individual transformations. The National Merit semifinalist who never did anything to get noticed by the dean of students one day decides to streak across campus. The jock now spends every afternoon tutoring middle school kids. Teenagers want to make a mark on their community. They want to take a flyer. In short, they now want to feel that they are grown-up—that they are adults. No wonder a teenage crush in this frame of mind (especially at the end of a long school year that has eroded everyone's boundaries) can imaginatively transform into the possibility of a sexual relationship with an adult. All this is to say that for an adult this is a time to be vigilant, a time to take special care for teenagers.

Speaking of time, second-semester senior time is very fluid. Past, present, and future—everything overlaps, and it almost becomes possible for teenagers to move into the future, relive the past, and hunker down into the present, all in the same instant. That's why deadlines are enigmas, why curfews become wishful, why first period never ends, and why graduation will never ever arrive.

Could It Be . . . Senior Year Is Overrated?

By the springtime of their senior year teenagers, even as they are furiously celebrating, grieve more than they may let on. The year began with high hopes and seemingly limitless possibilities. The school put on an assembly just for them and everybody looked to them for leadership. They would live up to the billing; they would put it all together. They would win the championship this year or get an A in Physics or be admitted to the college of their dreams.

Maybe they do win all the laurels, and maybe they get the grade and the fat envelope in the April mail. Amazingly, though, it does not seem enough. Somehow, anyway, the time seems laden with unrealizable expectations and vaguely lost opportunities. For what? It would be hard to say. The seasons, the days go painfully, tortuously, uneventfully by, and they suddenly grasp, to their sorrow and bitterness, that senior year is—overrated. They wonder who told them it was supposed to be otherwise, and they wonder if they were deceived by some conspiracy. They look to blame somebody. Teachers, who insist they do their work in order to pass their classes, are a worthy target. So are parents, who suddenly seem to want their teenagers' social life to revolve around the family. And so are old friends who have changed so much, for somehow they have let them down as well.

In the Shifting World of Being a Senior, Teenagers Count on Their Parents More Than They Can or Will Say

As parents, resolve not to become one more problem for them to deal with. If your relationship has been strong, they will overlook you during this time. Not out of disregard, quite the opposite; because they can count on your love and support, they can take you for granted during this overwhelming onslaught of mixed-up feelings, convoluted thoughts, fears, and fantasies. Give them quiet space and plenty of support, both verbal and nonverbal. Tell them you love them and are proud of them, and do this often. Take advantage of the chances they give you. For example, when they regress and want to stay home with a very mild case of the flu, take the day off, if you can, and pamper them anyway. If it helps, think of your presence as an early graduation gift. Your being there with them will mean as much as anything you say. And it will mean more than they can possibly tell you.

Another Conversation with the Class Dean

It's late August and Verna is getting packed for college when she runs into her class dean at the drug store, where Verna is doing some last-minute shopping. They haven't seen each other since commencement day.

—Emily, is that you? I never knew teachers shopped in drug stores.

—Amazing, isn't it? Usually I just send my butler, but he's got the day off.

—I think that was the first time I called you by your first name. Feels kind of weird.

—It's OK. I like my name, so feel free. How are you doing these days? Ready for college?

—*I* am. My parents? They're another story. They're stressing about everything. You'd think after high school they'd cut themselves a little break and relax.

—If I know you, Verna, you'll help them get through.

—OK, anyway I wanted to let you know what happened—about, well, you know who I'm talking about. I appreciate what you said to me that day when I was going off about him. I'm sorry if I was a little mean to you.

—So what happened?

—He and I talked.

—Really? You and Justin?

—Yeah. The day before graduation. I've never seen him nervous like that, but he was real clear. And he was nice about it, too. Even said he was flattered. Anyway, I understood and didn't make him give me the whole "I'm a teacher and you're a student" speech.

—Glad you two talked like that.

—Me too. Guess it was just one of those crazy ideas you get when you have to graduate. Hey, Emily, how are you going to get along without me next year?

—We'll struggle, but just like your parents, we'll manage.

17

Death and Rebirth

After great pain, a formal feeling comes—
The Nerves sit ceremonious, like Tombs—

> —EMILY DICKINSON, 431

I study myself more than any other subject. That is my meta-physics, that is my physics.

> —MONTAIGNE, "OF EXPERIENCE" (TRANS. DONALD FRAME)

Melvin's Conversation with the Counselor

This conversation took place years ago while Melvin was still in high school, shortly after his mother's death. He was in the counselor's office at the prompting of his vice principal.

—Very sorry to hear about your mom, Melvin.
—Yeah, thanks. Mrs. Scott told me to come by.
—I know, she said it would be helpful for us to talk.
—About what?
—About your mom, about your family, about school, about you.
—Maybe.
—I've got time right now.

—Guess I'm not all that sure it would do any good. My mom'll still be gone, no matter how much we talk, right?

—You're right, but that's not the reason we'd talk.

—So what would be the reason?

—As I said, it would be helpful. You've been through a lot and there's a lot more to go through still.

—I know that.

—Are you talking to anybody? Your dad? Your friends? Anybody at school?

—Dad's in his own world. They were together a long time.

—Friends?

—At first. But what can anybody say?

—Maybe they can listen.

—I'm talked out, nothing personal. I don't know that there is any help from you, from anybody, I could use now. Would you tell Mrs. Scott I came by?

—Of course I will. If something ever comes up, I'm here everyday.

—Me too, for another year and a half.

Enormous Changes at the Last Minute

Like all teachers, on the tough days I feel like a spectator of my students' lives. This is when I see that what they are doing (or not doing) is bad news. I notice distress signals flying everywhere. I watch that drifting look in their eyes and that cloud of sadness and anger rolling behind them wherever they go. For some reason, these are usually my favorite students, the ones I most want to speak to, the very ones I took up teaching for. The problem is, I want to *say* something, *do* something before they have made some unrectifiable mistake, before they have reached the point of no return. Only I can't figure out what. It's frustrating, like one of those dreams you can't dream your way out of. You keep clawing away at unconsciousness, and you wake up exhausted.

It's funny how your students can sometimes come into focus when you're off to the side or observing them from the distance. It's called perspective, I suppose. I'm thinking of one particular student. I am thinking about the tragedy that took place in his life and his unforgettable response to it, and what I learned about him—and from him.

A little over two years ago, in the middle of his junior year, Melvin's mother died. Her death was totally unexpected. At first, as anyone would expect, he was crushed. I feared he was going to pack it all in at school. Fortunately, though, he learned to open up and eventually he was able to talk to people he trusted, his friends and a few adults. His openness helped him deal with his loss—to the extent that anybody can ever be said to deal with a tragedy of this magnitude.

Yesterday Melvin came back to campus for a visit. It was good to see him, and I could tell he was doing all right. We were talking about his high school days, and I brought up in passing his puzzling academic career. He had changed in all sorts of ways during those last two years, but here's the bizarre part. Before his mom's death he was an average student. Then, and this always seemed telling to me, afterward he became a truly distinguished student, never receiving a final grade lower than an A. Who would have counted on that?

"Academic career?" He laughed. "You call that a career? That's a pretty fancy term for what I did in high school. First I couldn't get off the bench and then I got so hot they couldn't drag me off the court."

His forehead knotted up and he got a faraway look in his eyes. He was taking a long, long time choosing his words. He was visibly struggling. I offered to take him off the hook, telling him it was OK if he couldn't. But he shrugged me off.

"You know, to this day I guess I don't really understand. I just know that right after my mom died, doing well in school became the thing I needed to do. All of a sudden, school was important. Up until then I really couldn't be bothered. I had better things to do—whatever they were. But anyway, school had always been important to my mom and I guess it's almost like when she died she sort of passed that desire on to me. Maybe one of us had to keep the idea going. Or maybe I found a way to keep her spirit alive. Or maybe I was kind of doing it for her."

Experiencing this tragedy seemed to somehow draw him closer to his mother. Which struck me as strange and as beautiful enough to be true. I asked when it was that he had put all this together.

"Just this second, when you asked me." An apparition of a smile flashed across his face and then vanished. We both looked away, keeping silent, hoping somebody would track down a voice.

Those friends of mine who don't teach—I know they wonder. They don't come right out and ask me why I'm not doing something else with my life, but I can tell. Teaching's all right to do for a while, they imply, but isn't it about time I get over it already, go on to something more redeeming and worthwhile? They don't always mean money, but you can tell money is part of the equation. If they did ask why, though, I would point to a moment like this, with Melvin, when I find myself in deep, involved in mysteries of life and death and growing up, when I learn more than I can ever say. Now that I think about it, maybe that's how come these days most of my friends turn out to be teachers.

You know, in a way, Melvin's disclosure that he had just put it together surprised me even more than all the grades he had racked up. It made me want to know more about what he had gone through, now that he had gained a little distance. I asked him if he could say what had been helpful to him during that time.

"Definitely just talking to people helped a lot, especially in the beginning. But there is only so much talk you can do. What made a huge difference was the little things people did: friends who sent me cards, people who acknowledged the anniversary of her death, and especially people who brought food to our house!" Then after a moment he added, "Something else that helped a lot was that people kept the same expectations for me. I didn't want anyone feeling sorry for me—or going easy on me."

I wanted to know some more.

"Well, there was this one teacher who told me I didn't have to worry about the next couple of papers. All I had to do was talk to her about the books and she would give me my regular grade. Normally you would think I would be all grateful and like, 'Gee, thanks a lot!' But it had the opposite effect. I got angry with her and told her that there was nothing wrong with me and that I didn't need her pity. Looking back, I see her intentions were good, and I might have hurt her feelings. One day—who knows—maybe I might try to apologize to her."

Instantly we both realized that he probably wouldn't do this, at least not this time around. Still, here's an old lesson I keep relearning about schools, how kids at various times in their lives need various types of adults. Sometimes they need the warm and fuzzy ones who help them express themselves and hold their hands through an ordeal, but other times they need adults who care about them at a little distance, who give them privacy.

"So cutting you slack was the last thing you needed." My statement must have come out as a kind of question.

"Weird, huh? The best way to help was to let me go about my business and not assume I was weak because my mother died."

My eyes welled up and his did, too. He went on: "I really valued the way you treated me afterward. You never went easy on me in class, and you always listened outside of class. You know, I bet sometimes it wasn't so easy for you, either. Hey, I thought I just came here to say hi. I think I should be saying thanks. Give me a second, and I will."

He was right; it hadn't been easy for me to witness a good kid grieving. But that was my chance to thank him, and I did. I wanted Melvin to hear from me that he wasn't the only one who had been changed.

Notes Home

No Teenager Is Prepared for a Death in the Family

Teenagers usually take years and years to come to terms with family or personal catastrophes—disasters such as a fire or an earthquake, disease, divorce, job loss. Perhaps nothing rivals the death of a loved one, however, especially the death of a parent. Most surviving teenagers desperately struggle just to keep their heads above water in school. Some compensate madly. Some throw it all away. Others hear a call to faith, still others give in to cynicism. The only universal is this: the teenager's world is turned upside down and his or her life is never the same.

Death in a family uproots all the markers by which we organize and delineate what we consciously know of our life, especially when it comes about so dramatically, without warning. No teenager is prepared to find his own way in his disorientation, no matter how mature and experienced he may be. After a while, he will eventually feel a well-intentioned pressure from every corner in his world to relocate his previous life, even as he finds himself frozen in space and time. He is surrounded by people—family, friends, teachers, coaches—who may truly care about him but find it agonizing to stand alongside him in his suffering. These are people who may try to distract him from his pain, encourage him to move forward, or advance all sorts of compensatory strategies. None of this will prove very effective, except possibly in part, and then only fitfully and unsatisfyingly. The grief, the guilt, and the anger surrounding his mother's death will periodically overwhelm and dizzy him.

Driving Without a Map:
Following a Teenager's Lead

When a teenager returns to school after a death in the family everything may feel foreign, threatening, or pointless to him. Alert, sensitive adults will not fail to catch this. At the same time, no adult, no matter how well-meaning or how close to the teenager before the tragedy, can do anything to assuage the grief of one who has suffered such a shock. This recognition of limitations goes against the grain of those who work with teenagers. Didn't they respond to a calling to know, and, yes, even to mend kids who are torn by tragedy, by disappointment, by loss, by whatever crises befall them? What may guide adults working with somebody like Melvin in extreme circumstances? Among other things, they must remember to follow the teenager's lead.

Because a parent's death is the most disruptive of events, the teenager's world has irrevocably changed, and his relationships are radically altered as a result. Teachers wonder if they are now expected to become a kind of peer, parent substitute, or psychologist. If they do not pay attention to what the teenager needs from them, they might resort to one stock alternative or another: either rigidly adhering to the past, as if nothing had changed, or abandoning the old connection in favor of being a kind of helper, therapist, or grief counselor. Adopting either of these stances will not prove very useful for the teenager, his continuing education, or their evolving relationship. The problem is that both teenagers and adults in this circumstance are looking for authentic ways to act and authentic ways to be. But death, particularly the death of a parent, threatens to disrupt their development. The world they once knew is gone, and the selves they once were are now imperiled.

Growing Pains

Until adolescence, and even through early adolescence, children consciously experience emotions one at a time, in a distinct sequence that is comprehensible and connected. For instance, an eight-year-old gets angry and throws a temper tantrum. A five-year-old gets sad and cries. This lucidity, explainability, and sequentiality of emotions is something about elementary school kids that their teachers embrace. If it is missing, there is usually sound cause for concern, if not alarm. For this phase of life, during which emotions are experienced in discrete outlines, lays the foundation for the child's developing the articulate and sophisticated emotional world of an adult.

Mature adults experience several (usually conflicting or contradictory) emotions simultaneously—or at least in such proximity to one another as to feel they are simultaneous—and bear with this transitory, emotional disequilibrium (which is experienced as anxiety) for as long as it takes to sort out what they are feeling. (This is different for the immature adult, who is unable to brook this emotional disequilibrium and instead acts inappropriately, compelled by unconscious conflicts.) Strategies of negotiating such disequilibrium vary from person to person. In the extreme some may rely upon addictions or obsessions, some of which are socially acceptable to one degree or another (workaholic patterns or fastidious control fixations, say); others which are quite dangerous (like alcoholism or depression). Unfortunately, the consequence for the adult who is neither conscious of his anxiety nor able to cope with his emotional conflicts is that he is doomed to self-destructiveness and deflected rage. The goal of psychological health, then, is not to dispose of anxiety, the existence of which is a given, but to learn how to transform such anxiety—and to direct that energy into work, art, relationship, or some kind of meaningful engagement with the world. That is, the way adults act on this anxiety is both the measure and the means of their health and productivity. Healthy, productive adults virtually swim in a tempest-tossed ocean of emotions because they live rich, compelling, or, in other words, conflict-ridden lives.

Adolescence is the transitional phase between childhood and adulthood. Although it is a little bit of both, it is also a lot of neither. A teenager is not a small adult, nor is he a big child, even though he may play both parts from time to time. Not yet in possession of adult consciousness, teenagers nonetheless endure adultlike anxiety. This is the fierce paradox of adolescent development: teenagers need maturity to deal with the anxiety of life, and they must undergo the anxiety of life in order to develop the maturity necessary for them to grow into healthy adults. This paradox agitates the turmoil of adolescence. But when they are disrupted by psychic upheaval, teenagers benefit by the presence of mature, caring adults in their lives, who by their example and presence demonstrate how to confront the conflicts in their own lives.

Death Transforms a Teenager into an Adult

Back to Melvin. As a high school junior, sixteen or seventeen years old, he had been thrust headlong, and brutally, through the death of his mother into the world of adult emotion and anxiety. The guilt, the sadness, the confusion, the regret—these emotions assumed unprecedented formations and juxtapositions within him. He had no experience managing such conflicts at such intensity and depth. With some adult attention (and with the good fortune of having adults around him who understood what he was going through), however, he acquired such awareness. (When people look back over their adolescence, these are exactly the kinds of moments that might be said to have deepened their character and caused them to grow up.) Here Melvin chose an impressive, surprising, and yet pragmatic mode of confronting his mom's death. He increased his responsibility in and for himself, particularly in and through his academic work, which seems fitting insofar as a parent's death throws us, abandoned, upon ourselves. But still, there seems something more involved in the turn in Melvin's life.

Some might call Melvin's response an escape from the pain of loss, or an act of sublimation. Others might see it as an example of the discontinuous growth of personality, one of those moments we all recognize, when life mysteriously changes and we cannot go back to what we once were. Perhaps this behavior is an escape, but is it an escape *from* or an escape *to*? And how and when would we be able to answer that question? To speak of this adjustment in another way, it seems to be a nearly instantaneous surge of self. But is it an integration of all that has gone before or is it a sacrifice of his own previously conceived gusto for life, when he used to have, in his words, "better things to do"? It takes Melvin years, as the story shows, for him to understand exactly what it was he went through at the time. And this explains why it is hard to know, in the first flush of suffering and loss, how Melvin is doing. At the onset of grief, it is simply a matter of his getting through day by day. Healing, like self-understanding, cannot be rushed.

Grieving, Coping, Dreaming

Coming to grips with a parent's death entails years, if not a lifetime. Melvin cannot stop contemplating his loss. For the rest of his life his mother will be dead. This existential ordeal is difficult to articulate for any adult, never mind any teenager. Nonetheless, Melvin will be surrounded by many who offer up their versions of the meaning of life. Painful as it will be to listen, he will hang on every word, for a while. After all, he is looking for some all-inclusive vision to help him make sense of his life. For his mom's death reconstructs his home, his entire family, and his conception of himself. But his healing cannot take place until he finds for himself the meaning of *his* life.

For months Melvin might be looking down the hallway at home for his mother to come around the corner. He might even hear her moving about. He might think that if he is still enough or if he turns quickly enough, he can catch a glimpse of her. At the same time, he knows that this is impossible.

Normally, teenagers take a step backward or struggle to maintain their previous levels of involvement and achievement for about a year after the death of a loved one. (Interestingly, it takes just as long for them to adjust to divorce—and for similar reasons.) Most will experience their concentration and attention levels as frustratingly low. With the best intentions to read their history assignment, they will find themselves staring at the same page for a half hour, with absolutely no comprehension. This powerlessness frightens them. They wonder, "Will it always be this way?" Some question their past: "Was it ever not this way? Are my memories accurate?" With most teenagers this concentration loss is temporary. Their focus comes back with the passage of time and with psychic reorganization. For a teenager who looks to his parents for guidance—whether admitting it or not—the loss of a parent creates a void. Where there was once someone who could provide meaning, there is now no one. Melvin's task is to create a more mature and personal meaning for himself, to make something out of the emptiness formed in the wake of his mother's death.

For Melvin, it's the absence of his mother that hurts him so profoundly. And though he can never make her materialize again, he realizes that he can do something about that terrible absence. What he can do is sustain his relationship with her—which in a later conversation with a former teacher is exactly what he realizes he has done. Is Melvin indulging in magical thinking? To the extent that the question is relevant (not greatly), the answer is no. He earned all the As (he did the work, no magic there), and he did feel closer to his mother.

An Immortal Contract

Many teenagers find, if not consolation, deep or renewed meaning in their religious or philosophical tenets, and they act accordingly, embracing new or familiar rituals to sustain them in this hour of need. Similarly, others rage with bitter disappointment and reject their faith and family practices. But why did Melvin respond as he did? Nobody can claim to know for sure. His strategy (though that is not quite the right word) is something imaginatively shaped out of his experience, his family, his friends, and his own personality. Is his a conventional or normal response to the death of a parent? No. And that seems fitting somehow, for death, the only universal of human existence, destroys the very notion of convention. Nothing is conventional about the death of a loved one, and there is no conventional response to it. It simultaneously flouts and confirms our cherished assumptions. Particularly in the case of a teenager like Melvin, it subverts the myth of his personal exceptionality—that somehow he is invincible.

If this teenager's response to his mother's death is not a conventional one, is it wildly extraordinary? No, it is not that either. Melvin has diverted his grieving into his own self-creation. In fact, he realizes later that all along he had been creating a new self (symbolized by his reincarnation as a committed student) through the pursuit of relationship—first with his mother and then with understanding teachers. These are the adults who will allow him to be true to his relationship with his mother—by insisting that he meet expectations and by not indulging or accommodating him, which would taint his achievement both in his own eyes and (as he imagines it) in his mother's. For Melvin can only keep his pact with his mother by doing it on his own terms and, in that way, keeping the contract—and her—immortal.

Breaking the Silence

When a family is visited by crisis, sometimes there is a tendency to circle the wagons, to contain the troubles within the domestic sphere. This plan rarely works, however, to the benefit of the adolescent, who wears his pain and suffering on his sleeve, especially when he is under the impression that he is masterfully covering up. Although it may seem difficult for you to make the call—to the dean, the teacher, the counselor, the employer, or the camp director—you will help your child immeasurably by keeping the crucial figures in your child's life informed. Divorce, job loss, illness, major problems with siblings—these issues affect your teenager's day-to-day life. The school cannot undo the tragedies and the hardships that have profoundly rocked your life. But what the school can do, should do, and will do in most cases, is provide a place for your child that is safer for having been informed. Your child, of course, may recoil—in fear and self-consciousness—at the thought of being exposed, being made the object of sympathy, or being set apart; but a good school can work with him in confidence. It is important that you always inform your teenager before you make the call and assure him that the information will remain confidential. In fact, it's best if your teenager is involved in the choice of the best person to contact—a vice principal, a dean, or an adviser. In so doing, you and your child will probably gain new allies, even if you didn't think you wanted or needed them.

There is one more consideration to keep in mind: during times of trauma, probably all teenagers benefit from counseling. This does not mean, however, that all will instinctively allow themselves to risk such vulnerable engagement or that all, or most, need counseling. Melvin himself passed on this option advised by the vice principal. But he allowed himself to sit down with that counselor, if only for a minute and if only to indicate that he didn't see merit in any conversation, at least for now. In fact, though, he did listen:

> —*Guess I'm not all that sure it would do any good. My mom'll still be gone, no matter how much we talk, right?*
> —*You're right, but that's not the reason we'd talk.*
> —*So what would be the reason?*
> —*As I said, it would be helpful. You've been through a lot and there's a lot more to go through still.*

It turns out that Melvin did follow the counselor's advice, as the teacher observed: *Fortunately, though, he learned to open up and eventually he was able to talk to people he trusted, his friends and a few adults. His openness helped him deal with his loss—to the extent that anybody can ever be said to deal with a tragedy of this magnitude.* The effects of that brief counseling session, in other words, were delayed but still crucial. What Melvin hears in his brief meeting with the counselor he enacts with others in his life, such as his teacher, and, we can imagine, his father and his friends.

Your Presence in the Void

When your family is struck by tragedy, you might be tempted to concentrate all your emotional energies either on the welfare of your teenager or on yourself. This is normal but is not a choice you should make. You need to take care of both yourself and your child.

Contrary to popular belief, in a crisis like Melvin's, a teenager does not need you to be stoic and controlled. If you convey the illusion that death does not devastate, that death does not cost, and that death does not cause chaos, your teenagers will be more terrified than ever, because that is something out of the realm of possibility for him. What he needs instead, and urgently, is your presence, your acknowledgment of confusing and conflicting feelings clashing with the reality of day-to-day demands, your resolve to get through this ordeal one step at a time. This is an implicit recognition of what he is coping with. In short, he needs appropriate vulnerability and appropriate fortitude from you. Correspondingly, you need people around you with whom you can let go—to explore your darkest fears in order to discover the hope that resides in the farthest corners. Doing all this, even in this agonizing time, you will be gratified to see how your relationship with your child will mysteriously grow and deepen.

Appendix A

"Where Am I?"

Being 14–15 Means . . .

- You're in the ninth grade and you suddenly feel lost. You have been pulled up by your roots. Now, all day long, you go around looking for signs to point the way, especially when you used to know where you were supposed to be. But wait a second. Here you are, set down on a new, heretofore unexplored planet—high school—with a bunch of strangers. They've given you a course schedule and a map of the campus, but where is your survival manual?
- You worry about lunch. Help! How are you going to get through lunch? Who will eat lunch with you? Should you make the first move? When did eating a stupid sandwich become so intense, and how come lunch has so little to do with food? Maybe you should just skip lunch altogether.
- You are wondering, gee, *you know*, about, *guess you'd have to say* . . . SEX! (*I have no idea what it is, I don't even know the questions, are you talking to me, oh, OK, never mind. But I still might try it.*)
- You are looking into the mirror more than you care to admit and more than you even realize. The escalating, complicating, enriching, exhausting self-consciousness!
- You are adjusting to revised and intensified expectations all around: schoolwork, sports, drama, art, community service. And of course these expectations bring along a host of corresponding emotions, such as excitement, anxiety, anticipation, ambition, fearfulness, remorse, hopefulness, usually several in combination.

- You feel mystified lots of the time. (By comparison with the ordinary fifteen-year-old, the paranoiac conspiracies infusing science fiction will seem tame. Ninth graders doubt themselves as well as their perceptions and conceptions of reality. Exactly what is going on? Is it even possible to find out? Whom should they ask?)
- You are struggling all day long to establish priorities in your own life— academics, athletics, family, personal, spiritual, and religious. Whose priorities rule? Is it OK if they're only your priorities?
- You are always asking yourself questions like, What am I supposed to wear? Are you supposed to care about what you are supposed to wear? But you have to dress in some way, right, so how to look?

For just about every teenager, the trauma of starting high school—or to view it from the related, equally valid perspective of leaving eighth grade—is difficult to overestimate. Yes, they know there is nothing left to learn, conquer, or endure in middle school, but that recognition only increases a ninth grader's sadness. And sadness it is, too, which can be overwhelming and poignant. Now they are compelled to make this dramatic transition. As they are doing so, they feel simultaneously banished from the old world they had labored to master and (talk about unfair) systematically excluded from a new one they aspire to enter.

By that first month of high school, teenagers are a perpetual heartbeat away from exhilaration, from tears, from laughter, from hyperventilation, from anger. The causes of any emotional reaction may not quite be clear to anybody, including themselves. A mere look from a classmate or a teacher can send them spiraling into depression or uplift them into the most rarefied realms of bliss. At home, there will be unaccountable mood swings. In their classes, they will strike their teachers in one moment as behaving like uncontrollable children and in the next impress them as being incredibly sophisticated "for their age." They will make tremendous strides intellectually, challenging adults with their honest questionings and strivings to understand. But they will also inexhaustibly ferret out the humorous potentialities, for example, in even the most oblique references to natural bodily functionings. They will thrill to the prospect of making new friends, of expanding their social world, even as some will cling to the cliques that they form as a buttress against the unknown. Still others will victimize their peers and find themselves victimized at the same time. Adults will be tempted to shake their heads, incredulous as to how kids can be so mean to each other or so dependent on each other, having momentarily forgotten that they all endured the same ordeal or perpetuated the same cruel survival strategies.

This is a time when kids require the clear voice and steady support of adults—parents, teachers, coaches—who establish boundaries that are reasonable and explained. That's because the whole year seems so confusing, and life seems played out on somebody else's terms. Their bodies aren't linked up with their minds yet. Classes don't seem to be aligned with their intellectual priorities—and how can they be, since these priorities continually skid and slide around? Some people, including members of their own family, don't quite yet understand or appreciate who they are or who they are trying to be.

Well, what else would you expect? They don't know either.

All this to say this year is a time when tact on the part of adults is most poignantly called for. In one moment, these teenagers will need to be treated almost as if they were still children—somewhat needy, dependent, and incorrigibly playful. Yet in the next moment, they will insist on being treated like proto-adults, wanting freedom and responsibility. Only at our own peril do we discount such a claim. Sometimes they will need to be treated with the formality and respect accorded a state dignitary, other times, extended all the patience and understanding that can be summoned up for a teething infant. (Try to manage that attitude without condescension. Lots of luck.) We do best by them when we hold them to reasonable expectations and patiently embrace them in our sympathetic understanding. The truth is, of course, new to their teenager identity, they are both children and adults, and both totally as well as provisionally.

Appendix B

"Who Am I?"

Being 15–16 Means . . .

- You got through last year, though you hope nobody asks you how. ("OK, at least now I know the ropes.") But now you start to question if you really fit in with the kids you call your friends. It's just that you're changing so fast and they all seem to be staying in the same place. But what's even crazier is that you act just like them when you are with them, even though that isn't who you are—at least anymore.

- At the same time you dedicate yourself to your friends. Passionate relationships, including passionate same-sex relationships, new friendships, form and flower. Sometimes they cause a family crisis. ("Where did you come up with him?" "What do you see in her?" "Must you spend every hour with them?")

- You take a hard look at yourself and it puts you in a panic. ("I guess I'm not going to win an Olympic medal or be a professional superstar athlete.")

- You keep thinking about . . . SEX! (*I have no idea what it means, but it sure sounds like fun. Don't worry, I have all the answers.*)

- A Car! Freedom. Independence. Your own music. You reprogram the station presets, you scrape their old decals off the windows and bumpers. An apartment on wheels!

- You ask yourself if you really should throw that party. You could get away with it if you time it just right. Or should you go to that party what's-her-name is having? (If there is one pretty near-certainty, if experience with just about every school in the country counts, this is what will

happen: Some sophomore will throw the Party from Parent Hell. With
good luck, someone will be tipped off just in time to stop it.)
- Your body is out of control. (*Help.*)
- You don't need any help. (*I got to go.*)
- Deep down, you believe your home is a safe haven (relatively speaking).
- Deep down, you believe your home is a prison (relatively speaking).
- You question authority everywhere: at home, in stores, and at school.
- Your Season of Experimentation begins.
- Your year comes in like a lamb and goes out like a lion.
- You ask yourself: Who are my friends? Do I have any friends? But most
  important, what is a friend anyway?
- Someday they'll probably make a movie of your life.

In philosophy, there is a venerable problem called the mind-body split. For
many centuries great thinkers have weighed in on this topic. As even the most un-
philosophical parents know, however, this split is being played out daily inside
most fifteen- and sixteen-year-olds. An amazing metamorphosis is taking place in
teenagers at this stage. They usually look something like children when the fall
term begins, and by final exams in the spring they look something like adults, or
at least more like their senior peers than the eighth graders who entered school
not so long ago. The revolutionary physical changes correspond to astonishing
cognitive developments: by the end of this year they are much more comfortable
with abstract thinking, much more fluent in their ability to make thematic, struc-
tural, intellectual, formal connections between works, disciplines, and traditions.
Their written and oral expression grows more complex and ambitious, sometimes
even running out of their conscious control. At the same time, they become more
passionate in their relationships, and friendships become precious and complicated. The prospect of romance looms for many of them; and, of course, heartbreak follows close on its heels (something that parents may be excused from
helpfully pointing out in advance). At home, they will advance the causes of justice and fairness and will argue for their rights and earned privileges with an increased cogency borne of that quintessentially coruscating teenage logic that is
guaranteed to drive their parents a little batty. They may maintain a public per-
sona of knowing everything that is to be known while privately worrying their
nights away, for example, rehearsing exactly how to look and what to say when
you-know-who passes by them on the street. For many families, as teenagers now
approach legal driving age, this is the point at which the automobile discussion
flowers—or fizzles—or flares, sometimes all in the same ten-minute span.

This is a time for adults to hold on, that is, to hold on as close as possible without smothering—an excellent trick well worth the massive effort you expend to master it. The trials will be coming for your teenagers soon, and once they start, they may temporarily show no signs of abating. This may be a time of experimentation that takes many forms, or at least a time when teenagers have to rule out consciously such experimentations—with drugs, with sex, with alcohol, with relationships, with their own bodies, with the boundaries of behavior. Testing the limits becomes quasi-religious in its allure for some teenagers. Adults may find sophomore self-absorption to be stunning in its totality, and yet this is also why schools find this time to be, perhaps amazingly, the best opportunity for challenging these teenagers with rising academic expectations and requirements, as well as increased responsibilities for community service. This is the time when, even as they pursue the act of shaping a self, they rise to the occasion, survive, and thrive—if we give them both clear limits and lots of room.

Appendix C

"What Are You Looking At?"

Being 16–17 Means . . .

- You are comfortable now with abstract thinking. It's the rest of your life you may not be comfortable with. You truly can't remember not thinking this way. You have sympathy for those poor fourteen-year-old youngsters.
- Your new brain power contributes to your all-consuming interest in questioning your parents, as well as all those brazen enough to assert authority, from a waiter to a traffic officer to a vice principal. This challenging approach to life simply becomes a staple of your life.
- You contemplate college, perhaps for the first time. Then, and almost instantaneously, college pressures weigh you down, coloring every decision. *(How will this affect my GPA? What do I need to do to get into a first-rate university? I won't get into medical school if I don't get an A in Biology.)*
- You meditate all the time on the deepest meaning of . . . sex. *(LOVE!)*
- If you're lucky, you possess your own wheels. If you are even "luckier," you don't have to sweat all the time about car repairs and insurance. Your car gives shape and direction to your whole social existence.
- You know you will never be mistaken for a little kid anymore—not even by your suddenly sentimentalizing parents. Every time your parent asks you, *Remember the time when . . .* , you wince and stare down into your cereal bowl and hope the story will be a short one.
- Your relationships intensify, and friends become more dependable. You, too, become a more dependable friend.

- Now you begin your idealization of certain people, such as an important coach, teacher, or boss. This may temporarily drive your parents nuts, which has the advantage, for you, of keeping them occupied.
- You develop a stronger personal identity while at the same time remaining fragile.
- You discover vehicles for your passions, not all of them (as you can almost admit to yourself at certain times) the appropriate ones.
- You begin to see your own families more clearly, or so you think. You're amazed they can't see their enormous character flaws.
- This is the time you believe you need to assert independence from the family.
- You wait and hope that your parents will back off a little. Overmanage at your own risk, you want to say. (*But don't back off too far . . .* , which is something you can't say.)

Juniors will usually exert a powerful influence on the whole high school universe. Juniors will aspire to be leaders, to make a difference in school organizations, and to perform community service. They will try to take over school publications, performances, and teams. They will have a vision. They will feel the power. So much else is going on, too. They will have a list of colleges they might consider blessing with their attendance. They speak to adults as if they were equals. And adults address them in nearly comparable fashion.

For all the talk about junior year being the toughest for kids, when standardized tests loom in greater importance, when the academic courses seem more challenging, when so much is expected of them in class and on teams and in extracurricular activities, this can also be the best of times. They see the light at the end of the high school tunnel, and the idea thrills them. They develop goals and work toward their dreams. They are romantic, in the broadest sense of the term, yearning for connection, knowledge, relationship, friendship, influence on adults, and power over their own lives.

It's a rare school where the faculty looks at the juniors and does not say, "This is going to be a great senior class." In other words, it's a year of hope and promise. And every parent gives thanks to be done with the sophomore year.

Appendix D

"Where Am I Going and Where Have I Been?"

Being 17–18 Means . . .

- You personally coin the expression *Seize the Day.*
- At last you are an adult. (Aren't you?)
- This is your time to be respected by one and all.
- Sex, sex, sex, sex . . . SEX! (*SEX!*)
- You can afford to be a little nostalgic about your childhood, defined as the period of your life that ended roughly yesterday but also seems like a hundred years ago.
- You are divided between feelings of total comfort around school and excruciating restlessness.
- You suffer a most un-Zenlike burning desire to leave an impression. You want to make yourself a few memories, and you want to be remembered.
- Your relationships are even more important, painful, and rewarding.
- What happened to your independent, accomplished, strong-willed, clear-eyed parents?! Now they start to be very clingy. (*What time are you coming home? Can I look at your application? Why do you need to go out on a weeknight? You wearing socks or not? How come you can't go to a movie with us?*)
- Is college for me? If so, where? If not, why not? And if not, then what?

- If you're college bound, a special bonus reward for you: incalculable first-semester stress in classes and throughout the entire application ordeal.
- My classmates are my world! And everything changes come June!
- You imagine that adults can be your friends. They're certainly your equals. *(Can we stay in touch after graduation?)*
- Time! There just isn't enough.
- Oops. Blip on the screen. Senioritis. *(What, me worry?)*
- Sometimes, in the middle of an afternoon class, you study watermarks on the ceiling and think, Why won't this year ever end?
- Oh, no, senior year is over already . . . How did that happen? Where did high school go? What did I miss? What *didn't* I miss?

Freshman year is a like a lyric poem. Sophomore year is like a short story. Junior year is like a play, sometimes Neil Simon, sometimes *Othello*. Senior year? Senior year is *War and Peace*. And there's no translation available, and you don't read Russian. (Of course, sometimes it's also one of those old Marx Brothers movies, too, or even one of those hilarious slasher movies best watched late at night all by yourself or with one good friend.)

Why all the complication, passion, and urgency?

Seventeen- and eighteen-year-olds, usually seniors in high school, are both savvy and naive, savvy about what they have accomplished and naive in that they think they now definitively know themselves. Most at least suspect, however glimmeringly, that this self-knowledge is not quite secure. Not only that, they have a hunch this self-knowledge will be less than comprehensive a few short months from now, after the last strains of graduation promenade music fades in the distance.

During this time, they are continually consolidating their adolescent experiences in preparation for one big leap into the future. They are rethinking who they are, who their friends are, what their family is, what is truly important to them, and, probably for the first time, their illusions about themselves.

Actually, senior year *fall* is different from senior year *spring*. In the fall, seniors are absorbed in and by the future. They are forward thinking and driven. In the spring, they are reaping the benefits earned in the past and they are anxious about decisions they have already made. They are nostalgic and sentimental, and definitely not driven.

This year is not a smooth ride for anybody. Not for somebody in a long-term relationship, not for a soccer star, not for the student body president, not for somebody early-admitted to a prestigious college, and not for somebody who gives hours every week to community service. Not for kids the school puts on a pedestal, not for kids with an armful of prizes and scholarship offers. Not for anybody.

At this stage, regression is a good bet, and so is a spurt of unprecedented growth. Parents may have slightly bizarre midnight conversations with their teenagers while standing around the refrigerator and rethink what is meant by the term quality time. On other fronts, there may be arguments that parents could have easily avoided. Parents will be proud, will be downcast, will be stunned, will be awed by the sensitivity of their beautiful children, and will be disgusted by the spectacle of what's been left on the kitchen counter.

Above all else, this is the moment for parents to tell teenagers they love them and believe in them. They'll need to be reminded. Because somehow your time together with them has been worth every ounce of energy and imagination and concern that you have invested. Though sometimes that is something you can only see in the rearview mirror. Step on the accelerator, though it breaks your heart, and go. But don't worry. Your teenager will always know where to find you down the road.

Bibliography

Ahrons, Constance. *The Good Divorce*. New York: HarperCollins, 1994.

Aronson, Elliot. *The Social Animal*. 7th ed. New York: Freeman, 1995.

Banner, James M., and Harold C. Cannon. *The Elements of Teaching*. New Haven: Yale University Press, 1997.

Beck, Aaron T. *Depression: Causes and Treatment*. Philadelphia: University of Pennsylvania Press, 1967.

Bell, Ruth. *Changing Bodies, Changing Lives: A Book for Teens on Sex and Relationship*. 3d ed. New York: Times Books, 1998.

Breger, Louis. *From Instinct to Identity: The Development of Personality*. Englewood Cliffs, N.J.: Prentice-Hall, 1974.

Brumberg, Joan Jacobs. *The Body Project: An Intimate History of American Girls*. New York: Random House, 1997.

Carey, Lorene. *Black Ice*. New York: Vintage, 1992.

Carse, James P. *Breakfast at the Victory: The Mysticism of Ordinary Experience*. San Francisco: Harper, 1994.

Dryfoos, Joy G. *Safe Passage: Making It Through Adolescence in a Risky Society*. New York: Oxford, 1998.

Epstein, Mark. *Going to Pieces Without Falling Apart: A Buddhist Perspective on Wholeness*. New York: Broadway, 1998.

Erikson, Erik. *Childhood and Society*. New York: Norton, 1963.

_____. *Identity: Youth and Crisis*. New York: Norton, 1968.

Fass, Paula S., and Mary Ann Mason. *Childhood in America*. New York: New York University Press, 2000.

Finnegan, William. *Cold New World: Growing Up in a Harder Country*. New York: Modern Library, 1999.

Fraiberg, Selma H. *The Magic Years: Understanding and Handling the Problems of Early Childhood*. New York: Simon & Schuster, 1959.

Furstenberg, Frank F., Jr., and Thomas D. Cook, Jacquelynne Eccles, Glen H. Elder Jr., and Arnold Sameroff. *Managing to Make It: Urban Families and Adolescent Success*. Chicago: University of Chicago Press, 1999.

Garbarino, James. *Lost Boys: Why Our Sons Turn Violent and How We Can Save Them.* New York: Free Press, 1999.

Gardner, Howard. *Multiple Intelligences: The Theory in Practice.* New York: Basic, 1993.

Gilligan, Carol. *In a Different Voice.* Cambridge: Harvard, 1982.

Giroux, Henry A. *Channel Surfing: Racism, the Media, and the Destruction of Today's Youth.* New York: St. Martin's, 1997.

Goffman, Erving. *The Presentation of Self in Everyday Life.* New York: Doubleday, 1959.

Goleman, Daniel. *Emotional Intelligence.* New York: Bantam, 1995.

Gurian, Michael. *A Fine Young Man: What Parents, Mentors, and Educators Can Do to Shape Adolescent Boys into Exceptional Men.* New York: Tarcher/Putnam, 1998.

Hallowell, Edward M., and John H. Ratey. *Driven to Distraction: Recognizing and Coping with Attention Deficit Disorder from Childhood Through Adulthood.* New York: Simon & Schuster, 1994.

Harris, Judith Rich. *The Nurture Assumption: Why Children Turn Out the Way They Do.* New York: Free Press, 1998.

Hersch, Patricia. *A Tribe Apart: A Journey into the Heart of American Adolescence.* New York: Fawcett Columbine, 1998.

Hine, Thomas. *The Rise and Fall of the American Teenager.* New York: Avon, 1999.

Inaba, Darryl S., and William E. Cohen. *Uppers, Downers, and All Arounders.* Ashland, Ore.: CNS Productions, 1983.

Jalloun, Tahar Ben. *Racism Explained to My Daughter.* New York: New Press, 1999.

Kegan, Robert. *The Evolving Self: Problem and Process in Human Development.* Cambridge: Harvard, 1982.

Kelly, Gary F. *Learning About Sex: The Contemporary Guide for Young Adults.* 3d ed. New York: Barron's Educational Series, 1987.

Kindlon, Dan, and Michael Thompson. *Raising Cain: Protecting the Emotional Life of Boys.* New York: Ballantine, 1999.

Kohn, Alfie. *Punished by Rewards.* New York: Houghton Mifflin, 1995.

Kübler-Ross, Elisabeth. *Death: The Final Stage of Growth.* Englewood Cliffs, N.J.: Prentice-Hall, 1975.

Lawrence-Lightfoot, Sarah. *Respect: An Exploration.* Reading, Mass.: Perseus, 1999.

Lefkowitz, Bernard. *Our Guys: The Glen Ridge Rape and the Secret Life of the Perfect Suburb.* New York: Vintage, 1998.

Levine, Mel. *Developmental Variation and Learning Disorders.* Cambridge, Mass.: Educational Publishing Service, 1983.

_____. *Educational Care: A System for Understanding and Helping Children with Learning Problems at Home and in School.* Cambridge, Mass.: Educational Publishing Service, 1994.

Maderas, Lynda, Dane Saavedra, and Ralph Lopez. *What's Happening to My Body?*

Book for Boys: A Growing Up Guide for Parents and Sons. New York: Newmarket, 1987.

Maderas, Lynda, Claudia Ziroli, and Jackie Aher. *What's Happening to My Body? Book for Girls: A Growing Up Guide for Parents and Daughters.* New York: Newmarket, 1987.

Males, Mike A. *Framing Youth: Ten Myths About the Next Generation.* Monroe, Me.: Common Courage, 1999.

Meier, Deborah. *The Power of Their Ideas: Lessons for America from a Small School in Harlem.* Boston: Beacon, 1995.

Newberger, Eli H. *The Men They Will Become: The Nature and Nurture of Male Character.* Reading, Mass.: Perseus, 1999.

Newton, Miller. *Adolescence: Guiding Youth Through the Perilous Ordeal.* New York: Norton, 1995.

Orenstein, Peggy. *SchoolGirls: Young Women, Self-Esteem, and the Confidence Gap.* New York: Doubleday, 1994.

Oster, Gerald D., and Sarah S. Montgomery. *Helping Your Depressed Teenager: A Guide for Parents and Caregivers.* New York: Wiley, 1995.

Palladino, Grace. *Teenagers: An American History.* New York: Basic, 1996.

Pinker, Steven. *How the Mind Works.* New York: Norton, 1997.

Pipher, Mary. *Reviving Ophelia: Saving the Selves of Adolescent Girls.* New York: Putnam, 1994.

Pollack, William. *Real Boys: Rescuing Our Sons from the Myths of Boyhood.* New York: Random House, 1998.

Ponton, Lynn. *The Romance of Risk: Why Teenagers Do the Things They Do.* New York: Basic, 1997.

Reinisch, June M., with Ruth Beasley. *The Kinsey Institute New Report on Sex.* New York: St. Martin's, 1991.

Riera, Michael. *Uncommon Sense for Parents with Teenagers.* Berkeley: Celestial Arts, 1995.

———. *Surviving High School.* Berkeley: Celestial Arts, 1997.

Rose, Mike. *Lives on the Boundary: A Moving Account of the Struggles and Achievements of America's Educational Underclass.* New York: Penguin, 1989.

Rubin, Nancy. *Ask Me If I Care: Voices from an American High School.* Berkeley: Celestial Arts, 1994.

Ryan, Joan. *Little Girls in Pretty Boxes: The Making and Breaking of Elite Gymnasts and Figure Skaters.* New York: Warner, 1995.

Sacks, Oliver. *An Anthropologist on Mars: Seven Paradoxical Tales.* New York: Knopf, 1995.

Sadker, Myra, and David Sadker. *Failing at Fairness: How America's Schools Cheat Girls.* New York: Scribners, 1994.

Shandler, Sara. *Ophelia Speaks: Adolescent Girls Write About their Search for Self.* New York: Harper, 1999.

Sizer, Ted. *Horace's Compromise: The Dilemma of the American High School.* Boston: Houghton Mifflin, 1985.

Sullivan, Harry Stack. *Interpersonal Theory of Psychiatry.* New York: Norton, 1968.

Sulloway, Frank. *Born to Rebel: Birth Order, Family Dynamics, and Creative Lives.* New York: Pantheon, 1996.

Takaki, Ronald. *A Different Mirror: A History of Multicultural America.* Boston: Little, Brown, 1993.

Tannen, Deborah. *You Just Don't Understand: Women and Men in Conversation.* New York: Ballantine, 1990.

Tatum, Beverly Daniel. *"Why Are All the Black Kids Sitting Together in the Cafeteria?" and Other Conversations About Race.* New York: Basic, 1997.

Trillin, Calvin. *Family Man.* New York: Farrar, Straus, Giroux, 1998.

Vida, Vendela. *Girls on the Verge: Debutante Dips, Drive-bys, and Other Initiations.* New York: St. Martin's, 1999.

West, Cornel. *Race Matters.* New York: Vintage, 1994.

Wheelis, Allen. *How People Change.* New York: Harper, 1973.

White, Michael, and David Epston. *Narrative Means to Therapeutic Ends.* New York: Norton, 1990.

Wolf, Anthony J. *"Get Out of My Life, but First Could You Drive Me and Cheryl to the Mall?" A Parent's Guide to the New Teenager.* New York: Noonday, 1991.

Notes

Chapter 1

1. *New York Times*, 6 April 1999, D6, national ed.
2. *San Francisco Chronicle*, 30 September 1998. American Academy of Pediatrics Press Release: "AAP Releases New Findings on Teens and Underage Drinking," 30 September 1998.
3. "Do Parents Count," *New York Review of Books*, 5 November 1998, 19.
4. Office of National Drug Control Policy and U.S. Department of Health and Human Services.

Chapter 2

1. Joan Ryan, *Little Girls in Pretty Boxes* (New York: Warner, 1995).

Chapter 5

1. Daryl S. Inaba and William E. Cohen, *Uppers, Downers, All Arounders* (Ashland, Ore.: CNS Productions, 1983), 178.
2. Shedler and Block, "Adolescent Drug Use and Psychological Health: A Longitudinal Study."
3. *San Francisco Chronicle*, 2 September 1998, A6.

Chapter 6

1. Beverly Daniel Tatum, *"Why Are All the Black Kids Sitting Together in the Cafeteria?" and Other Conversations About Race* (New York: Basic, 1997), 53.
2. Dan Kindlon and Michael Thompson, *Raising Cain* (New York: Ballantine, 1999), 241–242.

Chapter 8

1. Quoted by Lawrence H. Diller, "Running on Ritalin," *Doubletake,* Fall 1998, 53.
2. *The New York Times,* 5 May 1998, B12, national ed.
3. Mel Levine, *Educational Care* (Cambridge, Mass.: Educational Publishing Service), 256–258.
4. Ibid., 271.

Chapter 10

1. Constance Ahrons, *The Good Divorce* (New York: HarperCollins, 1994), 79.
2. Mary Pipher, *Reviving Ophelia* (New York: Putnam, 1994), 136.
3. William Pollack, *Real Boys* (New York: Random House, 1998), 364–388.

Chapter 11

1. *The New York Times,* 9 May 1999, sec. 4, 1, national edition.
2. *The San Francisco Examiner,* 9 May 1999, A1.
3. James Garbarino, *Lost Boys* (New York: Free Press, 1999), 14.
4. Dan Kindlon and Michael Thompson, *Raising Cain* (New York: Random House, 1999), 4.

Chapter 12

1. *San Francisco Examiner,* 26 July 1998, D1.
2. William Pollack, *Real Boys* (New York: Random House, 1998), 210.

Chapter 14

1. June M. Reinish and Ruth Beasley, *The Kinsey Institute New Report on Sex* (New York: St. Martin's, 1991), 262.

Chapter 15

1. Miller Newton, *Adolescence* (New York: Norton, 1995), 197.
2. Gerald D. Oster and Sarah S. Montgomery, *Helping Your Depressed Teenager* (New York: Wiley, 1995), 44.
3. "Push to Prevent Suicide," Associated Press, 28 July 1999.
4. "Use of Anti-Depression Medicine for Young Patients Has Soared," *New York Times* 10 August 1997, national ed.: A1.
5. Mary Pipher, *Reviving Ophelia* (New York: Putnam, 1994) 151.
6. Lynn Ponton, *The Romance of Risk* (New York: Basic, 1997) 6–7.

Index

intuition about teens, 50–51
learning disabilities in teens,
135–136
low self-esteem in teens, 130
motivating teens to achieve, 29–31
parent-teacher relations, 148–150
response to cheating, 58–59, 63–64
teen conflict and, 91–93
teens' falling in love, 232–235,
241–242
teens' response to death of parent,
273–277
understanding dishonesty, 59–60
See also Communication; Divorce
Parties, 139–142
ambivalence about, 144–145
letting teens make decisions about,
150–155
Peer issues, xxi, 34–35
drinking and driving, 1–19
drug use, 74–75
eating disorders, 110–112
illicit parties, 139–142
influence on teen decisionmaking,
11
trusting instincts about dating,
43–45
Piaget, Jean, 117
Pipher, Mary, 162, 254
Pollack, William, 45, 162–163, 206
Ponton, Lynn, 255
Power struggles
eating disorders and, 106–107,
113–114
over academic issues, 135
Psychotherapy, 254
See also Counseling

Quitting. *See* Decisionmaking

Race Matters (West), 100–101
Racism, 85–88
adult response to, 98–99

fighting intolerance and hate,
100–101
hate groups, 99–100
learning from conflict, 91–96, 98–99
personal identity and, 90–91, 93–95
teen response to, 88–90
Raising Cain (Kindlon and
Thompson), 96–97, 185, 254
Rape, date, 52
Real Boys (Pollack), 45, 162–163, 254
Reinisch, June, 240
Rejection, fear of, 35–36
as turning point for better
opportunities, 213–214
in homosexual teens, 196
Relationships, interpersonal, 288–290
adults' appropriate reaction to crisis,
48–51
breaking up, 225–232, 236–237
eating disorders and, 115–116
motivating teens to achieve, 29–31
self-esteem and, 129
talking about sex, 240
teacher-student relationships,
259–266
testing limits of, 268–269
Respect
as weapon against intolerance,
100–101
racism and, 90–91
Responsibility, 32–34
appropriate reaction to crisis, 48–51
drinking and driving, 17–19
drug use and, 78–84
illicit parties, 139–142
learning from mistakes, 90–93
making wise choices, 150–152
part-time jobs, 21–23
taking responsibility for mistakes,
54–56, 60–64
Reviving Ophelia (Pipher), 162, 254
Rites of passage, 259
Role models
as motivation to achieve, 31–32